THE ARCHIVABILITY
OF TELEVISION

THE PEABODY SERIES IN MEDIA HISTORY

SERIES EDITORS

Jeffrey P. Jones, *University of Georgia*
Ethan Thompson, *Texas A&M University, Corpus Christi*

THE ARCHIVABILITY OF TELEVISION

ESSAYS ON PRESERVATION AND PERSEVERANCE

EDITED BY **LAUREN BRATSLAVSKY AND ELIZABETH PETERSON**

THE UNIVERSITY OF GEORGIA PRESS | ATHENS

© 2025 by the University of Georgia Press
Athens, Georgia 30602
www.ugapress.org
All rights reserved
Set in 10.75/13.5 Garamond Premier Pro Regular
by Rebecca A. Norton

Most University of Georgia Press titles are
available from popular e-book vendors.

Printed digitally

EU Authorized Representative
Easy Access System Europe—Mustamäe tee 50, 10621
Tallinn, Estonia, gpsr.requests@easproject.com

Library of Congress Cataloging-in-Publication Data

Names: Bratslavsky, Lauren editor | Peterson, Elizabeth, 1968– editor
Title: The archivability of television : essays on preservation and perseverance / edited by Lauren Bratslavsky and Elizabeth Peterson.
Description: Athens : The University of Georgia Press, 2025. | Series: The Peabody series in media history | Includes bibliographical references and index.
Identifiers: LCCN 2024060699 | ISBN 9780820373881 hardback |
  ISBN 9780820373898 paperback | ISBN 9780820373904 epub |
  ISBN 9780820373911 pdf
Subjects: LCSH: Television archives | Motion picture film—Preservation | LCGFT: Essays
Classification: LCC PN1992.16 .A726 2025 | DDC 384.55—dc23/eng/20250311
LC record available at https://lccn.loc.gov/2024060699

CONTENTS

List of Illustrations   vii

Foreword   ix
CAROLINE FRICK

Acknowledgments   xv

Introduction   1
LAUREN BRATSLAVSKY

PART I. ACCOUNTING FOR THE WORTHINESS OF TELEVISION-RELATED MATERIALS FOR ARCHIVAL SPACES

Chapter 1. Considering the Archivability of Early U.S. Television Newsfilm   29
KATE CRONIN

Chapter 2. Heritage in Search of a Home: Archiving the Learning Designs and Artistry of Instructional Television of the 1970s and 1980s   59
OWEN GOTTLIEB

Chapter 3. Inventorying, Classifying, and Narrowly Interpreting Post-Broadcast Value: Research Leading Up to the Formation of the Museum of Broadcasting   86
LAUREN BRATSLAVSKY

PART II. THE ARCHIVE AS SOURCES OF AND INTERPRETERS FOR HERITAGE AND CULTURAL LEGITIMATION

Chapter 4. How an Award Created an Archives: Broadcasting History Unfolds in the Peabody Awards Collection   113
RUTA ABOLINS

Chapter 5. Local Value in the Television Archive:
The Media Archive for Central England   130
HANNAH SPAULDING

Chapter 6. Writing Tomorrow's History Today:
Lessons Learned from Pieces of the Past for
Tomorrow's Archiving and Exhibitory   148
WALTER PODRAZIK

Chapter 7. Television Archives in Australia:
"The Passing Down of Memory..."   166
LYNNE CARMICHAEL

PART III. TRANSFORMING THE EPHEMERAL INTO MORE VISIBLE AND LEGIBLE HISTORICAL MATERIAL

Chapter 8. Reviving Neglected Giants: Digitally Preserving
and Sharing Two Early Television Collections   183
ERIC HOYT, MARY HUELSBECK, AMANDA SMITH,
MAUREEN MAUK, OLIVIA JOHNSTON RILEY, MATT ST.
JOHN, PAULINE LAMPERT, AND LESLEY STEVENSON

Chapter 9. Preserving Campus Television; or, How an
Undergrad Found Willem Dafoe in the Archive   203
HUGO LJUNGBÄCK

Chapter 10. Archive Camaraderie: The Media Ecology
Project's Digital Queer Feminist Camp and Anti-
Racist Trans TV Post-Post-Production   222
QUINLAN MILLER

Chapter 11. Visibility and Value: A Citation
Analysis of Television Archive Materials   241
ELIZABETH PETERSON

Contributors   261

Index   265

ILLUSTRATIONS

FIGURES

Faye Emerson and her son Scoop, from Emerson's collection   186

A photograph from the production of *Men of Annapolis* from the Ziv-TV collection   187

A photograph of Faye Emerson from her collection   189

A telephone prop on the *World of Giants* set from the Ziv-TV collection   192

A fire extinguisher prop on the *World of Giants* set from the Ziv-TV collection   193

The WCFTR's Lasergraphics ScanStation   195

Still images from four of the productions featured on the *IML Composite* sample reel   208

Still image from *Nicaragua 1982*   209

A few of the one-inch Type C tapes in the extant collection   212

A mystery tape labeled only "Racism Tape 1" with no other identifying information   213

The new digitization setup in the old Cunningham studio control room   215

Still image from *Civil Commitment Hearings*   217

TABLES

2.1. The Institutional Evolution of AIT   62

11.1. Journal Titles Included in This Study   247

11.2. Number of Journals and Articles Reviewed   250

11.3. Geographic Representation of Archival Repositories Cited in This Study   251

11.4. Journals in This Study Containing Articles with Citations to Archival Material   252

11.5. Number of Articles Published That Cite Archival Material by Year   253

FOREWORD

Nearly twenty years ago, I founded the Texas Archive of the Moving Image (TAMI), an organization dedicated to preserving, providing access to, and educating the community about Texas's rich media legacy. Our team has traveled tens of thousands of miles across the state with a "bring out your film and video" campaign, discovering audiovisual artifacts that both complicate and confirm conventional understandings of the Texas past. Our website streams fully researched and vetted video content, of which broadcasting material plays an increasingly central role, garnering millions of views. TAMI's collections have been featured in high-profile media projects, including award-winning documentaries, and are used in K–12 classrooms around the state.

I am very proud of what we have accomplished thus far, but I often find myself regretting one key decision: the inclusion of "archive" in our organizational title. Labeling our work as "archival" has created significant confusion about our underlying intentions, the organization's abilities, and, just as importantly, our funding sources. TAMI is presumed to be a part of the Texas state government (it is not) and our mission assumed to be the physical conservation of film and video artifacts in perpetuity (which it isn't). What would be lost, however, with jettisoning the word "archive" from our name? Would we be seen as less serious? Less professional? Would our collections be less worthy of financial support should we be seen as just a group of well-intentioned, passionate hobbyists collecting what bits of the past we can find?

For *The Archivability of Television*, Lauren Bratslavsky and Elizabeth Peterson have convened a remarkable group of scholars and practitioners to address facets related to television preservation. As I reviewed the anthology's table of contents, I found my ongoing frustration with TAMI's nomenclature reflected in many of the essay titles and underlying themes—particularly those related to the value and perception of televisual artifacts. Where should historical television live, and what factors play into how to ensure that television is seen as worthy of long-lasting preservation? Early television studies scholars wrestled with similar concerns, echoing the pioneering film archivists and theorists before them. The twentieth-century solution, even if unfulfilled, advocated for the increased collecting of media artifacts by archives.

In the twenty-first century, however, an archive (or, for an increasing number of scholars, pundits, and artists, "*the* archive,") occupies a powerful, if largely imaginary, discursive space that appears increasingly fetishistic in approach and use. With the historiographical turn in film and media studies during the 1980s and 1990s, scholarly interest in archival collections grew significantly.[1] Pivoting from a focus on the aesthetics of the film or televisual text, academics in media departments increasingly turned to archival-based inquiry and, concomitantly, cultural theory as a method to help explain the inevitable experience of evidentiary absences.

The poststructuralist pivot in academic scholarship has created some unanticipated challenges for scholars and archivists alike. Increasingly in the humanities, the term "archive" has become, as Professor Michelle Caswell notes, "a Foucauldian or Derridean metaphor, an idea, rather than a material reality."[2] Academics, and indeed the general public, often conflate the notion of an archive with underlying assumptions related to power, privilege, and political intention. In October 2021 alone there were 2.6 million mentions of "the archive" in global social media, many mentions of which elide the pragmatic, slow-paced reality of preservation with abstract notions of power.

A quick glance at recent scholarly conferences and journal CFPs helps illustrate the trend as well: the University of London's Anarchival Materiality in Film Archives conference (2022); "Exploring the Digital (Im)materiality of the Moving Image Archive," *Frames Cinema Journal* 19 (2021); or the Orphans Film Symposium's 2022 theme, "Counter-Archives." In each, "the archive" offers a powerful strawman at which scholarly voices can voice frustration, and passionately argue to "unpack" and dismantle.

During this same period, academics began moving from a largely user and/or advisory role to more central, leadership positions in archival organizations such as the Association of Moving Image Archivists and, in the United States, the Library of Congress's National Film Preservation Board and National Recording Preservation Board. This trend proved logical as the key educational programs devoted to training moving image preservationists emerged first from humanities-oriented programs instead of traditional library science or archival studies schools.

The increased hybridization of these professions, of which I represent both sides, has allowed for great opportunities as well as challenges. Increased attention to preservation practice through academic discussions offers a dynamic and appropriate space for intellectual debate over the history and role of archives in society. Archivists and academics both have undeniably benefited from these conversations. At the same time, however, increased (and perchance over-) use of the term "the archive" in a largely theoretical sense by media scholars has created a tension, even if unintentionally, with practitioners. The true meaning of an archive has largely been diluted, resulting in the term being employed to describe a selected group of artifacts or texts under study.

During COVID, archive-related social media spawned frustrated posts about this disconnect (e.g., "The CDC recommends using the word 'archive' to refer to any loosely defined corpus of things"), somewhat ironically before the U.S. National Archives emerged in its conflict with the nation's executive branch over highly classified documents.[3] Indeed, the discussion of the standoff between the National Archives and the Trump administration brought much-needed attention to not just the stakes for government collections but the work of federal archivists themselves, often seen as the mere conduit or facilitator of the important work that is produced by researchers.

The stakes, like most academic stakes, appear small but can take outsized import. What kinds of jobs are available to graduates of educational programs, or how are funds from national endowments and initiatives being allocated? Who gets a seat around the table when priorities are being discussed and headlines being pitched? Despite the veneer of professionalism, morale and the emotional aspects of archival labor can appear at odds with academic colleagues especially when the amount of funding for historical preservation and research remains limited and stagnant. Sadly, these tensions can only prove detrimental to television preservation writ large, unless we proactively address them. As one practitioner noted about the debut of Netflix's *Archive 81* (2021), a series featuring a media archivist, amusedly tweeted about the program: "A historian [will get] all the credit, no doubt."[4]

Oddly, the representation of film and video archivists in popular media appears to be on the rise and, incidentally, helps illustrate long-standing frustrations. In the pilot of *Archive 81*, the media archivist is tasked with significant work to resurrect obsolete video formats; his work tedious, chemically laden (where is smell-o-vision when we need it most?) and requiring a significant montage to make it appear engaging. Most shows refer to media archivists figuratively and literally as basement dwellers. Peacock's *Poker Face* (2023) featured Luis Guzmán's studio archivist character being told to "get back in the f'ing basement" while in *Slow Horses* (2022) Gary Oldman evocatively described the basement-located records department and archives as "where all hope goes to die."

For the purposes of this anthology, however, HBO's *Hacks* (2022) appears to have the most illustrative nod to how broadcasting collections, particularly local affiliate content, are housed, collected, and processed—and by whom. A disgraced young comedy writer assists an aging comedian and is tasked with "archiving" the star's materials for an upcoming anniversary show. When she demurs, rolling eyes at the project, she states that she "just doesn't love running tech in the basement all day." She descends into said basement encountering varying video formats, papers, playback machines (notably not dusty and absurdly functional), boxes and boxes of documents, and just plain junk everywhere. I can assure you that this depiction best illustrates the real provenance of TAMI's broadcasting collections. They remain not because they were housed in "the archive" but by having been salvaged by stakeholders' interest and legacy, the product (and detritus) of a life and profession lived in a very real, material sense.

American television collections remain scattered across a vast terrain of historical societies, regional libraries, university special collections, corporate closets, and, yes, domestic basements. The obstacles to a united, proactive, and national effort remain as potent as they were in the 1970s when this crisis first was noted by media librarians and archivists. Is branding television "archivable" helpful in any concrete way to making these materials more accessible and relevant to contemporary society? Scholars and media archivists must work more effectively together to harness the public eye in an effort to champion the need to collect and preserve these materials before it is too late. The stakeholders well represented in this anthology, our colleagues, and our partners in the ever-changing televisual landscape must get out of the comfort zone of the academy to advocate, loudly, for attention.[5]

When I feel most despondent, however, I do wonder if, should this work prove too difficult, the lack of serious funding and proactive, organized collecting might prove a blessing: that television can continue to remain wild and unarchived. Television might just escape that discursive space where the archived becomes more exalted, possessing more import than what remains noncollected and nonprioritized; television can continue to be messy historical ephemera vs. staid preserved programming. As University of Wisconsin–Madison assistant professor Marius Kothor has noted: "The idea of 'the archive' is so seductive but it's an illusion. History is everywhere."[6]

CAROLINE FRICK

NOTES

1. See, for example, the work of Tino Balio, David Bordwell, Kathryn Fuller-Seeley, David Gomery, Lea Jacobs, Richard Maltby, Thomas Schatz, Janet Staiger, and the Orphans Film Symposium, among others.
2. Michelle Caswell, *Urgent Archives: Enacting Liberatory Memory Work* (New York: Routledge, 2021), 15.
3. Rachel Corbwomyn (@rachelcorbman), "The CDC recommends using the word 'archive' to refer to any loosely defined corpus of things," Twitter, December 29, 2021, 5:24 a.m., https://twitter.com/rachelcorbman/status/1476182441857536000?s=20.
4. Megan McShea (@meganmcshea), "and a historian gets all the credit, no doubt," Twitter, December 27, 2021, 7:43 a.m., https://twitter.com/meganmcshea/status/1475492567840083972?s=20.
5. Please join the efforts of the Association of Moving Image Archivists' Local Television Preservation Task Force: www.thechannelusproject.com.
6. Marius Kothor (@MariusKothor), "I use [*sic*] to spend so much time fretting about 'archival silences' but it was only when I realized that standard archives could never capture the dynamic lives of my actors that my work really began. The idea of 'the archive' is so seductive but it's an illusion. History is everywhere," Twitter, September 25, 2021, 5:47 a.m., https://twitter.com/MariusKothor/status/1441746173728108547?s=20.

ACKNOWLEDGMENTS

From Lauren: The labor to develop an edited collection is massive--and well worth it. I am grateful to Ethan Thompson for recognizing how my research would fit within the newly minted Peabody Series in Media History that he and Jeffery Jones founded. We talked out ideas for a book and thank goodness I opted for an anthology over a solo work. This collection was an opportunity to meet others with similar obsessions about archiving media. Crucially, to be successful, I needed a collaborator and knew the perfect person: Elizabeth Peterson, librarian extraordinaire and extraordinary friend. The cliché "this could not have happened without you" is a fact. Elizabeth has always been a part of my research interest in archives. My time as a graduate student at the University of Oregon was enriched with her encouragement and support. Conferences like AMIA, IAMHIST, and SCMS afforded us opportunities to see each other and kept our interests in archives alive. Each time I thought I was done with my projects on the history of archiving television, she persuaded me to continue. And I thankfully persuaded her to join this venture. Elizabeth--you saved my sanity many times over the years and steered our collaborative energies toward the completion of this project.

The majority of my research and conceptual development occurred as a doctoral student at the University of Oregon. For the sake of brevity, I'll point to the acknowledgments in my dissertation, with a shout-out to two librarians at Oregon State University, Tiah Edmunson-Morton and Larry Landis, who facilitated my entry point into the study of archives and the profession. Thank you to Cynthia Meyers for her support through various stages of my research and this book over the years. At my institution, Illinois State University, I thank my colleagues for their encouragement and the School of Communication for its support. I am grateful to Dr. Joe Blaney for taking me seriously when I casually joked about needing an accountability structure to support time dedicated to scholarship. The monthly writing days at the Milner Library and lakeside retreats were crucial in preparing and completing this book. Thank you to the Office of Sponsored Research and the College of Arts and Sciences for their book subvention grant as well as the dedicated resources they offered to those writing days.

Finally, thank you to my friends and family, for many, many, many moments of encouragement.

From Elizabeth: I am grateful to Lauren Bratslavsky for inviting me to work on this project. This collaboration started many years ago with long, animated conversations in the hallways and stairwells of the Knight Library as we discovered our mutual enthusiasm for archival media. It has been a delight to bring this collection to fruition with you. Thank you to Dr. Gabriele Hayden, head of Data Services in the University of Oregon Libraries, for her help and insights into citation analysis tools and strategies. I also acknowledge the University of Oregon Libraries for providing computational and institutional resources that enabled me to work on the book. Thanks to Lance Troxel for his ongoing and unflagging support.

On behalf of both of us, we thank the contributors for your expertise and experiences. This anthology exists thanks to your hard work and passions long before we sent out the call for chapters. The press is run by outstanding individuals, and it is an honor to work with you all. The importance of a university press cannot be overstated. The executive editor, Mick Gusinde-Duffy, gave us guidance and support throughout each stage, as did Ethan Thompson, who initiated this book as the coeditor of the series. Thank you also to the production editor, Jon Davies, and those who worked to coordinate the rounds of editing, contracts, marketing, and production.

# THE ARCHIVABILITY
OF TELEVISION

LAUREN BRATSLAVSKY

INTRODUCTION

I think of researching in an archive, especially researching something within the orbit of television, as fluctuating between two kinds of moments. There's the exhilaration of the hunt, acting on a hunch that somewhere there exists evidence of a program just as it aired, or a decision made by a writer or network executive, or the toils of an engineer or a regulator, or the reactions of a fan or censor—whatever it might be to illuminate an area of inquiry. Whether the evidence is in the form of carbon copy paper or a newly digitized tape, regardless of being intentionally or serendipitously located, there's a sense of excitement but also relief and maybe shock that such a record exists. Conversely, there's an exhaustion from the hunt, defeated that the desired evidence is not in the collection, not in this archive, or likely in any archive, let alone saved beyond the span of its use.

While such feelings are by no means unique to researching television history, these kinds of moments are cogent reminders about some of the thorniness of preserving television. The thrill of finding a document or program from the past within an archive, oftentimes at university, government, or nonprofit institutions, can be met with reverence toward all sorts of forces that made that archival encounter possible. From the fact that someone at some point thought to save that piece of evidence to the labor of those who archive and facilitate access—in addition to the obvious limitations of the technologies to transmit, record, and store television content—means that there were and are a variety of haphazard and formal structures capable of transforming what was once ephemeral and behind-the-scenes into material for the purposes of history.

What do we know about how television moved from ephemeral broadcasts, and mounds of paperwork documenting bureaucratic and creative processes, to become historical material housed in archives? Who made and continues to make decisions about the contents of an archive? What policies, structures, and professional practices govern decision-making with acquisitions and preservation projects? The more we know about the archival process, the better equipped we are as researchers to face the contents held in archives. With contextual knowledge about archives and the collections housed within them, we enhance our position to analytically understand why we have access to some materials and not others. Overall, how might scholars, archivists, librarians, media professionals, and others work together in order to continue to preserve and understand television and its relationship to culture and society?

The Archivability of Television critically engages and evaluates the archives and archival processes that collect, order, and preserve elements of television as historically, culturally, socially, politically, and economically significant material. The overarching intent of this anthology is to interrogate where television as historical material "lives." To do so, we bring together scholarship by academics, archivists, and practitioners to reflect on the processes and places that confer television with historical value.

ARCHIVABILITY: TELEVISION AS PRODUCTS AND PROCESSES THAT *COULD* BE ARCHIVED

Television's specificity in archival spaces—the challenges of its physical media, its distinctions from other media and yet its interrelations with other media, its history of marginalization as compared to other media and civic pursuits, among other concerns—can contribute more broadly to theories, histories, and practices of archiving. By focusing attention on the theories and questions about the archives, this anthology seeks to gain insights into such enduring media studies issues as the specificities of the medium, the relations between technology and culture, the political economy of the cultural industries, and the minutiae of television's "place" in society. After all, for television to enter archival spaces, people had to recognize reasons to pursue preservation projects, namely, to serve historiographic needs. More than recording events, programs and broadcast flows were and continue to be imprinted with the political overtones, economic structures, social tensions, and cultural milieu of a particular moment.[1]

These points of focus frame how we define and explore television's archivability, meaning the conceptual and pragmatic frameworks that facilitated television's direct and indirect paths into archival spaces. The term "archivability" tends to be used in a limited, technical sense about the storage of data: the capacity for a physical medium to be preserved to ensure longevity of the content stored on the medium. Examples of this include reports by the Ampex Corporation detailing magnetic tape as a recording medium, or the challenges posed by digital programming structures to preserve the completeness of digital content, such as a website.[2] This technical sense already lends itself well to questions about how television enters archival spaces and many of the challenges for the management and preservation of audiovisual materials in archives. The technological ability to record, preserve, maintain, and re-view television as it aired is essential in the *possibility* of developing archival holdings of recorded television.

There are two shortcomings, though, to focusing on the technological aspects. First, the technology is not so much a cause or effect for television's archivability; it is part of the structural conditions of television. While technologies of television transmission and reception preceded the development of content, as Raymond Williams argues, social and institutional processes drove the technological aspects of television. Technology is important, yet still superficial in light of the "restraining complex of financial institutions, of cultural expectations and of specific technical developments."[3] Williams's work defines television as a whole system, and thus television includes records and meaning generated at all points: from creation to broadcast to preservation and reuse. The archivability of television as a question of a physical medium holding content is only a fraction of what constitutes as television. When we limit discussion of television's archivability to the technology—as urgent and challenging as it is—we risk losing sight of the totality of television, and how the variety of records in all formats that constitute "television" make their way into archives. The specific questions about television's archivability also point to broader questions about how any kinds of materials move from initial uses and purposes to archival and historical uses.

In this sense, the term "archivability" draws inspiration from philosophical and critical takes about the archive. For instance, the political theorist Achille Mbembe writes, "In any given cultural system, only some documents fulfill the criteria of 'archivability.'"[4] While he was referring mostly to those documents made by the state, then selected and ordered for narrow uses, we can extrapolate broader questions about the rules and values of a cultural system. There must be some guiding forces for television to enter into archival spaces, especially formal institutional spaces. These spaces include university special collections, historical societies, cultural institutions, and national institutions. Each of these institutional spaces is part of and shapes cultural systems, specifically in relation to trends in historiographies, valuations of popular culture, and articulations of what constitutes evidence for knowledge production.

The archivability of television—and which parts of television—are undoubtedly tied to the physicality of the television product. Programs, or *products* of television, are what comes to mind for most people when considering how archives and archive-adjacent spaces, whether publicly accessible conventional archival institutions (e.g., university special collections) or digital spaces (e.g., streaming services or YouTube), preserve and make available television programming. Indeed, the archival, academic, and popular imagination often notes television's archival presence and absence simply in terms of the broadcasted shows—what was *on*, followed by the question, what can we still watch? For instance, there is an extensive Wikipedia entry devoted to lost television programs, and a separate entry focused solely on *Doctor Who*, which has a legacy of notorious loss and then recovery efforts by fans and the BBC.[5]

The products include the physicality of the programs and other content like advertising and interstitials, be it analog (e.g., film, tape) or digital preservation. To that we may add those more existential questions about the television text—how to preserve television flow, like the broadcast schedule. Another way to situate the television products for the archive is to consider the paper medium proxy for the audiovisual broadcast or recording: scripts. These have been and continue to be primary alternatives that archivists and scholars seek out when the ephemeral broadcast record, at worst, does not exist, or at best, is not readily accessible for reasons such as playback issues or an inability to physically travel to securely view the program. Additionally, in compiling those lists of missing or lost broadcasts, there is also a reliance on another paper medium—catalogs and TV listings. These traces point to the empty spaces in the television product records. But the questions of locating the products are far from enough to explore the criteria and the challenges for television to reach the status as not only possible to archive but worthy of being archived.

Less present in the popular imagination, and to a degree, the academic, are lamentations for all of the paper records surrounding television. From writers' notebooks to shooting scripts to memos to correspondence to budgets to internal reports and more, there are potential troves of archival evidence that document various aspects of television leading up to and extending beyond the programs. Such documentation reveals not only information about the production and circulation of television but also the ways in which television overlaps with institutions (e.g., politics, regulation, education, etc.), social systems, and culture. If the programs are the products, then these material traces represent television as *processes*, meaning the documentation about dimensions of industries, regulations, technologies, social roles, and creative endeavors. The paper records, what we conventionally think of as the contents of archival manuscript collections such as correspondence, memos, notebooks, ephemera, and so on, reflect television as processes. Viewed holistically, "television archives" consist of a myriad of formats and content that include programs as merely one component.

This collection offers various contextual explorations about some of the ways television entered archives and the professional, scholarly, and industrial practices to continue preservation efforts. Those of us who are television and media scholars tend to study the program, how programs were made, how individuals contributed their creative labor, or how audiences made meanings from shows—but we may take for granted the existence (or lack) of television materials and perhaps even the notion that we can use television as historical evidence. Studying how television entered archival spaces (e.g., traditional archives, libraries, museums, etc.) aids in furthering our understanding of how television came to be artifacts for studying a wide range of subjects, such as issues of representation, political trends, and so on. It is not uncommon for television to show up in historical and analytical projects, where television offers persuasive evidence about a time and place, such as postwar family roles or consumer society, to name a couple of examples.[6] Examining contemporary challenges about the preservation of television and, moreover, the findability and accessibility of television collections provides insights about a range of pragmatic and critical issues such as how to distribute scarce resources for preservation projects or how the contents of an archive are tied to the politics of memory and heritage. Overall, television's location in archives and the construction of various archives' specializations that relate to television (directly or indirectly) serve as indicators of television's worth as historical evidence, cultural legitimacy, and academic study.

Television's archival presence—and which aspects of television are present in archives—point to the ways in which archivists, academics, and those associated with the television industry have marked television as historical and cultural material. To draw on the work of Jeremy Packer in defining what an archive is for media history, who were the determinators (e.g., archivists, academics, industry professionals) to conceptualize television as archivable?[7] What factors enabled television to be archived, or hindered it? And which aspects of television more readily entered archival spaces over others? In a more contemporary string of questions, what choices and priorities are determinators making in how they manage long-dormant collections as well as new collections by making these more accessible—and legible—in the digital era?

A major component in the linkage between the logistics and logics of the archive and media studies scholarship is a groundwork of understanding the theories and practices of the archival profession. Likewise, there are some points of knowledge that media scholars take for granted pertaining to the complex dynamics of television. This anthology in no way purports to be both a comprehensive account of archival theory and a thorough overview of television studies. Still, the bulk of this introduction chapter offers a selective account of archival theory, which aids in grounding knowledge about the basics of the archival profession. This frames an overarching argument of the anthology about television's archivability from both the conceptual perspective—why would television belong in an archive?—and the physical considerations—how can television be housed in an archive? These accounts about archival theory, the archival collection of materials related to popular culture, and the specific challenges of television as an object for the archive comprise the next section.

ARCHIVES, POPULAR CULTURE IN ARCHIVES, AND TELEVISION IN PARTICULAR

Illuminating archival process supports understanding about how the archive's contents relate to knowledge production and the histories we write. We can engage with the archive on various levels. Archives are physical places, with real material considerations such as the allocation of money, labor, and storage. There is room for abstract understandings about the archive, specifically the spatial boundary of knowledge and who has the power to shape how users interact with the archive.[8] Engaging with the archive on a conceptual level invites a myriad of notions about history, power, and knowledge. Who has the power to define the contours of knowledge? How are materials selected and ordered? Which materials, or rather, which individuals, professions (such as politicians and businessmen), social realms, and aspects of culture do archivists privilege for selection? The archive, then, is not just a physical place but also a space that demonstrates a confluence of professionalized archival practice as well as the academic priorities that define the scope of materials counting as historical evidence.

This line of thinking represents a recent trend in taking a more critical, reflexive view of the archive. I begin with some foundational principles to define archives as the profession developed in the early twentieth century in order to situate the *archival turn*—meaning the ways in which literary and cultural scholars, social scientists, historians, and those in the library sciences focus on questions about the construction of archives, power, and impact on historiographies. To define archives by drawing on literature from the library sciences and archival theory is to ground archives as physical places with professionalized practice. This is followed by a brief discussion of how scholars have critically interrogated "the archive," especially those from within the archivist community where there are lively reactions to the archival turn. Depending on how one views what an archive *is* and its purpose will guide how an archive is managed. But more specifically for the purposes of this project about archiving television, the concept guides the sorts of records that are collected and the role of the archivist.

LEGACIES OF PROFESSIONALIZING THE ARCHIVIST AND THE ARCHIVE

The profession of the archivist and the institutional space known as the "archive" are fairly modern inventions. The philosophies, and thus practices, that guide archival procedure tend to be associated with two men who influenced the development of the profession in the early twentieth century. Chief among early archivists to consider the professionalization of the archivist and the institutionalization of the archive are Hilary Jenkinson and T. R. Schellenberg. Both drew on broader prevailing principles of the early twentieth century: applying scientific methods and reasoned objectivity to what archives are and what archivists do. Both concerned themselves with the development of an emerging profession and treated archives as institutions that hold records, but they differ on the underlying concept of the archive and the subsequent discussion about the function of an archive and the value of its records.

Jenkinson, representing the British tradition, defines archives as housing and managing records of "official transaction and ... preserved for official reference."[9] The archive is a repository, the records are materials created and used for government and legal purposes, and the archivist is the custodian, the keeper of records, and not responsible for selecting records beyond the needs of the institution.[10] Jenkinson spoke of archives (and of course, the archivist) as possessing the quality of impartiality, that the intentions of those who created the documents are completely separate from the archive itself, given that the archive is a neutral place entrusted with ensuring the authenticity and veracity of the original materials in their original order.[11] He initially meant for the archive to be a physical place that is internally oriented, meaning that the archive fulfills administrative, legal, and fiscal functions for a single organization, such as a corporation or a governmental institution. Still, the archive could also still be an externally oriented institution, such as a state's public archive, but nevertheless a place to primarily serve administrative needs while being publicly available.[12]

Schellenberg, an American historian, diverged from Jenkinson and influenced an alternate trajectory for the concept of the archive and thus the practice of the archivist, especially how archivists appraise value. He writes that "materials must be preserved for reasons other than those for which they were created or accumulated. These reasons may be both official and cultural ones." As records, the documents serve "official" functions or fulfill a specific purpose, such as providing *evidence* of these institutions' functions, purposes, policies, structures, legal obligations (and protections), and so on. As archives, the documents take on another, albeit secondary, value, serving for "purposes other than those for which they were produced or accumulated," such as for research.[13] Whereas Jenkinson saw little need to address value outside of official purposes, Schellenberg argued for the recognition of social and/or cultural purposes of records in addition to the evidentiary value of official transactions and administration. In this sense, "archival" can be "used generically to encompass manuscripts and manuscript collections as well as public and corporate records."[14] Archives could be understood as more externally oriented as places that accumulate and manage records from various organizations and individuals for the purposes of history, argued Schellenberg in *The Management of Archives*.

This contrast is significant because of the enduring legacy that each person had on how the theory of "the archive" and what constitutes records undergirds the institutional structure of an archive and, crucially, the methods of acquiring and ordering the contents of an archive.

In the discipline of archival sciences, one distinct way to frame these two legacies is to label Jenkinson's theories as influential on the *recordkeeping paradigm* and Schellenberg's writings as influential on the *archival paradigm*. The theoretical, and thus methodological, framework for the former claims impartiality and prioritizes the preservation of institutional transactions in the service of the institution, such as government or a corporation, while the latter recognizes archives as cultural and social resources containing vast evidence (or records) of human *and* institutional activity.[15] In the recordkeeping paradigm, the archive functions as an accountability mechanism and as repository for the institution, especially government. The archival paradigm is more aptly labeled as the historical manuscripts tradition given Schellenberg's influence in the development of archives in the United States through support of building separate institutions specifically for the collection and preservation of records for their historical value, or what he called secondary evidentiary value. The lack of centralized governmental archives (such as in England and France) and a flurry of local and state institutions committed to preserving records as historical milestones "set the precedent that in the United Sates archival agencies were largely about documenting history rather than documenting government's administrative actions."[16]

Such a contrast in archival traditions provides a glimpse into the questions about television and archives. The early establishment of the BBC's internal recordkeeping practices is a testament to Jenkinson's influence in modern records management as originating from *within* the institution and *for* the institution's administration and national functions. In contrast, there was no nationalized broadcasting system in the United States and no centralized institution for recordkeeping. We can see the influence of both Jenkinson and Schellenberg in the example of NBC's archive. NBC adhered to a records management system of a modern corporation to control its internally oriented archive to preserve only those records vital to the operation of the corporation without regard to any larger historical purpose. While a corporate archive might acknowledge the historical value of their records, that is not their priority. However, NBC came to see the broader value of their records in the 1950s when the State Historical Society of Wisconsin approached NBC to deposit their records as part of an effort to collect documents of modern businesses. NBC sent their noncurrent and soon-to-be-destroyed files to the society's archive. By selecting and acquiring NBC's institutional records, the society conferred new status on them as records with long-term historical and cultural value. Documents that were once part of NBC's bureaucratic structure are now accessible as historical evidence.[17]

These classic texts such as Jenkinson's and Schellenberg's influential writings "have shaped archival practice[,] but the evolution of communication technology and its impact on records and record-keeping, changing concepts of the nature and uses of memory, and shifting notions of authority, evidence, and truth severely undermine the ongoing relevance of these manuals."[18] This "old" paradigm, meaning the archival theories and practices of the mid-twentieth century and earlier for both records or historical manuscripts, taught a fairly narrow conception of what constitutes evidence and the value of said evidence. These teachings and practices involved conceptions of documents as static and as passive products of a particular time and place. The view held that archives are just places that manage and collect documents, caring for documents with a logical positivism that frames archivists as objective and documents as neutral. As the prominent archivist, Terry Cook, explains the transition: "Archival theoretical discourse is shifting from product to process, from structure to function, from archives to archiving, from the record to the recoding context, from the 'natural' residue or passive by-product of administrative activity to the consciously constructed and actively mediated 'archivalisation' of social memory."[19] The new paradigm, influenced by the postmodern milieu that questions meaning, facts, authority, and structures, suggests a reconceptualization of the archive and what it holds. Archives are dynamic environments or institutions. People make decisions and judgments as active agents in compiling records that help shape memory.

This line of thinking parallels academic trends across disciplines to interrogate the archive. Outside of the archivist profession, scholars explored questions about the archive. Notably, Foucault wrote about the archive as a mechanism to define boundaries of what can be known and should be known.[20] Conferences and collections about "the archive" peaked in the 1990s and early 2000s following Jacques Derrida's *Archive Fever*, which is cited as one of the key influences in reconceptualizing the archive by specifically calling attention to how the structure and origin of an archive shapes what *is* and *can be* archived, thus constructing history.[21] Derrida plays with the word "archive," noting the etymological roots of *arche* as "beginning" as a means to the formation of the archive as literally formative in building a historical memory, identity, rules, knowledge, and so on. A facet of tracing the formation and management of the archive is to interrogate how those who decide on the archive's contents and its ordering (as in, how records are categorized, privileged, and presented) hold the power of interpretation and can draw the boundaries on knowledge production.[22] Archives are figured—and refigured—in that forces of all kinds (e.g., political, economic, social, cultural), people, technologies, and more leave imprints on how archives are developed, who is in control, and what the archives contain.[23]

In reaction to the archival turn, or the "interdisciplinary wave" to research archives and knowledge production, the archivist R. C. Head summarizes how archives are "fascinating objects of study themselves, whose history and development speak to themes including memory, the exercise of power through knowledge, and the emergence of a distinctive, archivally based historiography."[24] However, what some scholars leave out of their critical inquiries about archives are the primary agents of these spaces: the archivists. The archive is a convenient frame for reflecting on the practice of writing history and the role of societal remembering, and in doing so, the archive is reduced as a showcase for semiotic musings about meaning while obviating the archivist's decisions, labor, and thoughts.[25]

WHAT IS EVIDENCE? VALUING POPULAR CULTURE AND TV IN ARCHIVES AND RECORDKEEPING

These debates and shifts inside and outside the archival profession are significant to track in the context of the archivability of television because much of the early and paradigmatic theories and practices of archives resulted in ignoring television in particular, and the materials of popular culture more broadly. The question of value—as in value for knowledge production—is among the core issues limiting popular culture and/or television in archival settings. Archival practice developed with a bias toward the medium of paper, and moreover, toward the records produced by institutions and prominent figures. Indeed, it is a profession born out of the need to manage documents in eras of textuality and literacy.[26] Additionally, the archival practice of acquiring, selecting, and ordering such material developed in tandem to the preferred knowledge structures. For example, if the dominant trends in historiography point toward the "great man" narratives or focus on histories of events that happened more than a century ago, then the structures and practices that guide archivists and archival institutions have less conceptual room or precedent to collect manuscript records from lesser-known people or from more recent events. For an archive to collect recent newspapers could be an easy fit given that (1) this form of mass media was already in a familiar paper-based format, and (2) this category of records was normatively known as first drafts of history. The more ephemeral and consumerist magazines of a time, or niche ethnic newspapers, or the records of a small-town newspaper would have been seen as less vital for collection on the grounds of disposability or lack of notoriety. Or in other words, such materials did not serve prevailing knowledge structures. On a more meta level, the archivist profession crystallized in an era of applying the objective, positivistic sciences to human endeavors, as illustrated by the discussion about Jenkinson's influence on the profession. Archivists ought to operate as value-neutral *facilitators* of how and why creators need to preserve their records.

The people guided by the old paradigms held limited conceptions of how television and modern popular culture could constitute valuable evidence. The archival profession did not naturally accept materials associated with popular culture or commercial culture as historical evidence. Archives and libraries sporadically collected the documents of popular culture, especially given that the academic study of popular culture was barely valid around the 1970s.[27] Archives dedicated to the collection and preservation of historical material rely on frameworks regarding what constitutes historical evidence: "If the archive cannot or does not accommodate a particular kind of information or mode of scholarship, then it is effectively excluded from the historical record."[28] If an archivist does not consider the merits of popular culture materials, such as the development and popularity of a television program, such material may not readily be available in a publicly accessible archive. Yet scholarly trends, institutional practices, and professional training change and grow, therefore precipitating shifts in the kinds of material actively collected.[29]

Histories of film archives are instructive, especially when considering discursive constructions of film as both mass, popular culture (e.g., nickelodeon theaters, Hollywood blockbusters, etc.) and art or high culture. Film archives did not begin in the conventional archive space led by people trained to handle and evaluate paper materials. It is noteworthy to consider that the professional knowledge to care for and preserve the film medium began to codify around the 1970s, after decades of several major periods in cinema's popularity and significance since the mass introduction of film in the 1890s.[30] The Museum of Modern Art's Film Library, established in 1934, was among the first dedicated film archives, along with similar art-related film libraries in Europe. Thus the film archive originated in a space devoted to the treatment of objects, alongside paper material documenting the lives of the creators and the creation of objects. As Haidee Wasson details, collecting film in an art museum meant not only treating film as creative and artistic objects but also recovering "a history that had been lost" by engaging in interpretation and preservation activities to cultivate senses of cinema's history alongside American history.[31] Caroline Frick argues that efforts to archive film required transformative frameworks to consider film along interrelated lines of historical evidence, artistic merit, and contributions to sense of national identity and heritage.[32] As the academic study of film codified, "historically specific notions of an academic field ('film as art') . . . [have] spilled over into archival preservation policy," which William Uricchio examines in order to critique absences in the archive.[33] The mix of acquisition, preservation, and interpretation practices mutually reinforced the conceptual mechanisms to value film for the archive, in close tandem with the legitimation of film studies and the professionalization of the *film* archivist.

Archivist (and historian) interest in popular culture and media-related material started to gain traction in the later decades of the twentieth century, as some academic disciplines increasingly sought out histories from the bottom up—histories greatly enriched by media and popular culture—and began to critique how archives skew toward the collection of records of those who hold disproportionate power.[34] Archivists needed to deal with what Hans Booms called "the preliminary question: what constitutes the documentary heritage of today and how does a documentary heritage come into being?"[35] From there it follows that the archivist considers the complexities of how to appraise the value of *all* material that contributes to the totality of records worth saving as cultural and political representations of a society, while balancing the economics of storing so much data.

The various paper records and other formats of media and popular culture could have evidentiary, informational, and enduring value for knowledge production. In the language of the archivist, this is about the appraisal of material: evidence of a record creator's purpose or structure, the informational value of the content within the records as unique and/or important, and the potential usefulness or significance for future generations as opposed to serving the record creator's needs.[36] Appraisals of popular culture records could not have happened without changes and shifts in both archival professions and academic pursuits. Some archivists challenged or broadened the appraisal criteria and collection development practices, in large part because it may have been impossible to ignore epistemological and ideological influences from critical theory and praxis in the academy. These shifts made by more activist-oriented and future-looking archivists, along with academic partners, meant greater embrace of collecting materials of popular, contemporary culture that had been largely ignored given a mix of dominant modes of doing history, archivist commitments to a sense of objectivity, and discursive constructs about popular culture as not compatible with preservation and serious study.

As such, some archivists more readily recognized the need to actively build collections that captured the present moment for future, unknown. For instance, the head of the State Historical Society of Wisconsin, an archival institution closely tied to the University of Wisconsin–Madison, explained in 1960 about integrating more mass media into archival collections: "It is not a traditional field of interest to the historian.... However, the historian of the future may be just as interested in the history of radio or of television ... and the respective impact of each on social, economic, and political life of this century."[37] Other institutions in the United States in the 1960s and 1970s actively developed archival holdings of popular culture materials, such as collecting popular music at Bowling Green State University and the eclectic entertainment holdings at the University of Wyoming's American Heritage Center.[38] However, the push to include more popular culture material still runs up against constraints that limit what comprises this documentary heritage. Hierarchies favoring the popular, the commercially successful, the "tasteful," and so on still played and continue to play a major role in the decisions as to which materials are appraised for selection into the archive and which holdings will be favored for preservation and accessibility projects. Even as television became represented within institutional holdings, certain genres and kinds of materials still remained outside of collecting. Elana Levine points to soap operas as "one of the clearest cases of this conventional archival neglect" given how little archivists and academics considered the long-denigrated genre as holding any sort of value or interest for contemporary and future researchers.[39]

Accounting for criteria of worthiness along axes of cultural relevance and historical worth are immensely powerful factors for television's archivability.[40] Yet what confounded archivists in the past and remains an enduring concern is the physical medium. Programs are television's most visible (meaning "salient," though pun intended) products. Thus, when we think of television and accessing its history, we tend to privilege the programs and search for the material record of ephemeral broadcasts. This merits a brief interlude about the physicality—or the lack thereof in the early years in particular—of television. For the sake of those readers who are encountering the basic technological questions about the television medium, the next section serves as a baseline introduction to the early broadcast technologies.

THE PHYSICAL MATERIALITY OF TELEVISION AND THE PRIORITIZATION OF THE VISUAL PRODUCT

The technology to transmit images and sound (and earlier, the radio technology to transmit sound) preceded the technology to record.[41] After all, television is a *broadcast* medium. In U.S. broadcast history, there were three main ways that a live program could be captured onto a physical recording medium and/or prerecorded prior to the digital era: 16mm kinescope film, 35mm film, and magnetic videotape. Early attempts to record live television used a process called kinescope recording. A 16mm film camera was placed near the viewing tube, called the kinescope. Quality was not as great as 35mm film, the Hollywood standard, but kinescope recordings (or kinescopes) got the job done if the goal was to record the content in the early to mid-1950s. In an era of live television, recordings were used largely for *retransmission* purposes, such as the transmission of a live East Coast broadcast to the West Coast. The kinescope recording also served as a relay function between stations lacking a cable connection as early as 1949. Occasionally, networks used kinescope recordings to screen programs for sponsors or for internal reference purposes.[42] Suffice to say, kinescopes served short-term commercial needs. Much more costly was the use of Hollywood-grade 35mm film. The possibility of future reruns and syndication offered high enough economic incentives to use the higher-quality film. Famously, Lucille Ball and her production studio, Desilu, filmed *I Love Lucy* with a commercial intent in mind, specifically syndication.[43] The earliest uses of magnetic tape in 1956 and onward were for time-shifting broadcasts, rather than as a mechanism of storing television programs for posterity. The technology to record "was seen as providing a clear and tangible benefit *right now*, not for the future."[44] In many cases, when the initial retransmission use was fulfilled, the recording medium was salvaged or reused. Thus, broadcasters were not concerned about long shelf life, and certainly not the long-term historical merit of one program or another. They were concerned about such issues as the durability to rerecord onto tape, and physically how much space film and tapes took in their storage rooms.

Even as industry practices to record television content on high-quality film increased and the technologies to prerecord or record live programs onto magnetic tape improved throughout the decades, preservation was hardly the primary goal for networks and production houses. Recorded programs could control costs, alleviate the problems of live production, improve quality, and ultimately boost profits. The industry viewed entertainment programming as ephemeral and not in anyone's interest to maintain preservation copies unless there were apparent commercial applications or legal reasons to maintain these records. News operations were an exception, though still limited to internal recordkeeping. The broadcast networks regularly started to save videotaped news broadcasts when it became cost-effective with the three-quarter-inch U-matic tape cassette in the 1970s. It was not until the technology was cheap that there was an incentive to save television's output. But as evidenced by the high-profile copyright litigation between CBS News and the Vanderbilt TV News Archive in the 1970s, networks held on to these recordings as corporate assets.[45]

The existence of the recorded product did not equal preservation. There were additional steps that needed to take place in order for the recorded programs to become archival, not least of all the need for someone to first save such recordings and then agree to donate or deposit them into publicly accessible archives. A 1971 survey of U.S. television libraries conducted by Ruth Schwartz, who headed UCLA's Television Library, found that about thirty institutions "were actively engaged in a television acquisition program" to support educational and scholarly goals. Most of the programs were procured by donation, purchase, local production, off-air recording, or copyright deposits, or as part of a larger collection. Very few of the institutions had consistent preservation policies, funding, and other material resources to manage these collections, and they struggled to secure resources given the status of television.[46]

By the 1990s it was no longer a question of television's value as historical and cultural material. Concerns about television in the archive shifted to the physical preservation of television's recorded output, balancing the needs to preserve old formats with the exponentially growing amount of television.[47] To address the increasing concern about television (read: the programs and even commercials, or more aptly, the broadcast flow) and its posterity for historical study, moving image archivists, academics, and others formed communities and organized conferences. The technologies of preservation and the inconsistencies of public as well as corporate archives to ensure the preservation of television's recorded output seemed to take center stage, overshadowing discussions about television's other material traces. This is best exemplified by the 1996 multistage study and hearings conducted under the direction of the Library of

Congress about television and video preservation. The testimonies, hearings, and eventual published report codified a history of television's inclusions in and exclusions from archival settings, focused almost exclusively on the audiovisual products. Story after story emphasized industry neglect, taping over programs, and outright destruction, such as the testimony by Edie Adams about how the networks dumped kinescopes of *The Ernie Kovacs Show* into the river. Technological limitations were certainly an obstacle to preservation, but more troubling was access. Television's past and present were increasingly preserved, but "retained in the custody of private corporations whose policies are subject to the ebb and flow of the marketplace."[48]

As more people working in academia, archives, and cultural institutions began to articulate the value in caring about television beyond the initial broadcast moment, the more attention was poured into articulating the challenges in collecting and preserving television's *products* because of the increasing recognition of a broadcast record's status in terms of content and physicality. The emphasis on the product homes in on the core tension, and a shortcoming, of this anthology. Despite the desire to interrogate the archivability of television in its entirety—as a holistic assemblage of audiovisual products and paper records documenting creative, industrial, national, and regulatory processes—the contributions remain skewed toward the preservation of the programs. This is a reminder of the great amount of precarity with the care of ephemeral and fragile visual products, alongside the evidentiary value of the product itself, which is arguably best ascertained by the researcher when being able to actually see the program for oneself.

SUMMARY OF CHAPTERS

The loosely defined categories of products and processes help demystify television as a homogenous entity and address dimensions of television's materiality. All the contributions engage with such materiality in order to interrogate the enduring social, cultural, political, and economic facets involved in the valuation of television as worthy of preservation and access for knowledge production. The concerns and approaches to addressing the precarity of television's products and processes as significant primary source material varies, as some authors write from positions as researchers, as practitioners working in archival spaces, or as both. As such, rather than organize this collection of essays along the lines of the researchers who hunt for and use archival collections and the archivists who build and preserve such material, the organization reflects unifying, predominant themes.

The collection brings together scholarship and personal experiences by academics, archivists, and others to reflect on the processes and places that confer television programs and related materials with value. To account for value is to broadly ask why someone at some point would devote time and effort to somehow ensuring that some portion of television resides in an archive. Value, though, as examined earlier, is oftentimes contingent on a shifting constellation of professional training, historiographic paradigms, the needs and foresight of creators, and the needs and imagination of users. Emerging from the following chapters is a conceptualization of building blocks to value television, particularly as distinct from its iterations of commercial value, and articulate historical, cultural, social, political, and other intangible values. The ways in which people and organizations attend to television-as-history can be roughly parsed into three segments: deciphering television's worthiness for preservation (and thus formulating which parts of television and for what purposes), how institutions legitimate and frame television's value, and the work of making primary sources more accessible and usable for knowledge projects.

The first section focuses on the archivability of television from the perspectives of needing to recognize, define, and argue for television as historical material worthy of preservation. The section begins with an examination of broadcasting's commercial structures as it relates to newsfilm, a type of broadcast content that one might expect to have been obvious for preservation from the start. Kate Cronin focuses on how the NBC and CBS film libraries operated in relationship to their respective network news departments, and how that relationship shaped the archival and historical value of early television newsfilm. The next chapter shifts to noncommercial television. Owen Gottlieb chronicles the struggles and eventual success of one producer to find a home for educational television. His chapter highlights how the precarity of television's past can be mitigated when people advocate for finding homes for distinct and comprehensive collections, and moreover, places where related sorts of archival material already live. Concluding this section is my research about the formation of the Museum of Broadcasting (now known as the Paley Center), which developed out of a multiyear study to first investigate the quantity and quality of television tapes and films found in academic and cultural institutions as well as corporate holdings in the United States, and then devise methods to ascertain historical value for the purposes of forming a new institution.

The second section features stories of how institutions, specifically archives associated with academic and government sites, shape and frame television *into* valued historical and cultural material. Ruta Abolins details the chronology of the University of Georgia's Peabody Collection and the Media Archives, thereby codifying a history of how various stakeholders built, maintained, and fought for this unique archive. Hannah Spaulding turns critical attention to regional collecting and analyzes how the organizing principles of a British regional archive articulate the value of regional television, particularly those programs that do not align with the criteria of the BBC's national collecting efforts. Walter Podrazik, drawing on his experiences in curating exhibits and participating in industry-archive outreach, addresses how archival institutions may invest in public-oriented activities as a means to showcase their assets. In other words, Podrazik demonstrates the ongoing value of creating retrospective and exhibition content with archival material in order to both highlight television's past and also publicize institutions' holdings. Lynne Carmichael draws on her career as the music coordinator for the Australian Broadcasting Corporation to discuss the challenges of archiving a specific genre of 1950s television broadcasts—musical performances. While focusing on a niche genre, her chapter illuminates the close ties of the policies of national broadcasting systems as well as national archives and how notions of identity and cultural hierarchies can motivate the preservation of television.

The third section features perspectives that ultimately address questions of access, interpretation, and building new knowledge. Eric Hoyt and Mary Huelsbeck, as director and assistant director of the Wisconsin Center for Theater and Film Research, with the collaboration of film archivist Amanda Smith and graduate students Maureen Mauk, Olivia Riley, Matt St. John, and Pauline Lampert, write about the work to revive television programs buried within the center's vast collection. The chapter details how obstacles of access, from locating materials, to the preservation work to access the programmatic content, to researching copyright, are well worth the effort to broaden scholarship, especially when developing publicly accessible exhibits. Hugo Ljungbäck likewise draws on his experience in which he saw an opportunity to establish a collection and faced the technological, financial, and conceptual obstacles that may resonate with others working in such spaces. His case study about campus television services illuminates many of the common challenges of television's archivability, observing that even within a "safe" institutional context of higher education, precarity and questions of value permeate the entire life cycle of the materials. Whereas the authors of these first two chapters in this final section share their experiences of methods to encourage the use of materials that already reside in the archive and demonstrate generative uses of such material, the authors of the two remaining chapters interrogate the use of television's archival records. Quinlan Miller takes a self-reflexive and critical look at the *unarchivable* by discussing the incompleteness of what seems like a complete and publicly accessible collection when posing questions about tagging, description, and thus interpretation. Elizabeth Peterson's bibliographic analysis of television historiography concludes the collection. She systematically examines a sample of recent television scholarship published in popular journals in order to analyze the prevalence of how researchers use television archives in their work, and which repositories are represented in these articles. The results suggest that even with an abundance of online finding aids and digital access points, television's archival records remain underutilized by television scholars.

Each author contributes to a larger picture about television's archivability by discussing details about when, how, and why archivists, creators, academics, and others working in archival contexts invested time, money, and substantial effort to deal with the vastness and varieties of television. Inherent throughout these chapters is the underlying assumption that television *is* worthy of preservation. Many of our contemporary questions are not focused on whether we ought to preserve television but rather how to continue preservation activities, broaden the scope of what is collected in formal and informal places, and encourage the use and interpretation of materials. Across institutions, there are common challenges around resources: whether we have people, equipment, money, storage, rights, and so on. These are the kinds of concerns dealing with what it will take to get a collection described and accessible, thereby discoverable and usable for scholars and others. After all, the stronger the descriptions of and access to what might be *possible* to find in archives, the stronger our chances of identifying potential linkages across collections and broadening our scope of primary sources. Missing from this anthology are the parallel (and intersecting) stories of how people outside of institutions devote their energies and resources to archiving television. As Elana Levine writes of her experiences researching soap operas, "fans and collectors are the most vital archivists of media that are more valued by audiences than by institutions; their passion and their generosity make research into such subjects possible," namely, subjects that are "marginalized cultural forms, whether marginalized by medium, by funding structure, by social positioning, or by cultural status."[49]

Relatedly, another persistent set of questions is how to decide what is worth saving, especially in tandem with the allocation of resources. This collection is not an attempt to set a tone for making such decisions of worthiness. However, by gathering past and contemporary stories of collecting, preserving, and accessing television's *past*, there are interventions about the archivability of television's *present*. What are the ways in which people are preserving recent television, including the much broader and generous identification of what counts as television (e.g., web series, disappearing videos made by people on social media that may be akin to how public access television served as a publicly accessible platform for anyone to "make" TV, etc.)? For example, many of us already experience the precarity of a program suddenly leaving a streaming platform, which magnifies long-standing tensions of television's commerciality (programs are corporate assets) as well as precarity of how we watch television and can (or cannot) "save" television for future viewings. Moreover, as we stress about the preservation of and access to television *products*, the gulf of documenting television's *processes* further widens. What are present-day strategies for acquiring manuscript collections? Are we to rely on trade press, social media, and perhaps even leaked documents, without the possibility of also diving into an author's or an executive's manuscript collection? Anecdotally, a cable television executive told me about an annual "document destruction day" to discard memos, pilot scripts, reports, and other kinds of documents that are the sorts of primary source gems located in those hunts through archives; the executive recalled how that was generally viewed as a gleeful event for them. The kinds of records found in the NBC collections at the University of Wisconsin may never happen again. But what can we all be doing—as researchers, archivists, curators, students, teachers, creators, and fans—to advocate for the collection and preservation of some slice of the present? Will our future archives be heavily skewed toward certain kinds of genres and documents? The records of television's first few decades are undoubtedly sparse and fragmented. The reasons, though, are tied not just to technological limitations but more so to conceptual reasons whereby people and institutions did not deem television as worthy of long-term historical uses. The same cannot be said of today. It is the goal of this anthology to continue to instigate and foster preservation efforts by way of learning from past examples and current experiences.

NOTES

1. Fay Schreibman, "A Succinct History of American Television Archives," *Film and History* 21, nos. 2–3 (1991): 89–95; Paddy Scannell, "Television and History: Questioning the Archive," *Communication Review* 13, no. 1 (2010): 37–51.
2. Neal Bertram, *Recording Media Archival Attributes (Magnetic): Final Technical Report, Covering the Period May 30, 1978–Nov. 30, 1979* (Ampex Corporation, 1979); Mat Kelly, Justin F. Brunelle, Michele C. Weigle, and Michael L. Nelson, "On the Change in Archivability of Websites over Time," in *International Conference on Theory and Practice of Digital Libraries*, ed. T. Aalberg, C. Pappatheodoru, M. Dobreva, G. Tsakonas, and C. J. Farrugia (Berlin: Springer, 2013), 35–47.
3. Raymond Williams, *Television: Technology and Cultural Form* (New York: Schocken, 1975), 31.
4. Achille Mbembe, "The Power of the Archive and Its Limits," in *Refiguring the Archive*, ed. Carolyn Hamilton, Verne Harris, Jane Taylor, Michele Pickover, Graeme Reid, and Razia Saleh (Dordrecht, Netherlands: Kluwer Academic Publishers, 2002), 19.
5. See "Lost Television Broadcast," Wikipedia, last modified July 20, 2024, https://en.wikipedia.org/wiki/Lost_television_broadcast; "*Doctor Who* Missing Episodes," Wikipedia, last modified July 21, 2024, https://en.wikipedia.org/wiki/Doctor_Who_missing_episodes.
6. For example, see Stephanie Coontz, *The Way We Never Were: American Families and the Nostalgia Trap* (New York: Basic Books, 2016); Lizbeth Cohen, *A Consumer's Republic: The Politics of Mass Consumption in Postwar America* (New York: Random House, 2003).
7. Jeremy Packer, "What Is an Archive?: An Apparatus Model for Communications and Media History," *Communication Review* 13, no. 1 (2010): 88–104.
8. Francis X. Blouin and William G. Rosenberg, "Archives in the Production of Knowledge: Introduction," in *Archives, Documentation, and Institutions of Social Memory: Essays from the Sawyer Seminar*, ed. Francis X. Blouin and William G. Rosenberg (Ann Arbor: University of Michigan Press, 2006).
9. Hilary Jenkinson, *A Manual of Archive Administration* (London: P. Lund, Humphries & Co., 1937), 4.
10. Frank Boles, *Selecting and Appraising Archives and Manuscripts* (Chicago: Society of American Archivists, 2005), 15.
11. Terry Eastwood, "Reconsidering Archival Classics: Jenkinson's Writings on Some Enduring Archival Themes," *American Archivist* 67, no. 1 (2004): 31.
12. Jenkinson, *Manual of Archive Administration*; Margaret Cross Norton, *Norton on Archives: The Writings of Margaret Cross Norton on Archival and Records Management* (Carbondale: Southern Illinois University Press, 1975).
13. T. R. Schellenberg, *The Management of Archives* (New York: Columbia University Press, 1965), 13, 16.
14. Richard C. Berner, *Archival Theory and Practice in the United States: A Historical Analysis* (Seattle: University of Washington Press, 1983), 5.
15. For discussion about the legacies of these archivists and the naming of these paradigms, see Mark Greene, "The Power of Meaning: The Archival Mission in the

Postmodern Age," *American Archivist* 65, no. 1 (January 1, 2002): 42–55; Norton, *Norton on Archives*; Luke J. Gilliland-Swetland, "The Provenance of a Profession: The Permanence of the Public Archives and Historical Manuscripts Traditions in American Archival History," *American Archivist* 54, no. 2 (1991): 160–75; Frank Boles and Mark Greene, "Et Tu Schellenberg? Thoughts on the Dagger of American Appraisal Theory," *American Archivist* 59, no. 3 (July 1, 1996): 298–310.

16. Boles, *Selecting and Appraising*, 16.
17. Lauren Bratslavsky, "The Archive and Disciplinary Formation: A Historical Moment in Defining Mass Communications," *American Journalism* 32, no. 2 (April 3, 2015): 116–37, https://doi.org/10.1080/08821127.2015.1032865.
18. Terry Cook and Joan M. Schwartz, "Archives, Records, and Power: From (Postmodern) Theory to (Archival) Performance," *Archival Science* 2, nos. 3–4 (2002): 3–4.
19. Terry Cook, "We Are What We Keep; We Keep What We Are: Archival Appraisal Past, Present and Future," *Journal of the Society of Archivists* 32, no. 2 (2011): 4.
20. Michel Foucault, *The Archaeology of Knowledge* (New York: Vintage, 1972), 128–29.
21. Louise Craven, "From the Archivist's Cardigan to the Very Dead Sheep: What Are Archives? What Are Archivists? What Do They Do?," in *What Are Archives? Cultural and Theoretical Perspectives: A Reader*, ed. Louise Craven (Aldershot, U.K.: Ashgate, 2008), 7–30; Marlene Manoff, "Theories of the Archive from Across the Disciplines," *Portal: Libraries and the Academy* 4, no. 1 (2004): 9–25.
22. Jacques Derrida, *Archive Fever: A Freudian Impression*, trans. Eric Prenowitz (Chicago: University of Chicago Press, 1996).
23. Antoinette M. Burton, *Archive Stories: Facts, Fictions, and the Writing of History* (Durham, N.C.: Duke University Press, 2005); Carolyn Hamilton, Verne Harris, and Graeme Reid, "Introduction," in Hamilton et al., *Refiguring the Archive*, 7–18.
24. R. C. Head, "Preface: Historical Research on Archives and Knowledge Cultures: An Interdisciplinary Wave," *Archival Science* 10, no. 3 (2010): 191–94.
25. Joel Wurl, "Reviews-Dust: The Archive and Cultural History," *American Archivist* 66, no. 2 (2003): 335; Mark A. Greene, "Archive Stories: Facts, Fictions, and the Writing of History (review)," *Biography* 30, no. 3 (2007): 397–99. Greene, the director of the University of Wyoming's American Heritage Center, critiques the tone of "exposing" the archive as "figured," which "almost completely ignore[s] the role—much less the thoughts and analyses—of archivists . . . and archivists have been wrestling with their own historicity for some time" (399).
26. Hugh Taylor, "Opening Address," in *Documents That Move and Speak: Audiovisual Archives in the New Information Age; Proceedings of a Symposium*, ed. Harold Naugler, National Archives of Canada, and International Council on Archives (Munich: K. G. Saur, 1992), 18–29.
27. Lucy Shelton Caswell, "Donors and the Acquisition of Popular Culture Materials," in *Popular Culture and Acquisitions*, ed. Allen W. Ellis (New York: Haworth,

1992), 13–22; Michael Schudson, "The New Validation of Popular Culture: Sense and Sentimentality in Academia," *Critical Studies in Mass Communication* 4, no. 1 (1987): 51–68.

28. Manoff, "Theories of the Archive."
29. For critical reflections about the development of archives and shift in archival practice, see Cook and Schwartz, "Archives, Records, and Power"; Gilliland-Swetland, "Provenance of a Profession"; Hugh A. Taylor, Terry Cook, and Gordon Dodds, *Imagining Archives: Essays and Reflections by Hugh A. Taylor* (Lanham, Md.: Society of American Archivists / Association of Canadian Archivists / Scarecrow Press, 2003).
30. Notable texts that helped establish moving image preservation as a specialized field are Ralph N. Sargent, *Preserving the Moving Image* (Washington, D.C.: Corporation for Public Broadcasting / National Endowment for the Arts, 1974) and Sam Kula, *The Archival Appraisal of Moving Images: A Ramp Study with Guidelines* (Paris: Unesco, 1983). Kula's book emerged out of an international effort for film preservation and the work of the International Federation of Film Archives formed in 1938, to share knowledge and develop professional standards.
31. Haidee Wasson, *Museum Movies: The Museum of Modern Art and the Birth of Art Cinema* (Berkeley: University of California Press, 2001), 29.
32. Caroline Frick, *Saving Cinema: The Politics of Preservation* (New York: Oxford University Press, 2010).
33. William Uricchio, "Archives and Absences," *Film History* 7, no. 3 (1995): 256–63.
34. Warren Susman, *Culture as History: The Transformation of American Society in the Twentieth Century* (New York: Pantheon, 1984).
35. Hans Booms, Hermina Joldersma, and Richard Klumpenhouwer, "Society and the Formation of a Documentary Heritage: Issues in the Appraisal of Archival Sources," *Archivaria* 1, no. 24 (January 1, 1987): 75–76.
36. See Schellenberg, *Management of Archives*; Boles, *Selecting and Appraising*; F. Gerald Ham, "The Archival Edge," *American Archivist* 38, no. 1 (1975): 5–13; Helen Willa Samuels, George Orwell, and Arthur C. Clarke, "Who Controls the Past," *American Archivist* 49, no. 2 (1986): 109–24.
37. Les Fishel, "Working Papers for a Conference on Mass Communications History," April 1960, 17, Office Files (unprocessed), Mass Communication History (Background), Wisconsin Center for Film and Theater Research, University of Wisconsin–Madison.
38. Bonna J. Boettcher and William L. Schurk, "From Games to Grunge: Popular Culture Research Collections at Bowling Green State University," *Notes* 54, no. 4 (1998): 849–59; D. Claudia Thompson and Shaun A. Hayes, *University of Wyoming American Heritage Center: Guide to Entertainment Industry Resources*, 2009, https://www.uwyo.edu/ahc/_files/collection_guides/ent-ind-guide-2009-ed_Jan_2017.pdf.
39. Elana Levine, "Alternate Archives in U.S. Daytime TV Soap Opera Historiography," *JCMS* 60, no. 4 (Summer 2021): 174.
40. For a detailed case study, see Lauren Bratslavsky, "The Archival Value of Televi-

sion in the 'Golden Age' of Media Collecting," *Film and History* 47, no. 2 (2017): 12–27.

41. Chuck Howell, "Dealing with Archive Records," in *Methods of Historical Analysis in Electronic Media*, ed. Donald G. Godfrey (Mahwah, N.J.: Lawrence Erlbaum, 2006), 305–48.

42. Jeff Martin, "The Dawn of Tape: Transmission Device as Preservation Medium," *Moving Image* 5, no. 1 (2005): 45–66; Richard J. Goggin, "Television and Motion Picture Production—and Kinescope Recordings," *Hollywood Quarterly* 4, no. 2 (1949): 152–59; Derek Kompare, *Rerun Nation: How Repeats Invented American Television* (New York: Routledge, 2005).

43. Syndication of *I Love Lucy* began in 1955. Gary R. Edgerton, *The Columbia History of American Television* (New York: Columbia University Press, 2007), 139.

44. Martin, "Dawn of Tape," 56, emphasis in original.

45. See Kompare, *Rerun Nation*, for more about industrial strategies for recorded programs; Schreibman, "Succinct History," about the shortfalls of the industry to care about preservation; William T. Murphy, *Television and Video Preservation 1997: A Report on the Current State of American Television and Video Preservation* (Washington, D.C.: Library of Congress, 1997), 111, about news preservation as well as more context about the state of preservation; and Lucas Hilderbrand, *Inherent Vice: Bootleg Histories of Videotape and Copyright* (Durham, N.C.: Duke University Press, 2009), for his chapter about this copyright battle.

46. Ruth Schwartz, "Preserving TV Programs: Here Today—Gone Tomorrow," *Journal of Broadcasting* 17 (1973): 287.

47. Schreibman, "Succinct History"; Sarah Ziebell Mann, "The Evolution of American Moving Image Preservation: Defining the Preservation Landscape (1967–1977)," *Moving Image* 1, no. 2 (2001): 1–20.

48. Murphy, *Television and Video Preservation 1997*, 9.

49. Levine, "Alternate Archives," 179, 175.

PART I

ACCOUNTING FOR THE WORTHINESS OF TELEVISION-RELATED MATERIALS FOR ARCHIVAL SPACES

CHAPTER 1

KATE CRONIN

CONSIDERING THE ARCHIVABILITY OF EARLY U.S. TELEVISION NEWSFILM

In August 1949 Russ Johnston, an executive in the NBC Film Department, sent a concerned memo to his supervisor: "The thought just occurred to me that, to my knowledge, we have no insurance on the several million feet of film in the library at 106th Street unless it is covered by some standard company policy. I do not know what valuation we put on the library, but I should like to point out that film can be damaged in a great many other ways than fire or explosion."[1]

While Johnston was clearly referring to the financial value of the NBC film library, he had inadvertently articulated a pressing existential puzzle confronting early U.S. television newscasters: How should they value the millions of feet of television news footage steadily accumulating in their film libraries? Was it news? A corporate asset? A historical document? A cultural artifact? Some combination thereof?

During the first decades of television news production, television networks provided varying answers to this important question. In press releases to the public and communications with regulatory bodies, network executives emphasized the informational value of news footage and espoused their intentions to cater to a nebulously defined public interest. In contrast, corporate memoranda reveal heated arguments over the most efficient way to monetize that very same footage. At the heart of this debate was a new intranetwork operation: the television film library.

Television was still a fledgling medium in 1949 when Johnston sent this memo, and television news was likewise a rookie in comparison to print or radio news, still working to calibrate the aesthetic promise of television news with the vocational responsibility of journalism as an independent profession. During the first two decades of television news production, network film libraries were a central battleground for this struggle, the traces of which were embedded in the organization and description of the material newsfilm itself.

In practice, television network film libraries were large collections of broadcast network newsfilm staffed by teams of informational professionals. While the networks referred to them specifically as "film libraries," these operations embodied characteristics of both libraries and archives: like libraries, they facilitated access to a collection of reference materials; like archives, they served as a repository for records produced throughout the course of administrative or corporate activity. The film library was responsible for the physical and intellectual control of all newsfilm footage produced by network news departments; they tracked, shipped, sorted, edited, cataloged, and oversaw the preservation or destruction of all newsfilm. Moreover, film libraries were a primary source of audiovisual background for both planned and breaking news stories, commercial stock footage operations, and, later, documentary production. In this way, network film libraries quickly evolved from a necessary administrative resource into an active and creative collaborator with clear editorial responsibilities, not to mention a vital component of the early network business model. Significantly, the organizational policies and workflows established during this process of identifying and exploiting both the news and the commercial value of newsfilm shaped how future broadcast news was made, framed, and marketed, as well as what footage was preserved or destroyed.

On a purely practical level, this chapter spotlights television news because most early television film archives were almost entirely made up of newsfilm, that is, news footage purchased from theatrical newsreel companies or produced in-house by fledgling television news departments. The network film library emerged from a basic need to reliably circulate and repurpose an ever-increasing supply of newsfilm footage within the expanding television news departments of NBC and CBS and fast evolved into the administrative hub of television news production and distribution. To make good on the obvious advantage television news could claim over earlier news formats—the live synchronization of image and sound—network news departments required an immense volume of incoming celluloid film to pair with the stories of the day. Even a short fifteen-minute broadcast might combine live studio broadcasting, live pickups from bureaus in big news cities, and two or three filmed advertisements with *hundreds* of feet of prerecorded, pre-edited newsfilm, often pulled from the network film library. While directing the live broadcast of all these different media elements was an immensely complex organizational task, so too was the more invisible labor performed by the network film librarian—the timely acquisition, processing, inspection, cataloging, storage, and retrieval of all incoming and outgoing newsfilm.

Although there is a robust body of media studies literature addressing how archival acquisition in a historical context has shaped entire disciplines and subfields,[2] there is considerably less written about the work of information professionals like these early film librarians: media workers who marshaled the material and ideological contours of television during its earliest years.[3] Accordingly, this chapter asks: how does a historical case study of newsfilm libraries *within* the U.S. television industry itself inform our understanding of television's archivability more broadly?

As illustrated through corporate memoranda, trade press, promotional materials, and network-sponsored guidebooks, both NBC and CBS, the dominant early networks, operated with a clear commercial mandate but adopted starkly different initial strategies in the creation and subsequent use of their respective newsfilm collections. For NBC, newsfilm was first and foremost a corporate asset that could be used to generate short-term profits from direct sales. For CBS, newsfilm and the network film library were both a practical necessity and a strategic investment in further developing their reputation as a serious news brand.

At first, many journalists within both networks resented these more commercial valuations of newsfilm on the grounds that they were objective newsmen with a professional imperative to resist all commercial influence. But as the film libraries standardized the workflows necessary to process the rapidly accelerating volume of daily newsfilm, executives and newsmen alike were forced to adjust their initial valuations of newsfilm. Indeed, as television newsmen continued to experiment with different material configurations of news and public affairs programming, the film library turned stock footage archive emerged as an indispensable programming resource with clear editorial responsibilities. Producers relished the opportunity to produce sponsored documentaries inspired by film library footage while executives discovered that asserting the historical value of their film libraries was an effective strategy to capitalize on both the long-term commercial value and news values of the film reels contained therein.

Crucially, the information management infrastructures they assembled in the process—carefully designed to exploit the myriad values of network newsfilm—laid material and ideological groundwork for the much-heralded golden age of news and documentary television that followed.

THE COMMERCIAL VALUE OF NETWORK NEWSFILM

The TV producer on the phone sounded desperate. "I've gotta have some stock footage. An atomic bomb exploding. About 20 seconds' worth."

"That shouldn't be difficult," said Barbara Weiner, chief index supervisor of NBC TV Film Library, mentally thumbing index cards marked Disasters (explosion—atomic). "What sort of shot did you have in mind?"[4]

NBC was the first major network to seriously consider both the news and commercial value of material newsfilm. NBC could easily have outsourced their newsfilm gathering to newsreel production companies, as they did for most of their sponsored entertainment programming. Instead, NBC's newsmen—most of them veterans of the newsreel industry—chose to compete with the newsreels and newswires looking to break into television. In so doing they cleared the way for the other networks to do the same and prevented the theatrical newsreels and newswires from dominating the newsfilm market. While it seems obvious to us today that television networks would produce as well as distribute their own news, that was by no means a foregone conclusion during the earliest years of television's development. If not for the NBC News Department's early gamble on celluloid film as a feasible medium for television news production, the network-era television news industry might have developed very differently.

Another major consequence of NBC's decision to invest in celluloid film and in their own news-gathering operation was the expansion of their hybrid network film library/stock footage archive. NBC's first newsmen insisted on the importance of a newsfilm library on their arrival, and over the course of a decade, that library evolved into an essential network resource as well as a profitable, independent operation. When CBS followed NBC into the newsfilm game, they quickly realized, as NBC had a decade earlier, that a robust, well-maintained film library was the key to expanding both their news gathering and their news distribution infrastructures.

From the outset of their pioneering newsfilm-gathering operations, NBC newsmen and executives justified both the establishment of an in-house network newsgathering team and a film library to manage the newsfilm they produced as long-term material investments that would increase in financial value over time.[5] In 1947, frustrated former newsreel producer turned NBC newsman Paul Alley wrote John Royal, NBC's vice president of television, the following missive:

> The demands being made upon the Film Department are greater than ever before. It is physically impossible for the staff to turn out the work it is being asked to do.... With some 5,000 cans of film in its library, NBC Television has no one to list this material when it goes to vault; no one to handle the daily flow of film (which is amounting to 10 & 20 thousand feet a week). In other words: When YOU want a scene or a story, we have no way of finding it. Perhaps my presentation of our needs has not been sufficiently urgent. Perhaps my requests have not been sufficiently eloquent. When I came with NBC in 1944, I said that a LIBRARIAN was one of the most important jobs in the Film Department. As of June 1947 we still have no Librarian.[6]

Alley was the second-in-command for NBC News at that time. He had complete editorial control of NBC's weekly newsreel and would later produce *The Camel News Caravan*, a sponsored nightly news show that effectively subsidized the News Department for the first three years it was on the air. So it is notable here that the majority of his early memos to network executives are not long, philosophical pontifications of the potentials and limitations of television news from an editorial perspective but furious declarations of the importance of a film librarian to newsreel production.

Spared from Alley's fate of digging through mountains of unlabeled newsfilm, programming executive Noran Kersta took a slightly more entrepreneurial (and diplomatic) approach in his efforts to convince the network to fund and properly staff a film library:

> In addition to the day-to-day value that the Film Library has to present NBC Television operations, there are supplementary avenues of revenue which can be realized from this Library. Basically, the value of the library might be appraised as something in the order of $250,000. However, a film library increases in value as time goes on.... The price of stock film for a commercial show increases proportionately according to (a) scarcity of the subject desired, and (b) commercial importance of the sponsor. On the basis of these prices, our Library might have a top value in the order of $2,000,000.[7]

These memos making the case for network-level investment in the nascent NBC film library reflect an industry-defining, calculated risk on the part of NBC News: a bet that celluloid film would continue to be the most important material media format to television news production and distribution for at least a decade, and that newsfilm would have some financial value even after its initial use. They also reflect some of the earliest attempts of NBC newsmen to articulate the organizational and financial value of a well-maintained film library to a broadcast network. While the newsreel team treated the film library as a critical component of their production and distribution infrastructure, they also recognized its potential as a lucrative stock footage operation. Management was convinced, and later that year the NBC news film operation got their librarian, an assistant, and a vault clerk.

The first roadblock NBC encountered in their early efforts toward a newsfilm library/stock footage archive hybrid was a small legal complication. While NBC did not need to procure civil rights releases (i.e., written permissions) from individuals filmed in footage they planned to use for "pure news" programming, they did need civil rights releases in order to reuse newsfilm for non-news-related commercial purposes.[8] Likewise, they could not sell newsfilm to an outside client intending to use it for commercial or advertising purposes without first procuring written permission from all of the individuals and organizations depicted in the footage. To do so would expose NBC to significant legal and financial liabilities. Thus, to maximize the amount of newsfilm they could legally repackage as stock footage, NBC changed both their newsgathering and their film library workflows.

First, they equipped all NBC news cameramen with pocket-sized pads with short-form civil rights releases and encouraged them to obtain the signatures of all individuals they captured on film, "in every case where they can possibly do so."[9] Although a small adjustment to newsgathering workflows, it enacted a significant shift in how NBC newsmen were trained to value the material news footage captured by their expanding news operations. While NBC newsmen were theoretically guided by editorial principles of the NBC news department, they were also encouraged to do everything in their power to facilitate the commercial resale of the footage they captured. Once the NBC newsmen began acquiring civil releases for all newsfilm, the film library began to reorganize their holdings into two main categories: film for which they had civil rights releases, and film for which they did not. Ray Kelly, the manager of the Film Operations Division, reasoned that these adjustments would allow the NBC film library, over time, to "develop into a substantial library on which we could draw for film to be used for other than straight 'news' purposes."[10]

While the film library was still a critical component of network production and distribution processes, this reorganization established the commercial resale of network newsfilm as their initial organizational priority. Moreover, it marked the first of several times the commercial mandates of the film library would materially impact editorial oversight of NBC newsgathering and production workflows.

This initial for-profit orientation of the NBC film library inspired a creative accounting setup that bolstered the popular fiction that network news was inherently unprofitable. NBC News prioritized novelty and freshness in their newsfilm, and the NBC accounting department incorporated this value system into their ledgers. Specifically, they reasoned that the act of broadcasting effectively stripped newsfilm of all financial and news value. Thus, the financial value of all NBC newsfilm after its initial broadcast was officially recorded in NBC's accounting ledgers as zero dollars and cents.[11] The newsfilm was then gifted to the NBC film library, who controlled its commercial and editorial value throughout its extensive afterlife. Through the cataloging process, a librarian would assign each reel of newsfilm a new financial and thematic value in accordance with its salability to outside clients or potential future news value. The NBC News and Special Events Department received no portion of the profits made from the resale of the newsfilm they had originally paid to produce, and they were required to purchase any newsfilm they wanted to use for future broadcasts back from the NBC film library.[12] Moreover, NBC required all programming departments to look for background footage in the NBC film library first before consulting external sources, reasoning that "charity should begin at home."[13]

In practice, this arrangement produced a kind of hostage situation that benefited the NBC Film Division, which housed the film library, and disadvantaged the News and Special Events Department. NBC News had to pay twice for the same footage—first to create it, and second to buy it back from the NBC film library—and were only able to offset those production costs through sponsorships or by selling ad time. In contrast, the NBC film library had both a guaranteed supplier of recent newsfilm as well as a guaranteed buyer for that same supply of newsfilm in the NBC News and Special Affairs Department. When the NBC News Department expressed their dissatisfaction with this system to the executive in charge,[14] he outright dismissed their complaint that this accounting practice materially disadvantaged NBC News, replying: "The purpose of the joint library operation is the most effective and widespread marketing of our film library material. Since the intention is to gain a financial return to NBC I feel that failure to credit this revenue to the News Department is only an academic consideration."[15]

This elaborate creative accounting setup is just one example of what Michael Socolow has described as broadcast networks' efforts to convince the public and the FCC that their news departments were unprofitable.[16] It was a savvy public relations strategy to claim they only produced news content out of their selfless desire to serve the public interest; however, in order to do so, they had to hide their considerable profits from the ancillary sale of newsfilm in the balance sheets of different network departments. This meant that while the film library was undoubtedly an essential production tool for the News and Special Events Department, it was also a convenient place to hide the ancillary profitability of network newsfilm from regulators and the public.

Soon after the NBC film library's organizational transfer from the NBC News Division to the NBC Film Operations Division in 1948, NBC invested heavily in marketing the film library's services to external clients in order to, in the words of Frank Lepore, "stimulate the sale of stock footage." They felt that by not fully exploiting the full commercial value of NBC newsfilm in its afterlife, they were leaving easy money on the table.[17] Thus they spent thousands to produce an extensive film library handbook listing the 2,200 main subject terms in the library catalog and detailing exactly how to locate, order, and purchase specific footage for films, commercials, documentaries, and so on. NBC's film library advertisements boldly proclaimed their broad range of stock footage—"From Academy to Zululand ... it's in the NBC Film Library"[18]—and by 1956 they had garnered a reputation as the most active film library in the business, as well as one of the largest, most comprehensive, and affordable stock footage archives in the United States.[19]

By the time CBS launched their in-house newsfilm production in 1953, the NBC film library had already been operating as an independent film library and a commercial stock footage archive for several years. But whereas the commercial resale of newsfilm was the primary objective of the NBC film library, CBS instead approached the resale of newsfilm as a moderately profitable side hustle. CBS's film library was housed within their News and Public Affairs Department, and all profits from outside sales were eventually funneled back into the CBS News Division and were used to directly offset the substantial costs of newsfilm-gathering for television.[20] It is unsurprising, then, that NBC and CBS would adopt markedly different strategies for marketing both their newsfilm and their film library services.

While NBC treated all NBC newsfilm as potential stock footage, the CBS film library organized their collection into "pure news" and "stock footage." Film that was deemed to have "permanent news value" was cataloged and filed as news, and film with no "residual news value ... (sunsets, jet planes taking off, submarine surfacing, etc.)" was filed and cataloged as stock footage. Film that was determined to have value as neither news nor stock footage was destroyed in order to make room for incoming footage with either greater news value or greater retail value.[21] By 1956 CBS was netting approximately $1,000 a week from the resale of their library footage with "no residual news value."[22] Rather than concentrating their efforts on building up a lucrative stock footage operation, over the course of the 1950s they concentrated on operationalizing a robust library of newsfilm that would help CBS newsmen turn images into ideas. Unsurprisingly, this material would find a rich second life in independent and network documentary production from the late 1950s through the 1960s.[23]

CBS advertised its services as a stock footage archive quietly within trade publications and were careful to protect the CBS News brand in the process. While they would often sell news and stock footage to outside clients, they placed restrictions on buyers, prohibiting them from naming CBS as the source of the footage if they felt public knowledge of the sale might hurt the CBS brand. In fact, while they were happy to take money from politicians looking to purchase footage for their campaign advertisements, CBS placed clear restrictions on the use of that newsfilm so that no one could accuse them of partisanship.[24] But these smaller stock footage sales were never the focus of their commercial operation. Instead, they focused on the sale of their daily syndicated newsreel, *CBS Newsfilm*, and advertised access to their film library as a fringe benefit to affiliates and subscribers.[25] Rather than market the commercial versatility and thematic range of their film library as NBC had done, they were selling the CBS News brand writ large.

Thus NBC and CBS adopted inverse strategies when marketing library newsfilm, both in their regular news programming and as an independent product. NBC intentionally downplayed their own use of library film in promotional materials, even though they regularly integrated library newsfilm into both their live and syndicated news and public affairs programming. Instead, they marketed NBC News as the go-to network for the "hottest," best-quality documentation of domestic and international news, while also emphatically marketing their vast library of old newsfilm to outside networks and clients. CBS, in contrast, very publicly emphasized their commitment to "visualizing ideas" as the primary rationale behind their news programming decisions, engaged in less sensationalized marketing of their newsfilm to outside clients, and more closely associated their film library with their daily news programming and syndication service.

This small difference in how (and to whom) NBC and CBS exploited and advertised the commercial value of their film libraries had a major influence on the organization and description of each collection. Specifically, NBC's organization and description of its collection initially prioritized maximizing profits from sales to outside clients. While CBS also sold newsfilm as stock footage to outside clients, their quieter sales pitch and explicit distinction between "news" and "stock footage" within the library catalog itself indicates that the film library was first and foremost an extension of the CBS News brand. However, in both cases the ancillary sale of newsfilm in the form of stock footage and syndicated news content was a key component of each network's larger business models. At both networks, these profits were used to directly offset the considerable cost of their newsgathering operations, despite NBC's best efforts to disguise those profits.[26]

THE PUBLIC PERSONA OF THE NETWORK NEWSMAN: "HE FINDS DRAMA IN THE NEWS"

During the earliest years of network television news, newsmen and executives alike were primarily concerned with the logistical albatross of material newsfilm production. But as workflows eventually standardized and profits began to grow, they were finally able to turn their attention from the visual images their cameramen captured on film and reflect on the more abstract public image of their respective news brands.

At CBS, this manifested as a calculated, network-wide effort to reconcile the professional imperative of objective news coverage with a "distinctive but not distasteful" on-air personality who would appeal to sponsors and audiences alike. Short of an explicit editorial policy guiding CBS's news production, perhaps the closest articulation of what specific characteristics made up the "attitude" of a CBS newsman are public ruminations on what made for an ideal CBS news presenter. In his famous 1954 "Road to Responsibility" speech to the National Association of Radio and Television Broadcasters, Sig Mickelson emphasized objectivity as the dominant professional ethos of the television newsman:

> In both news and news analysis, the goal of the news broadcaster analyst must be objectivity. I think we all recognize that human nature is such that no newsman is entirely free from his own personal prejudices, experience, and opinions and that accordingly, 100 percent objectivity may not always be possible. But the important factor is that the news broadcaster and the news analysis must have the will and the intent to be objective. That will and that intent, genuinely held and deeply instilled in him, is the best assurance of objectivity. His aim should be to make it possible for the listener to know the facts and to weight them carefully so that he can better make up his own mind.[27]

Here, Mickelson acknowledges the impossibility of complete objectivity on an individual level but emphasizes the professional imperative to strive for it all the same. Writing more informally and for a much different audience, John F. Day, the director of CBS News, had his own idea of the kind of person best suited to be the face of CBS News. In a 1955 article for *Broadcasting* magazine, Day wrote,

> Television news, to reach any sort of perfection, requires a type of human being that to my knowledge has not yet appeared on the scene. He would be a sort of a paragon who not only could dig up, write and report the news but on top of that he would look like a veritable Clark Gable on the television screen; he would be a sort of walking or, perhaps sitting encyclopedia as the case may be, and he would be a marvelous public speaker who could simply forget about a script and discuss the subject at hand with conviction and meaning and persuasiveness.[28]

Taken together, Mickelson's and Day's visions provide a sense of what CBS envisioned the ideal kind of news coverage to be (objective and impartial), as well as the kind of person best positioned to lend that coverage authority and credibility (an eloquent, all-knowing Clark Gable). As one CBS executive put it: "I think we should add on-air personnel with very special and distinctive attributes. I have in mind not only a warm and pleasing manner, but a sense of insight and understanding and authority."[29] In other words, while CBS embraced a professional ethos of objectivity and impartiality, their news brand was firmly rooted in the genial attitude of authority embodied by the celebrity persona of one of Hollywood's foremost leading men.[30] So while CBS newsmen behind the camera routinely dismissed celebrity news as fluff, they also took great pains to cultivate and market the leading man celebrity persona for their on-air "talent."

At NBC, this tension between the commercial and professional mandates of network news was articulated—both publicly and internally—most explicitly in terms of who was not a newsman, and what was or wasn't newsworthy. In both cases, "serious" news was characterized as an inherently masculine genre for a well-educated audience. For example, an NBC Press Office press release promoting NBC's Daily News Service described the work of their only female news editor as follows:

> Marcia Drennen has brunet hair, a trim figure, winning smile—and a direct hand in editing and servicing some 130,000 feet of news film a year. Attractive as those items are to discuss, it's the latter figure, the 130,000 feet of news film, that must take first consideration in a news story. . . . Handling fast-breaking stories that might come in from any corner of the globe is a far cry from Miss Drennen's introduction to the news business of the *Ohio State Journal* in Columbus, her home town. For five years she labored unhappily on women's page assignments, itching to get a crack at a straight news story.[31]

While this press release is clearly intended as a celebration of Ms. Drennen's work, it is also framed as an invitation to view her as an oddity within the early television news industry: a woman involved in daily news production and not women's features! Moreover, the press release makes a clear distinction between the "women's page" and "straight news," a contrast that is further emphasized by the fixation on Ms. Drennen's "trim figure" and "winning smile." Here, the description of her physical appearance together with the note about her years of laboring "unhappily on women's page assignments" in order to earn the privilege of editing the *Daily News Service* underscores the attitude within early networks that hard news was, by default, a masculine endeavor.

Internally, this gendered rhetorical distinction between what was and wasn't news was articulated along similar lines. Specially, NBC's newsmen sought to affirm their position as serious newsmen by elevating "hard" news coverage of politics and industry from the "news features" targeting female, rural, and working-class audiences. Just one such example: while NBC's News Department was largely staffed by former theatrical newsreel men, the NBC marketing department took great pains to distinguish NBC as a rising star in the "highly specialized field of TV news," as opposed to theatrical newsreel coverage of "the annual convention of twins, a freckle contest, sheep-shearing time in Montana, girls underwater basketball and publicity clips about movie caravans."[32] That is to say, women's sports, agricultural news, and human interest stories did not qualify as "serious" television news. Along the same lines, NBC's own newsmen drafted blunt critiques of NBC programming, complaining, for example, that the fashion features of *The Today Show* could not possibly be anything other than a brazen effort to increase the show's sex appeal, an objective that could "better be accomplished by the permanent presence of a sexy girl." In his response, a *Today Show* producer countered drolly: "I contend that fashions are legitimate news to the 45% of our audience who happen to be women. Both the Times and the News carry fashions. I also wonder what the sexy girl would do on the show. Bumps and grinds?"[33]

On balance, CBS's positive ideal of a Clark Gable–like newsman could have been printed directly from NBC's negative image of who a serious newsman wasn't. There were, of course, clear tonal and personality differences between CBS and NBC news personalities; while CBS's Douglas Edwards was praised for his solemn, earnest nightly news coverage, NBC's Huntley and Brinkley—John Cameron Swayze's successors—were hired to add warmth, wit, and a dash of spontaneity to NBC's nightly newscasts.[34] Indeed, all of the earliest television news personalities at the national level—Swayze, Edwards, Huntley, Brinkley, Murrow, and Cronkite alike—cultivated their own unique personas and approaches as newsmen. However, the unspoken anchor of their ideological authority as "serious" newsmen was their discursive claim to hard news as the prerogative of white, well-educated men. That's not to say that NBC and CBS *only* addressed the interests of an assumed white male audience in their news and public affairs programming. Rather, in the wake of an explicit editorial policy within either network, it was exclusively white, college-educated men who were entrusted with the editorial authority to determine what was or wasn't newsworthy. So, while both networks produced reporting for and about nonwhite, female, and working-class audiences, the newsworthiness of that reporting was, despite the networks' professional commitment to objectivity, usually framed in relationship to the dominant subject position of the newsmen in front of and behind the camera.

NEWSFILM AND THE NEWSMAN

While the evolution of NBC and CBS's various newsmen personae informed the ideological thrust of news programming throughout the network era, it also manifested in more material terms. Above all, NBC and CBS newsmen were always braced to defend the integrity of their newsfilm against what they saw as the evergreen threat of commercial contamination. At NBC, such objections were most clearly expressed in response to the fusion of NBC newsfilm with NBC's entertainment programming, whereas at CBS, newsmen were routinely dismayed by news coverage they felt was pandering to a generalist audience, incurious about the world around them.

Perhaps the most spirited example of NBC newsmen's objections to the fusion of news and entertainment programming was their overt disdain for *The Today Show* in its earliest iteration. In 1952, directly after its launch, several NBC News and Special Events Department employees compiled a comprehensive critique of *The Today Show*. Their primary criticism was its synthesis of hard and soft news, a heartfelt assertion that "you can't mix astrophysics and hillbilly music." Clearly having some fun with their commentary, the NBC newsmen teased: "Garroway comes on the screen... is it news or is it Dial Soap?"[35]

A producer for *The Today Show* responded gamely to these critiques. "This is a valid criticism from a news point of view," he conceded, "but hardly from an advertising point of view. On the day that the audience knows it's going to be Dial Soap, Garroway's effectiveness as a salesman will be cut in half. The whole principle of TODAY's commercial pattern is skillful integration." He responded with similar candor to their complaint about mixing "astrophysics and hillbilly music": "I think you can. In fact, I think you must provide extremely varied fare in order to get an audience.... The newspapers do... to the best of their printed ability. *Today*'s editorial format is that of a daily *Life Magazine* with spot news added. *Life* can't mix astrophysics and hillbilly music only because they can't play music. But they can mix it with cheesecake and sports and comedy."[36] Here, the *Today Show* producer stresses that there is no one single editorial approach to reporting the news and that *The Today Show* very much saw itself as taking a magazine approach, which included a blend of newsfilm and live entertainment, along with public affairs programming to solicit the broadest possible audience.

For all intents and purposes, *The Today Show* was no more or less commercial than NBC's prized nightly news program, *The Camel News Caravan*, sponsored by R. J. Reynolds, maker of Camel Cigarettes. In fact, the producers of *The Camel News Caravan* were so thoroughly beholden to their commercial sponsor that they had to ask for special permission every time they wanted to broadcast newsfilm of Winston Churchill, one of the most important historical figures of the postwar period, simply because he was almost always filmed while smoking a cigar and R. J. Reynolds would only allow Camel cigarettes to be shown.[37] Thus, it was not the commercial sponsorship of news programming that the NBC journalists objected to here but rather the lack of an explicit, albeit subjective, distinction between subjects they saw as newsworthy and subjects they deemed frivolous. In other words, NBC's television journalists felt their professional status was diluted by *The Today Show*'s willingness to give science journalism, Dial soap, and a musical genre with cultural ties to poor, rural audiences equal weight and airtime.

At CBS, arguments over the commercialization of newsfilm were likewise focused on the network's efforts to curate the broadest possible audience for its news programming. While CBS cultivated an image as the most serious U.S. news brand, they were also careful to anticipate audience expectations. Heated debates between assignment editors and correspondents over the focus and level of detail required for CBS's international news coverage were a regular feature of CBS's early newsfilm clinics. Assignment editors regularly chastised correspondents for pitching international stories that required even moderate familiarity with the geography and politics of the world outside of the United States and Europe: "Sometimes it appears that you fellows overseas lose sight of the fact—maybe I am wrong—that actually interests in this country are quite narrow, and things look very big to you." These reminders to correspondents that *CBS Newsfilm* had to please sponsors as well as critics were not warmly received. CBS correspondents resented what they viewed as an intentional dilution of critical international news coverage to pander to an incurious U.S. audience. One correspondent dryly articulated his frustrations with the network's efforts to make international news coverage palatable to Americans, asking: "In interviews we understand that you do not want people with thick accents. What about foreign language? Suppose a man is in the news?"[38]

While these saltier objections to commercial influences on network news coverage came in response to specific programming decisions, NBC and CBS newsmen also wrestled with the industrial imperatives of television newsfilm production in material terms.

NBC's newsmen with origins in theatrical newsreels heartily embraced the technological affordances of celluloid film that allowed them to broadcast documentation of breaking news within hours of its original recording. NBC invested heavily in cutting-edge newsfilm-gathering infrastructure: they shot on 35mm film rather than 16mm in order to produce the best quality newsfilm possible in terms of image, they built out the largest early kinescope operation of any of the national networks, and they published rapid-fire press releases emphasizing the sheer volume of celluloid film that passed through NBC News cameras on a given day.[39] Their foremost objective, as well as their sales pitch to affiliates and potential sponsors, was their unique ability to get high-quality visual documentation of breaking news on U.S. television sets quicker than any other network. In this way, the NBC News and Special Events Department embraced novelty and timeliness as their predominant news values and imbued the material newsfilm itself, prior to its initial broadcast, with inherent news value. After its initial broadcast, and once it was cataloged within the film library, its news value was no longer its novelty but rather its potential to provide relevant background, context, or visuals for future news stories or commercials.

CBS, in contrast, was more reluctant to fully embrace the visual affordances of newsfilm, and they incorporated that reluctance into their carefully curated news brand. While not quite ready to articulate what television news was, CBS was adamant that television news was not a newsreel, a format they described as a technique "adequate for the disasters, dog and pony shows, animal acts, seven-day bicycle races and speeches of the newsreel era" but not "adaptable to the constant hard news and idea reporting needs of television." NBC's Television News Department had been built and staffed by mostly former newsreel men who prioritized novelty, timeliness, and volume. In contrast, CBS trained their correspondents, cameramen, and editors to distinguish between a newsreel feature and hard television news: while a newsreel used images to illustrate an event, hard news strategically deployed moving images to communicate ideas. In Mickelson's words, "What we were projecting was an organization vastly more complicated and designed to deliver substantially more product than even the most productive of newsreels and to aim primarily at hard news and interpretation rather than feature items." Thus, correspondents and cameramen were asked not just to illustrate and document but to intuit what kind of images would facilitate a deeper understanding of and interest in stand-alone and developing news stories on a conceptual level. In a presentation to the CBS Television Division Budget Department, Mickelson described this endeavor as "a cooperative effort with the best brains and techniques of the three men in the unit—correspondent, camera reporter, and sound technician—to convert both hard news ideas and abstract developments, behind locked doors news-making into pictorial reporting which will be interesting and meaningful to the American viewer."[40]

In other words, for CBS newsmen, newsfilm did not itself possess inherent news value. The news value of newsfilm was entirely dependent on its potential to provide background or context that would aid in their larger goal of "visualizing ideas." But while CBS newsmen enjoyed debating the appropriate ratio between newsfilm and words in a television newscast, this strategy was as much commercial as it was philosophical. In the words of one news executive: "In many respects the character of CRD [CBS Radio Division], CTD [CBS Television Division], and CBS, Inc. is set by the serious program schedule delivered by CND [CBS News Department] and I suggest that this character or corporate image very probably has a dollars and cents value in terms of both sales and ratings."[41] So even while NBC newsmen exchanged memos mocking CBS's *Douglas Edwards with the News* for its lack of original newsfilm,[42] CBS viewed their more measured incorporation of newsfilm into their news and public affairs programming as a long-term investment in the sustained profitability of their broader network brand.

This explicit internal and external emphasis on prestige meant that CBS's corporate culture encouraged and embraced a certain aura of professional superiority. Indeed, while CBS newsmen with editorial responsibilities were usually more than ready to complain about the hassle of teaching mere "technicians" to capture "ideas" in the form of images,[43] when administrators or technicians tried to talk to newsmen about how slight changes in technology or administrative logistics might likewise improve news coverage, they ran up against what an external consultant euphemistically referred to as "some of the rough personality edges that the newsroom now possesses."[44]

In order to communicate the intricacies of their new newsfilm-gathering operations to CBS newsmen without puncturing their image of themselves as the "idea men" driving television news, CBS executives drew clear distinctions between the administrative, technical, and editorial contours of newsfilm production. They adopted an elaborate series of metaphors—blending the rhetoric of industry and artistry—to articulate an unofficial departmental hierarchy. Staff with editorial responsibilities were "newsmen," and their work was described first and foremost in the realm of the conceptual. Executives focused on how those who reported, edited, or researched news contributed to CBS's broader goal of producing critically respected news programming. CBS staff who worked primarily with film technologies were next in the professional hierarchy and were alternately referred to as "technicians" and "craftsmen."[45]

At the bottom of the hierarchy were the administrators, who were usually described in starkly industrial terms, especially those relating to manufacturing. Newsfilm was deemed "the raw materials" of television news production, the film library became the newsfilm "supermarket," and administrators functioned to "design, install, lubricate and eternally modernize the machinery" that controlled the material flow of newsfilm.[46] In a 1955 strategy session, one CBS executive suggested holding regular workshops for CBS newsmen with editorial responsibilities, to which Mickelson replied with concern that CBS newsmen who considered themselves professional journalists might "react pettishly" to the suggestion that they attend a clinic. A potential solution, Mickelson countered, would be to "entice them into a round table discussion every three months" so that they did not feel that their identity as "idea men" and professional journalists was under threat.[47] Thus, in an effort to soothe their newsmen's discomfort with the more industrial aspects of network news production, CBS adopted both rhetorical and organizational distinctions between the editorial and the administrative functions of news production, despite their obvious mutual influence.

Clearly, newsmen from both networks struggled to reconcile their professional identity as journalists with the inevitable industrial imperatives of material newsfilm production. While NBC adapted by embracing the novelty of material newsfilm as a news value unto itself, CBS was careful to distinguish between news and newsfilm in its internal messaging and in terms of its carefully cultivated news brand. These very different strategies, in turn, informed the standards and practices adopted by their respective film libraries, organizations both networks had initially written off as purely administrative in nature.

DOCUMENTARY PRODUCTION AND EDITORIAL PRESTIGE

While NBC and CBS regularly incorporated library film into their nightly news broadcasts, in both cases film libraries were acknowledged primarily as an administrative support when they were acknowledged at all. But over the course of the 1950s, as news and public affairs programming expanded, both networks' film libraries evolved into active programming partners and editorial resources for their respective news divisions.

Last-minute scrambles to construct obituary film reels for ailing public figures were an early indicator to newsmen and librarians alike that film libraries could be a programming resource as well as a newsfilm repository. The deaths of King George VI in 1952 and his mother, Queen

Consort Mary of Teck, a year later, were an early catalyst for this kind of editorial labor on the part of the film library. NBC and CBS editors and correspondents were in regular contact with their international counterparts, especially the BBC in London. They traded leads and tips, and in early March 1953 a BBC contact informed NBC and CBS that it was likely Queen Mary would soon pass away, little more than a year after the death of her second son, King George VI.[48] While Queen Mary was not a wildly popular celebrity within the United States by any means, she was a symbol of Great Britain's international standing on the world stage, and her death had news value insofar as the United States and England, especially in the wake of World War II, continued to enjoy a "special relationship." Her death, as well as the death of her son the year before, also signaled to NBC News producers that framing the death of an international figure in visual terms would require considerably more proactive news routines than would have been necessary for the more reactive radio coverage of the same event. In fact, when George VI died in February 1952, one NBC editor sent a relieved memo to his supervisor noting that they had only just happened to have footage of King George in the film traffic rack for another story that week, and it was merely a lucky coincidence that they were able to put together a quick newsfilm obituary to play in conjunction with their correspondent's report.[49] A year later, when George's mother passed, the editors gave the film library the morbidly practical go-ahead to begin working with a team of editors to produce preemptive obituaries for Winston Churchill, Pope Pius XII, and Herbert Hoover as well . . . just in case.[50] Learning from this experience, NBC and CBS both incorporated the regular production of potentially relevant newsreels into their daily news routines. Networks compiled "VIP" lists of prominent figures and had visual obituaries of the ones they deemed most likely to pass away first ready to broadcast at a moment's notice.[51]

Soon the networks expanded this practice into the proactive production of newsreels for other major news events, not just the deaths of public figures. While "a nose for news" had usually referred to the ability to sense what might make a compelling news story, in the NBC and CBS film libraries, a "nose for news" grew to mean someone who could anticipate which library film would be most relevant to ongoing as well as breaking news stories.[52] In this respect, both networks took to building out reels of relevant political, social, and historical context in anticipation of expected news. As one CBS correspondent explained:

> About every three or four months in the last ten years, a government has fallen in Paris, and you can be sure it is going to happen again fairly soon. I could do a fairly tight analytical piece, but in a pictorial way, which would give Eric an opportunity to explain why French governments fall. He can update it when a government falls and have it ready to run. This might be an example of how an abstract idea can be handled intelligently. I would like to do one like that, because I know you can put that one in the bank and use it absolutely any time.[53]

Likewise, NBC editors also began assembling "for immediate use brief film packages which set the locale and picture background for a news break," reasoning that, for example, "if Tito is assassinated, we would supplement the bare news with an expert on Yugoslavia and maps, showing its strategic location, followed by an aerial picture of Zagreb, followed by closeups of the city, the surrounding country, the people, the customs, etc."[54] Networks regularly edited together such packages to "set the stage" in anticipation of expected news items, to commemorate the anniversaries of important events and public figures, to supplement light news days, and to provide pictorial metaphors for ongoing news stories.[55]

Critically, this practice of proactive anticipation of the news within the film libraries marked a small but significant shift in the working relationship between network newsmen and film librarians. In the earliest days of both NBC's and CBS's film libraries, the communication went one way: assignment editors and producers put in requests for film librarians to locate specific background footage without requesting input or feedback from librarians. But as the film library holdings multiplied, and as incorporation of background footage into network news programming evolved from single shots to fully edited reels of background and context, network film libraries and librarians became increasingly important programming resources, whether or not they were acknowledged as such.

One of the first long-term programming collaborations of this sort was a thirty-minute NBC Korean War retrospective in 1951 called *The Beaten Path*, pitched in anticipation of a potential (ultimately unsuccessful) peace treaty later that year in Korea. Frank McCall, vice president of news and special affairs, kicked off the project with the following suggestion:

> I would like to propose that we start working on a program, at least in basic outline, that can be thrown in hurriedly in case rumors of a negotiated peace in Korea come to fruition. This program could consist of films

showing the history of the war, with live commentary projecting the situation into the future. I think if this were gotten together it might form an attractive commercial offering to some sponsor. All this could be suggested even before the war comes to an end on the supposition that sooner or later it will, and then we will have a good story.[56]

While the Korean War would not end until 1953, the news department and the film library worked together closely to identify, package, and market extensive Korean War footage to sponsors and outside clients throughout the course of the war. This established an important precedent within both the NBC News Department and the film library when assessing the potential future news value of incoming newsfilm. While the newsfilm had immediate news value on its initial broadcast, as well as secondary commercial value as stock footage printed from the original negative housed in the film library, it *also* had a long-term news and commercial value as the raw material for documentary production.

By the mid-1950s both the NBC and CBS film libraries were regularly partnering with assignment editors, producers, and film editors to produce extensive, elaborately edited reels of library film for nightly news and weekly public interest programming. They were still turning respectable profits from stock footage sales to outside clients, but it had become clear that stock footage sales would only ever be a modestly profitable revenue stream. What is more, by the late 1950s independent documentary production for television—much of it spearheaded by former newsfilm librarians turned documentary producers such as Sherman Grinberg—had expanded considerably, garnering both critical and financial success through independent syndication.[57] In this context, network executives began to wonder if stock footage sales were the most efficient way to maximize profits from their film library holdings. NBC in particular decided to funnel their library newsfilm toward television documentary production rather than selling it as stock footage on a first-come, first-served basis. Irving Traeger described the rationale behind this shift as follows:

> There is a growing realization of the importance of the Film Library as a resource for building programs and series for network broadcasting, local broadcasting, and syndication. At present, this resource is treated more or less as a public domain into which any NBC operator can dip at will. A continuation of this practice can result in dissipating the values of the Film Library, whereas the establishment of a regular channel and system for ex-

ploiting these values can lead to wider and more profitable use of the material, inside and outside of NBC.[58]

In order to maximize their film library's editorial value as an in-house programming resource, NBC established an interdepartmental working group including representatives from the film library, the Program Department, the Public Affairs Department, and independently owned and operated (O&O) stations dedicated to documentary development. This group debated ideas and prepared scripts with considerable input from the NBC film librarians. Then a small group of editors assigned to the film library would work with the librarians to locate and edit together the most relevant footage.[59] While CBS had initially focused on outside sales of edited reels of library newsfilm, they soon pivoted to in-house production as well.[60] Both networks still operated as commercial film libraries and stock footage archives, but this was no longer the dominant feature of either of their business models, or of their public relations strategies with affiliates. In fact, by the late 1950s, neither NBC nor CBS were purchasing independently produced documentaries from external sources. Instead, they were investing heavily in their own award-winning documentary series: *NBC White Paper*, *CBS Reports*, and *The Twentieth Century* most prominently.[61]

In his expansive and nuanced analysis of the era of documentary production that followed, Michael Curtin has argued that this shift was both commercially and professionally motivated. Television networks—once again in competition with the floundering theatrical newsreel companies who had pivoted to feature documentary production—sought to box emerging independent documentary producers out of the television market. They also embraced the increased demand for television documentary production as an opportunity to publicly affirm the editorial judgment and journalistic integrity of their respective news divisions. CBS and NBC both invested heavily in their respective news divisions, and the decade of documentary production that followed proved to be the most prolific and lucrative era of U.S. television documentary production to date.[62]

Unsurprisingly, network film libraries would continue to be critical editorial and administrative partners in this endeavor. Using their extensive cross-indexed subject card catalogs, they were able to identify relevant supplemental newsfilm for the documentaries in production at a moment's notice, and they also maintained intellectual control over the material end products: outtakes, edited negatives, positive prints, and kinescopes. In-house documentary production was an obvious solution for network executives and newsmen alike, who were struggling to reconcile the commercial and news values of network newsfilm in its afterlife; for at least a few years, in-house documentary production allowed them to capitalize on both.

From a programming perspective, this golden age of documentary production has largely been characterized as an abrupt departure from the decade of television news service that preceded it,[63] but from a perspective grounded in the material artifact, it is not so surprising. Network news and television executives long puzzled over how to exploit the millions of feet of newsfilm in their respective film libraries to their fullest potential. At first, NBC focused on selling newsfilm to outside clients, while CBS managed their film library as a tool to enhance their prestigious news brand. Despite these different approaches, by the late 1950s both networks had amassed millions of feet of high-quality newsfilm, all of which was cataloged and elaborately cross-indexed by subject. They had also established daily interdepartmental collaboration between film librarians, editors, and programmers, and they had almost a decade of proof that the reuse and resale of network newsfilm could generate *both* profits *and* prestige. Thus, both networks had inadvertently established the organizational, informational, and industrial groundwork necessary to support the impressive volume of documentary production in the decade to come.

"FILM OF EVENTS AND MEN"

For the earliest U.S. television network newscasters and librarians, the preservation of newsfilm for historical purposes was little more than an afterthought. While networks came to appreciate the editorial value of network newsfilm in the years leading up to the golden age of documentary production, it was only through a series of accidents, innovations, and fortunate coincidences that they began to consider its historical value as well.

At NBC, this revaluation of the historical value of network newsfilm played out, once again, via the battle between the News and Film Divisions over the jurisdiction of the NBC film library. When the film library was first incorporated into the Film Division in 1948, the News and Special Events Department had been assured they would have final say in what footage was kept and what footage was destroyed.[64] In practice, however, the film library routinely destroyed 30 percent of the incoming news footage that they did not consider to be "satisfactory for library use."[65] During one episode that generated significant internal debate, employees of the News and Special Events Department were outraged to find that librarians had destroyed 250,000 feet of footage from the 1952 United Nations Assembly meetings in Paris on the basis that the footage merely recorded "speakers talking in foreign languages" and "went on endlessly."[66]

Soon after this discovery, NBC enacted three major changes. First, they formalized procedures to give the News and Special Events Department final say over whether the negatives for specific newsfilm could be destroyed.[67] Second, the film library was instructed to partner with the News and Special Events Department to complete a retroactive assessment of their entire collection, identifying any major historical gaps in coverage, and to order footage to fill those gaps from external sources.[68] Third, they established a procedure for the News and Special Events Department to request kinescopes for archival purposes be made of any upcoming news programming they anticipated as having historical value.[69] When the in-house kinescope recording division quoted them upward of $50,000 per year for this service, the News and Special Events Department reached out to CBS and ABC to propose they split the costs of a cross-network historical archive. Neither network was interested, so, to avoid the embarrassment of an incomplete historical record of their own coverage, NBC News began to fund an in-house kinescope archive of news footage they deemed to have long-term historical value.[70]

At the time, these changes were seen as a slight jurisdictional victory for the News and Special Events Department over the NBC Film Division. They were also, however, a tacit recognition of the inevitable editorial intervention of information management work. Critically, the department with the power to rationalize what film should be kept and why would shape the historical trajectory of the network newsfilm collection as a whole. For this reason, the NBC News Department, frustrated that the film library's commercial mandate had led them to prioritize secondary stock footage sales over the future news value of their newsfilm collection, demanded, and were granted, final authority to pass judgment on the historical relevance of NBC newsfilm.

However, much like their earlier objections to *The Today Show*, the NBC News Department's preservation efforts up to that point had been no less commercially motivated than the NBC film library's. Indeed, it is largely because of its initial sponsor, R. J. Reynolds, that any kinescopes of NBC's first nightly news program, *The Camel News Caravan*, were ever made in the first place. While NBC oversaw the show's day-to-day production in New York City, the show's sponsor, R. J. Reynolds, was headquartered in Winston-Salem, North Carolina, and could not access the live broadcast. In order to show the executives at Camel Cigarettes what their $10,000 a week was funding, NBC newsmen would point a film camera at a television screen when *The Camel News Caravan* came on and make a single, blurry kinescoped recording of the program, which they would then mail to R. J. Reynolds headquarters.[71] A few of these early kinescopes survive, and at least two have been digitized and made available on YouTube, a lucky break for researchers interested in early TV history and early TV news. So, while NBC's newsmen insisted that they were the best arbiters of newsfilm's historical value because they were not motivated by commercial interest, the historical preservation of television news has *always* been determined by an untidy confluence of historical and commercial value, even as justifications for its preservation tend to emphasize the former.

In contrast, CBS's recognition of the historical value of its newsfilm collection was both less contentious and less intentional than NBC's ongoing feud. CBS began their own newsgathering operations almost a decade later than NBC, and their film library, firmly under the jurisdiction of CBS News, distinguished between footage with "pure news" and footage with secondary commercial value as soon as it entered the library. As their holdings expanded and the film library became a critical programming partner within CBS News, the "pure news" value of network newsfilm became more or less synonymous with its historical value.

This slippage between CBS newsfilm's news value and its historical value is most clearly articulated in a television news handbook that CBS produced for classroom and newsroom use in 1958: *CBS News: Television News Reporting*. Reflecting on the relationship between present-day news value and history, the author writes:

> What is the most universal film? The film you cannot resist using? There must be several thousand individual subjects that answer this description, film of events and men—of history—which cannot be forgotten by any person living in this time. It is film which fits the definition of film for film's sake.... It is concerned with great events, ideas, defeats, disappointments, victories of our civilization.... These examples indicate what manner of men and events have figured in the universal television film of our time.... By its very subject matter, or its remarkable photographic integ-

rity, it smacks of bigness, is in a class of greatness, it is timeless film. Rather than decreasing in value as time passes, it becomes all the more valuable. Film of such caliber will be used over and over again.[72]

Notably, while the CBS News employee who wrote this passage never concretely articulates what makes something newsworthy or not, they describe the *historical* value of newsfilm as the inevitable continuation of its news value over time. In other words, newsfilm that the CBS News Department incorporated into its broadcasts again and again had historical value for its continued relevance. But while the author describes this film as "universal," "timeless," and "in a class of greatness," it is also important to recognize the wholly subjective editorial influence of CBS and NBC newsmen in the initial determination of a given film's news value. And as neither NBC nor CBS had explicit editorial policies mapping out their criteria for what made something newsworthy until the following decade, this meant that the news value of specific stories, and by extension their historical significance, was often up for debate.

This elision of the editorial labor necessary to determine what is and isn't news—and by extension, history—echoes the dilemma Michael Curtin describes in his analysis of the documentaries produced during the era that followed the first decades of television news production. While networks justified their decision to only broadcast their own documentaries by asserting the editorial acumen of their news professionals, they justified that professional status by pointing to their commitment to objective reporting. As Curtin notes, the impossibility of exerting editorial judgment while also remaining objective produced a decade of fascinating documentaries, full of "contradictory meanings" and "ideological gaps and ruptures" ripe for historical interpretation.[73] Similarly, within network film libraries, the dueling imperatives of editorialization and objectivity meant that subjective news values were often archived as objective historical documentation.

Although television newsmen saw themselves as objective, impartial reporters, and while their networks marketed them as such to critics, regulators, and audiences alike, the dueling commercial and journalistic mandates of early network television meant that television news was always both a commercial and a public service enterprise. Inevitably, this dual mandate shaped the afterlife of the newsfilm itself.

At NBC, newsfilm was initially described in a way that would appeal to the target demographics of midcentury advertising executives. At CBS, newsfilm was described in accordance with the dominant news values and popular subjects of the time. In both cases, this evolving process of organization and description was a practical necessity as well as an inherently ideological process of assigning value to material media artifacts. Thus, when they eventually developed criteria for preserving television newsfilm on historical grounds, both NBC and CBS prioritized hard news programming targeted to and associated with an explicitly male audience—international news, politics, business news, and so on—as the most historically relevant. Likewise, the organization and description of this newsfilm systematically reproduced the subject position of NBC's and CBS's carefully cultivated, public persona of the network newsman. News footage was assigned news value and/or resale value accordingly, thus dictating how it would be prioritized, organized, described, and made available within each network's film library.

So, while the material loss of and lack of public access to surviving early network news footage is undoubtedly a profound historical loss, it is not the loss of empirical visual documentation of the past; rather, it is the loss of history as told from a specific worldview, one that naturalized white, well-educated men as arbiters of both the public interest and the historical record. In this way, a material interrogation of the archivability of early television news expands our understanding of how news was physically made and who was actually *making* it. NBC's and CBS's ambitious and creative forays into television news necessitated an intricate synthesis between prerecorded and live elements on a massive scale, and within both networks it was film librarians—employees neither credited nor compensated as "newsmen"—who made the first three decades of television news and documentary production both possible and profitable.

NOTES

1. Russ Johnston to Carleton Smith, August 31, 1949, U.S. mss. 17AF, box 590, folder 4, National Broadcasting Company Records, Wisconsin Historical Society (hereafter NBC Records).
2. Lauren Bratslavsky, "The Archival Value of Television in the 'Golden Age' of Media Collecting," *Film and History* 47, no. 2 (2017): 12–27; Caroline Frick, "Manufacturing Heritage: The Moving Image Archive and Media Industry Studies," in *Media Industries: History, Theory, and Method*, 1st ed., ed. Jennifer Holt and Alisa Perren (Malden, Mass.: Wiley-Blackwell, 2011); Caroline Frick, *Saving Cinema: The Politics of Preservation* (New York: Oxford University Press, 2011), 13–20; Lucas Hilderbrand, *Inherent Vice: Bootleg Histories of Videotape and Copyright* (Durham, N.C.: Duke University Press, 2009), 117–55; Lynn Spigel,

"Our TV Heritage: Television, the Archive, and the Reasons for Preservation," in *A Companion to Television*, ed. Janet Wasko (Oxford: John Wiley & Sons, 2005), 71–74; Haidee Wasson, *Museum Movies: The Museum of Modern Art and the Birth of Art Cinema* (Berkeley: University of California Press, 2005).

3. Eric Hoyt, *Hollywood Vault: Film Libraries before Home Video* (Berkeley: University of California Press, 2014). Hoyt situates media libraries explicitly in a market context of supply and demand. Although Hoyt is primarily concerned with libraries of commercial feature films, for the purposes of my project, his work points to a promising reframing of media libraries as instruments that facilitate the full life cycle of audiovisual records, not just their afterlife. See also Travis Vogan, *Keepers of the Flame: NFL Films and the Rise of Sports Media* (Urbana: University of Illinois Press, 2014). Vogan addresses the essential role media archives play in industrial production processes. Taking the NFL Films Archives as a case study, Vogan shows how commercial media archives are essential to the continued financial success of the NFL as a media company. He effectively demonstrates that in a business where audiovisual content is collateral, understanding how commercial archives operate can illuminate how the media industries themselves function.

4. "157 Million Feet of Stock TV Film: Are You Getting the Most Out of It?" *Sponsor*, December 14, 1953.

5. Noran Kersta, "Report on the NBC Television Film Library," February 21, 1947, U.S. mss. 17AF, box 585, folder 38, NBC Records.

6. Memo from Paul Alley to John Royal, June 25, 1947, U.S. mss. 17AF, box 585, folder 38, NBC Records.

7. Kersta, "Report on the NBC Television Film Library."

8. Ray Kelly to Robert Meyers, August 12, 1949, U.S. mss. 17AF, box 590, folder 4, NBC Records.

9. Kelly to Meyers, August 12, 1949.

10. Ray Kelly to Robert Meyers, August 11, 1949, U.S. mss. 17AF, box 590, folder 4, NBC Records.

11. Frank McCall to Ray Kelly, July 15, 1953, U.S. mss. 17AF, box 368, folder 18, NBC Records.

12. Memo from L. Vaughn to Frank Lepore, April 8, 1952, U.S. mss. 17AF, box 279, folder 7, NBC Records.

13. Frank Lepore to Wile, April 4, 1952, U.S. mss. 17AF, box 279, folder 7, NBC Records.

14. Adolph Schneider to William Brooks, November 8, 1948, U.S. mss. 17AF, box 590, folder 12, NBC Records.

15. Ray Kelly to Carleton Smith, November 11, 1948, U.S. mss. 17AF, box 334, folder 16, NBC Records.

16. Michael Socolow, "'We Should Make Money on Our News': The Problem of Profitability in Network Broadcast Journalism History," *Journalism* 11, no. 6 (2010): 675–91.

17. Frank Lepore, July 21, 1950, U.S. mss. 17AF, box 200, folder 1, NBC Records.

18. "NBC Film Library Handbook," 1, 2 (quotation).

19. "157 Million Feet of Stock TV Film," 62.

20. Boyce Nemac, "Report on Management Survey of the Television News Film Operations of the News and Public Affairs Department," 1956, D-4, box 4Zd488, Sig Mickelson Papers, Briscoe Center for American History Repository (hereafter CAH).
21. Nemac, "Report on Management Survey," D-4.
22. Mickelson to Van Volkenburg, August 26, 1953, box 1, folder 13, Sig Mickelson Papers, 1947–1975, Professional Papers Series, Wisconsin Historical Society (hereafter Mickelson Papers).
23. Michael Curtin, *Redeeming the Wasteland: Television Documentary and Cold War Politics* (New Brunswick, N.J.: Rutgers University Press, 1995).
24. Emile de Antonio, "Interview with Emile de Antonio and Mark Lane," *Film Comment* 4, nos. 2–3 (Fall/Winter 1967): 12.
25. "CBS Newsfilm," box 1, folder 14, Mickelson Papers.
26. "1955 CBS News Clinic," box 1, folder 4, Mickelson Papers.
27. William S. Paley, "The Road to Responsibility," May 25, 1954, box 1, folder 13, Mickelson Papers.
28. John F. Day, "Growing Pains of Television News: Still an Infant, It Faces Many Problems," *Broadcasting*, August 29, 1955, 64.
29. Ackerman to Mickelson, October 14, 1955, box 4Zd488, Sig Mickelson Papers, CAH.
30. Next to Rhett Butler, Gable is probably best known for playing a wisecracking newspaper reporter in *It Happened One Night* (1934).
31. "Meet Marcia Drennen: Capable Newspaper-Trained Miss Who Edits 130,000 Feet of NBC News Film a Year," *NBC Trade News*, May 7, 1953, Internet Archive, https://archive.org/details/nbctraderelease1953nati_3/mode/2up.
32. Green to Keever, November 7, 1951, box 310, folder 8, NBC Records.
33. Charles Barry, June 16, 1953, box 279, folder 57, NBC Records.
34. Charles L. Ponce de Leon, *That's the Way It Is: A History of Television News in America* (Chicago: University of Chicago Press, 2015), 35.
35. Barry, June 16, 1953.
36. Barry, June 16, 1953.
37. "Reuven Frank," Television Academy Interviews, October 23, 2017, https://interviews.televisionacademy.com/interviews/reuven-frank.
38. "1955 CBS News Clinic," 15, 75.
39. "Joint Committee on Television Film Usage Minutes," August 26, 1949, box 118, folder 20, NBC Records.
40. Sig Mickelson, "Outline for the CTD Budget Presentation," November 30, 1960, box 1, folder 2, Mickelson Papers.
41. "CBS News Division Budget Meeting," February 2, 1958, box 1, folder 2, Mickelson Papers.
42. Barry, June 16, 1953.
43. "1955 CBS News Clinic," 65–67.
44. Nemac, "Report on Management Survey," 61.
45. "1955 CBS News Clinic," 3, 37–70.
46. "CBS News Division Budget Meeting," February 2, 1958; Organizational Chart,

January 2, 1954, box 1, folder 13, Mickelson Papers; Nemac, "Report on Management Survey," 29.
47. "Minutes of Television News Conference," September 8, 1955, box 1, folder 2, Mickelson Papers.
48. Meyers to Taylor, March 9, 1953, box 368, folder 18, NBC Records.
49. Schechter to Lyman, February 8, 1952, box 311, folder 32, NBC Records.
50. Meyers to Taylor, March 9, 1953, box 368, folder 18, NBC Records.
51. Colledge to Taylor, box 2778, folder 1, NBC Records.
52. Nemac, "Report on Management Survey," D1–D7.
53. "1955 CBS News Clinic," 38.
54. "Today Show Meeting Minutes," December 14, 1953, box 278, folder 1, NBC Records.
55. *CBS Television News Reporting* (New York: McGraw-Hill, 1958), 35.
56. McCall to Taylor, May 16, 1951, box 277, folder 1, NBC Records.
57. "The New Life in Old Film," *Broadcasting*, December 9, 1963, 27–30.
58. Irving Traeger, January 15, 1953, box 122, folder 23, NBC Records.
59. Traeger, January 15, 1953.
60. Draft of Memo to Messers. Van Volkenburg and Jones, box 1, folder 4, Mickelson Papers.
61. Curtin, *Redeeming the Wasteland*, 139.
62. Curtin, *Redeeming the Wasteland*, 120–38, 8. Between 1955 and 1979, over seven thousand individual programs and over 120 documentary series aired on U.S. network television, the majority debuting during the 1960s. See Daniel Einstein, *Special Edition: A Guide to Network Television Documentary Series and Special News Reports, 1980–1989* (Lanham, Md.: Scarecrow Press, 1997).
63. Eric Barnouw, *A History of Broadcasting in the United States*, vol. 3: *The Image Empire, from 1953* (New York: Oxford University Press, 1970), 42–43; Ponce de Leon, *That's the Way It Is*, 1–39.
64. Ray Kelly to Carleton Smith, November 11, 1948, U.S. mss. 17AF, box 334, folder 16, NBC Records.
65. E. Madden to Lyman Munson, March 12, 1952, U.S. mss. 17AF, box 569, folder 25, NBC Records.
66. Memo from Frank Lepore to Stan Osgood, March 7, 1952, U.S. mss. 17AF, box 569, folder 25, NBC Records.
67. Pinkham, March 13, 1952, U.S. mss. 17AF, box 569, folder 25, NBC Records.
68. Taylor to Lepore, September 21, 1951.
69. McCall, September 14, 1951, box 272, folder 46, NBC Records.
70. Lepore, September 26, 1951, box 272, folder 46, NBC Records.
71. "Reuven Frank."
72. *CBS Television News Reporting*, 35.
73. Curtin, *Redeeming the Wasteland*, 51.

CHAPTER 2

OWEN GOTTLIEB

HERITAGE IN SEARCH OF A HOME

ARCHIVING THE LEARNING DESIGNS AND ARTISTRY OF
INSTRUCTIONAL TELEVISION OF THE 1970S AND 1980S

PRELUDE: WHAT WILL HAPPEN TO IT ALL?
BLOOMINGTON, INDIANA, 2013

David Gudaitis did not know what he could do, but he wanted to do something. The entire library of television programs from his production company was at risk of being discarded and destroyed. It was keeping him up at night—David had been a producer at the Agency for Instructional Technology (AIT) for more than twenty-five years, having arrived in the late 1980s. AIT's history stretched back to the early 1970s, and in earlier incarnations with different names, back to the mid-1960s. At the heights of the achievements of the instructional television (ITV) genre in the 1970s and 1980s, AIT had produced and distributed hundreds of television programs broadcast into classrooms over the Public Broadcasting Service (PBS) in the United States and stations in Canada.[1] The programs were shown by legions of teachers to millions of students. Those programs included Emmy Award winners; for example, *Inside/Out* (1973), an aesthetically arresting and emotionally powerful program that taught affective health education, what we now refer to as social and emotional learning, to fourth and fifth graders. It won an Emmy in 1974 over the giants of children's educational television including *Sesame Street*, *Mister Rogers' Neighborhood*, and *Schoolhouse Rock!*

But by 2013 the days of instructional television and AIT's heights had long passed. Few nonprofits have a budget or plan for archiving their material, and AIT was not one of those few. Given that AIT was likely to soon close its doors for good, there certainly would not be space or resources to preserve its library. David worried: without a steward, would all those decades of television programs, scripts, awards, photos, and all the research that had been conducted on the programs, just go into a dumpster? Would the entirety of the agency's body of work just be discarded? What could he do to stop it all from disappearing?[2] David's next decision set in motion a chain of events. I return to him later in this chapter after exploring a story that stretches back two decades earlier: the story of a search for an archival home for instructional television and radio.

This chapter traces the stories of two collections. One collection, mostly of paper documents, remains a critical remnant of a once much broader plan to save instructional television and radio. The other collection story is that of the formation, preservation, digitization, and then scholarly exploration of a rare and voluminous archival collection of AIT television programs and text materials. These collections are invaluable for understanding the use of media in classrooms in the United States and Canada in the latter half of the twentieth century. The bulk of the second collection went a quarter century without an archival home and easily could have been destroyed at any point along the way. In fact, some of the Emmy Award–winning programs of the original collection have been lost. The stories wind through hopes and dreams of some of the people who created the programs, the struggles to safeguard the materials, and even the recovery of an otherwise damaged episode from almost ten thousand miles away. The stories map shifting institutional identities, the contestation over ITV's relationship to "Public Broadcasting," two university presidents with intersecting visions, painstaking and dedicated work of archivists, and numerous remarkable and fortunate convergences of circumstances across the decades. From these tales we might learn how to better promote the archiving of television in ways that leave less to chance and synchronicity. This is particularly important today as the programs and records of noncommercial, instructional, and local television are rapidly and continually being discarded and destroyed.

ITV AND AIT—THE AGENCY FOR INSTRUCTIONAL TELEVISION (LATER TECHNOLOGY)

In the 1970s and 1980s, ITV programs, specifically intended for use in classrooms, were broadcast into classrooms in the United States and Canada. The ITV of this period was built on hard-won lessons of the 1950s and 1960s, including overcoming the earlier production approaches of long, studio-bound lectures as well as technologies ranging from closed-circuit television to transmission into classrooms from airplanes in flight.[3] The new wave of the 1970s and 1980s, led by AIT, featured fifteen- to twenty-minute programs wrapped into classroom curricula with teacher guides and sometimes teacher trainings. Their creators brought bold new aesthetics and instructional designs. AIT teamed young filmmakers equipped with 16mm cameras, capable of on-location shooting, with instructional designers and researchers. These teams collaboratively developed increasingly more sophisticated approaches to media design for learning, which were then made available to any classroom with access to a television cart. That television could be simply switched on at the scheduled broadcast time each week; no longer was there the need to thread up, maintain, and run a 16mm projector.

Edwin "Ed" G. Cohen was a leader in educational and public television—specifically instructional television—since his career began in the 1950s, including work at NET in New York. He was the founder and long-term executive director of AIT as the genre of ITV blossomed in the 1960s and 1970s. And he led AIT through the treacherous 1980s when educational budgets were slashed or eliminated from the federal level down, and when demands for personal computers and software, rather than television, had radically altered the ITV landscape. Cohen was at the helm as AIT evolved through a number of institutional changes. It originally started out of the National Instructional Television Library (NITL), a "demonstration project" funded by the U.S. Department of Education and "contractually supported" by National Educational Television (NET) in New York. In 1962 Cohen, already having built a career in ITV, became the director of the new organization.[4] In 1965 NITL moved to Bloomington, Indiana, in coordination with Indiana University, where Cohen had earned his PhD years earlier. There Cohen transformed the organization into one that distributed *and* developed programming, thereby dropping the "Library" from the original name. The organization was renamed the Agency for Instructional Television in 1973 when it went independent from Indiana University, meaning it no longer received funding from the university's foundation. In 1984 AIT changed "television" in its name to "technology." For a map of the institution's history, see table 3.1.

At the core of the organizational magic of AIT during Cohen's time as executive director had been their homegrown consortia model of producing television. Since the early 1970s, NIT, and then AIT, raised money to fund sizable budgets for extraordinary instructional television by forming consortia of (U.S.) state and (Canadian) provincial educational agencies. In 1967 Cohen brought aboard Bob Fox, who by the 1970s would become associate executive director for development. Fox flew around the

TABLE 2.1

The Institutional Evolution of AIT

Date	Organization	Function	Auspices	Funding source
January 1, 1962–April 30, 1965	National Instructional Television Library (NITL)	Distribution	National Educational Television and Radio Center	U.S. Office of Education
May 1, 1965–August 31, 1967	National Center for School and College Television (NCSCT)	Distribution	Indiana University Foundation	U.S. Office of Education
September 1, 1967–June 30, 1973	National Instructional Television Center (NIT)	Development and distribution	Indiana University Foundation	Indiana University Foundation/users/grants
July 1, 1973	Agency for Instructional Television Center (AIT)	Development and distribution	Independent	Users/grants
1984	Agency for Instructional Technology (AIT)	Development and distribution	Independent	Users/grants

This table is slightly expanded from an original table in "The Genealogy of the Agency for Instructional Television," on page 13 of John Middleton's *Cooperative School Television and Educational Change*, and includes information regarding the 1984 shift in name from the expanded notes from University of Maryland's biography of Edwin Cohen in the Edwin G. Cohen Papers. I have added the term "grants" to note contributions from corporate, foundation, and Corporation for Public Broadcasting grants.

United States and Canada building relationships and partners for each consortium.[5] I refer to this as a federated network. This federated system meant that the agency and consortia could produce higher-budget and higher-quality programs than individual local stations could. This allowed AIT's programs to compete in terms of quality with the best of Children's Television Workshop's work (for example, *Sesame Street* had received considerable federal funds through Head Start). The significantly larger budgets would break the mold that had helped stigmatize locally produced ITV of earlier decades. Discussing the first of the AIT consortium-funded programs, the series *Ripples* (1970), Cohen reflected in an oral history, "These programs really were evidence that instructional television had turned the corner from inexpensive, boring, studio lectures to what instructional television proponents had always maintained it could be—that is, engaging programming that really brought the student and reality together."[6] The consortia system put AIT on the map and kept it vibrant through the 1970s and even into the mid-1980s.

AIT programs spanned subject areas from mathematics to language arts to history to world cultures. This was engaging television for learning with thicker content than preschool preparatory programs such as *Sesame Street*. Beyond recognizing letters and numbers, these programs taught schoolchildren a range of rich subject matter, including social and emotional learning in *Inside/Out* (then known as affective education), language arts in programs like *Wordsmith*, how to make decisions in economics in the program *Trade-offs*, and reasoning and problem-solving skills in *ThinkAbout*. Many of these series were funded using the innovative consortia model.[7]

The ITV programs of this period, born of these collaborations, and the related materials discussed in this chapter provide documentation of significant design precedents for the creation and use of media and technology in the classroom. The aims, the intentionality, the aesthetic innovation, the research brought to bear on program development, and the evaluation of the programs set them apart from every other genre of television. In addition to the depth of content, these programs and lessons were often developed in the context and consciousness of democratic practice and citizenry—how learning the skills and knowledge in various subject areas was key to being a better, more active citizen in a democracy.[8] The remaining AIT collections allow for preserving the history of a key period of media instructional design, one that, for a variety of reasons, has been chronically understudied.[9] The ability, afforded by this collection, to address these lacunae in the history could have significant implications for the design of learning media in its current forms of interactive media and video games for learning as well as the development of the next evolution of learning media and technology.

THE DASHED VISIONS OF AN ITV+RADIO ARCHIVE: COLLEGE PARK, MARYLAND, 1992–1995, 1997

In 1992, twenty-one years before AIT producer David Gudaitis contemplated how to preserve AIT's materials, Cohen set out on a similar but broader quest. Once he retired in 1990, he had a new mission. Donald R. McNeil (board member of PBS) had recently led the formation of the National Public Broadcasting Archives (NPBA) at the University of Maryland. Cohen saw the archives as an opportunity to safeguard the long and nearly unknown history of the fields of instructional television and radio. Via methods he had used successfully for decades for ITV financing and production, Cohen brought together experts to build ambitious, collaboratively supported plans to preserve the history of instructional television and radio. He raised funds from the Corporation for Public Broadcasting (CPB) to conduct an extensive research report on what it would mean to have an instructional television and radio collection formally held at the new NPBA. CPB awarded Cohen with both a planning grant for the proposal in 1992 and then a project grant in 1995. It was a comprehensive approach: Cohen involved ninety-four experts to consult on, review, and comment on the plan. Some served on a three-day advisory panel at the NPBA along with the archive's curator and Cohen.

In consultation with these experts, Cohen constructed detailed chronologies of the history of instructional radio and television, which to this day may very well be the only such chronology in existence. He presented acquisition criteria and prioritized key materials to acquire. He noted dozens of "essential" and "desirable" oral histories to record, as well as an appraisal of acquisitions that had already been made or were in process. Acquisition criteria in the 1992 plan include:

> IMPORTANCE—landmark, standard setting, award-winning programming; key procedures, practices, developments, organizations; prominent individuals; key statements; major legislation.
>
> REPRESENTATIVENESS—samples from a cross section of academic levels and subjects, instructional approaches and formats, related to regional and local service organizations; materials for exceptional learners, such as special needs students.
>
> COMPLETENESS—materials providing a view of all aspects of development and use of key programs—"needs determination, instructional design, production, formative evaluation, teacher training, summative evaluation, and budget"; materials documenting all aspects of creation of key organizations, policies, and legislation; data on practices that did not work with evidence regarding failure.
>
> PERISHABILITY—priority given to the material most at risk of "destruction or decay" and to bringing in older material first, with "blanket" priority for materials before the mid-1970s.[10]

Cohen's 1995 report determined the needs: space in the archives, staff (one full-time staff member to oversee), financing, and commitment of the University of Maryland and the archives. Determination of financing needs was specifically left to the assessment of the University of Maryland: "The precise cost of fully activating an instructional archives can be determined only by the University of Maryland at College Park Libraries. In general, however, its cost should be appreciably lessened because [an] instructional collection already exists and considerable additional acquisitions are underway. Of equal importance the present and projected integration of an instructional collection within NPBA should minimize start-up costs."[11] Cohen suggested key selections of materials from AIT including selections from nine key programs of the 1970s, including episodes of *Inside/Out* and *ThinkAbout*. He suggested oral histories with some of the core team. The scope of the project was far broader than just AIT, though chronologies note key contributions of AIT to instructional television.

The response Cohen received from the curator at the University of Maryland, Lauren R. Brown, six months later on April 28, 1995, expresses gratitude for the project.[12] The letter notes the value of the proposal itself but also points to the lack of resources unless Cohen were to raise outside funding. "The detailed chronologies you have included could by themselves serve as a valuable aid for ITV research," he wrote, and he continued: "On the matter of oral history, I certainly agree with you on the importance of gathering the historical recollections of the individuals you have identified in your report. The cost of good oral history is high however and could not be undertaken given the present NPBA budget. If you have any ideas on how to locate outside funding for this project, please share them with us; perhaps a cooperative endeavor is the best approach for completing the oral history component of your report recommendations." In terms of dedicated staff, Brown refers again to outside funding that could provide for such a staff member, but currently they have student assistants: "In the meantime, student assistants are and will be available for the basic work of creating inventories and other computer records for managing what has been received so far."[13]

It seems notable that Brown uses the term "cooperative," as it was by the cooperative consortia method that Cohen had produced television for decades, pooling resources from those with shared interests. Perhaps Brown noted the various series listed in the chronology that were cooperatively funded or had learned of the cooperative funding methods that Cohen and his team had pioneered in the early 1970s. The vision for a dedicated instructional television and radio collection at the University of Maryland seems to end with the letter. There do not appear to be subsequent grant proposals by Cohen, at least in the archives at UMD. Perhaps Cohen had determined he had reached the end of the line.

That said, numerous important elements related to Cohen and AIT do exist at the University of Maryland (UMD) Special Collections. These include Cohen's extensive papers (eighty linear feet, with over fifty boxes), the finding guide for which was completed in January 1999. Cohen also donated selected films and tapes for a number of AIT programs.[14] During one of my trips to the archive, Michael Henry of Special Collections at UMD discovered and shared with me an uncataloged, apparently unread, extensive oral history of Cohen conducted by Thomas Connors of the NPBA, contextualizing the collection—a resource that his been invaluable in conducting my research.[15] Years later, Saul Rockman, who led research at AIT for many years, donated his papers to the archive, though currently the Rockman papers have not yet been processed.[16] I have also found the papers of Robert D. B. Carlisle, a journalism and public broadcasting producer who often wrote historical materials for Cohen and AIT. Carlisle began donating his own papers to the NPBA in 1992. Cohen had included Carlisle in his proposal under the category of "essential oral histories" for higher education instructional television. Carlisle was one of the advisors in the three-day meeting or teleconference that Cohen convened, and he also reviewed the proposal. Though I have not yet found other sets of papers at the NPBA connected to Cohen's proposal, it is possible that others suggested in the Cohen proposals have also donated their papers. While the Cohen and Rockman papers do not represent the breadth or depth of the entirety of school television and radio, as Cohen had originally proposed, they do hold key historical records for AIT in its various incarnations through 1990. These include Cohen's handwritten detailed notes, files, research reports, strategic planning documents, and correspondence as well as even catalogs from other production companies like Great Plains National (whose library seems to be almost entirely lost). All of these materials are key for reconstructing ITV history.

THE INTERNAL DISCUSSIONS AT NPBA—
RESOURCES AND THE FRAMING OF ACQUISITION CRITERIA

Cohen may never have realized how far his proposal vision had come—from the initial, distanced concern among the NPBA archival team in 1993 all the way to the development and binding of Cohen's extensive oral history in 1997 led by Tom Connors. It appears that the UMD team grappled with the inevitable tensions organizations face between internal debate and external engagement. Documents shared internally at the NPBA in 1993 reveal that curator Thomas "Tom" Connors, then graduate student Mike Mashon, and curator Lauren Brown initially showed concern regarding Cohen's proposal. They were reluctant to even consider taking on additional instructional television and radio materials, despite already having a few ITV-related papers, including Cohen's own papers donated in 1991. They voiced concerns about the practicality of taking on such an endeavor and the fit of a substantial instructional television collection in the NAPB.[17]

In a memo to Don McNeil, founder of the NPBA, Connors expressed skepticism and concerns about the resources available and the means that Cohen intended to employ to garner the various data. Cohen proposed to CPB a large volunteer advisory council. Connors wondered, "Would there be any professional archivists on the team?" and "How these groups come together, how they will make decisions, how they will relate to one another should be clarified. It just seems to me that a lot of energy, time, and people are called for here. Need it be that involved?"[18] A week before, Connors wrote in a more blunt internal memo to Brown and two other colleagues that there was no space for such an endeavor. Furthermore, he commented on Cohen's plan of a volunteer council, an advisory council of experts, and a group representing end users: "I think the organizational structure he presents is hopelessly bureaucratic; I don't see how it could function effectively."[19] Connors's response is certainly understandable given the complicated and vast bureaucratic plan that Cohen set forth.

It seems that Connors was not yet familiar with how Cohen had navigated working with bureaucracies and large-scale coalitions for decades; years later Connors would eventually conduct the extensive oral history with Cohen about his career and AIT mentioned above.[20] Cohen and Bob Fox raised funding from partners in the consortia and beyond, creating highly improbable yet successful mass consensus-driven in-person decision-making sessions with dozens of state and provincial agency heads. Thus, Cohen and Fox had been making the improbable into the possible for a long time by conducting a vast orchestra of stakeholders in large gatherings—and harnessing that energy into great instructional television. Cohen, though, was apparently unaware of Connors's worries at the time of delivery of the initial planning proposal. Eventually, a curator from the University of Maryland would be on the team of the second CPB grant for the project stage. Perhaps this inclusion was in response to Connors's concerns about whether a professional archivist would be on the team.

In two 1993 memos, Connors referred to Lauren Brown's fear regarding lack of space for this proposed collection. Subsequent to the concerns Connors expressed about how realistic Cohen's plan was, there were issues of space and staff. The curators had help in evaluating Cohen's proposal: Connors enlisted the help of Mike Mashon, then a graduate student. Mashon was not, at the time of the letter, listed as a curator or employee of the University of Maryland. Mashon had access to and quotes from Cohen's initial planning proposal to CPB.[21]

In his letter to Connors about Cohen's proposed instructional television collection, Mashon concluded that the proposed collection was not a "fit" with the National Archives of Public Broadcasting.[22] He described how the 1967 Carnegie Commission that formed public television had separated ITV and "public broadcasting." Cohen notes in the oral history that the narrow focus of the Carnegie Commission made the Public Broadcasting Act possible.[23] I theorize, based on similar moves in the mid-1960s by the Ford Foundation, that the commission made this distinction to avoid saddling the broader mission of then-nascent "public television" with the stigma of the then well-known boring lectures—a stigma that has followed conceptions of ITV to this day—despite the remarkable examples of ITV that flourished in the 1970s and 1980s.[24] At the same time, the commission could avoid being seen as attacking the core mission of what had been "educational television"—part of the core of the argument for the public good of government investment in television.

Cohen understood ITV as a key part of PBS history, as had Saul Rockman.[25] AIT programs, for example, were broadcast across the United States on PBS stations through the 1970s, 1980s, and into the early 1990s; for some stations, AIT content occupied most of the hours between 10:00 a.m. (after *Sesame Street*) until the end of the school day.[26] Often, smaller PBS stations did not broadcast overnight, making ITV an even greater proportion of their broadcasting day. In his July 13, 1993, letter assessing Cohen's proposal, Mashon demanded a distinction—that carrying the programs was specifically "carriage" or as a "delivery system" for ITV programming—and argued that ITV constituted narrowcasting, like ITV's early days using closed-circuit systems, not public broadcasting. "These [ITV programs] are programs aimed at very specific audiences with particular results (mastery of subject) in mind."[27]

In considering the connections to the CPB aspect of ITV, Mashon argued that CPB had never funded instructional television, which would be a reason for exclusion from the NPBA collection. This last point was not in fact the case, as CPB had made a significant grant—$1.4 million on a $3.5 million budget—to the *ThinkAbout* series (1979) by AIT.[28] CPB also had contributed to the 1980 AIT series *On the Level*. Mashon also noted that Cohen's inclusion of extratextual materials such as teachers' guides—documents not distributed by public broadcasting (they were distributed at the state and station level)—would even further expand the bounds of the collection, later concluding that the entire proposal and collection, "in terms of our archival interests, it just doesn't fit." In a conversation with Mashon in September 2023 at the Century of 16mm Conference at Indiana University's Moving Image Archive, Mashon told me he was unaware of the funding by CPB at the time of the 1993 letter.

It is notable that the Mashon letter, while in most ways technically accurate, might also have been framed to justify the opposing perspective—that there was a fit. As for programs "aimed at very specific audiences with particular results in mind," this could have also been applied to flagship PBS programs such as *Great Performances*. William Hoynes and Laurie Oullette have pointed out that the target for much of PBS programming focused on those who donate during pledge drives.[29] My reading of the Hoynes and Oullette critiques is that there was an apparent focus on upper- and upper-middle-class viewers with attendant particular tastes and affinities (though I argue this also provided access to more diverse audiences who would otherwise not have access to such programming). As much as five hours out of a broadcast day on PBS (10:00 a.m.–3:00 p.m.) would be dedicated to instructional television, television that, by the mid-1980s, could be recorded and time-shifted by VCR. The programs could be viewed by children at home from school on snow days or teacher conferences, or viewed by stay-at-home parents. This availability also broadens the ideas about "narrowcasting." If *Sesame Street* was public broadcasting at 9:00 a.m., why must an ITV program at 10:00 a.m. be considered "narrowcasting"? If the broadcasting network sent the programs out to every television set and VCR within broadcasting range, can it truly be considered "narrowcasting" in the same way that closed-circuit, which strictly limited viewing, was narrowcasting? Mashon's argument about "carriage" holds greater strength than the narrowcasting argument—if the programs during ITV were not funded by CPB, then perhaps they were better aligned with the British imports on primetime PBS like *Masterpiece Theatre* and *Mystery*, programming not held in the NPBA archive. And yet, CPB *had* funded shows as evidenced by the large-scale grant to *ThinkAbout*. Does the exception prove the rule? Could the argument be extended to say that not enough of instructional television and radio had been funded by CPB to warrant inclusion in the NPBA? And yet, the archive already held non-CPB holdings in instructional broadcasting. The line drawn regarding fit must be considered in a broader context. The framing of the 1993 Mashon arguments, Connors's memos to McNeil and Brown, Brown's 1995 letter in response to Cohen's extensive CPB-funded study, the fact that there was already ITV material in the archive, and the fact that the NPBA eventually did accept more instructional material suggest that the acquisition criteria and the perceptions of fit may not always be cleanly compartmentalized from resource constraints.

Though we cannot know for certain, it appears that the primary driver of UMD's internal reluctance to establish a formal instructional television and radio collection in the NPBA, at least in 1993, is centered on serious resource limitations and process concerns. Space, staffing, and proposed large groups of advisors all appear as reasons to not engage in the broader project. The additional rationale, only discussed internally, regarding why an instructional collection may not be a good "fit" for a public broadcasting archive seems more permeable over time given the Cohen oral history and the limited inclusion of ITV programs and program-related materials. But the articulation of those concerns about fit brings into relief some of the misunderstandings of ITV as well as the long-standing outsider status that ITV has long held, even after decades of its most impressive productions were created and broadcast in the 1970s and 1980s, long after the Carnegie Commission. Though Brown pointed out that external funding brought by Cohen could have made a difference, is it also possible that a more detailed and up-front resource analysis at an early stage of Cohen's proposals have led to a different outcome?

Perhaps Cohen's initial proposal did not take into account enough of the fears, concerns, and interests of the curators and stakeholders at the University of Maryland, but the stance of the archives does seem to shift over time. Tom Connors, who was skeptical and even advocating against the collection to the founder of the NPBA, eventually conducted the 14.5-hour oral history with Ed Cohen, which was edited with Cohen, bound in two volumes, and given a comprehensive index. This project included Connors taking two trips from Maryland to Indiana to ask in-depth questions of Cohen. The archives at the University of Maryland housed and processed Ed Cohen's extensive paper collection of over fifty-two boxes, including materials such as selected teachers' guides, legislative history, and research studies, as well as Cohen's correspondence and handwritten notes. These materials, many of which would have been considered outside of the remit of the NPBA in the Mashon letter, preserve critical context for the AIT series, from financing to marketing to evaluation and research. For example, documents from the 1974 Emmy Award for *Inside/Out* exist in the Cohen papers that the National Academy of Television Arts and Sciences (NATAS) itself does not have on file.[30] Cohen's films and videos at NPBA, though they remain undigitized today, appear to contain particular prints that may preserve programs in full form elsewhere.

The process of delivering the CPB planning and activating grants, perhaps the fact that CPB funded both, and whatever relationship Cohen and Connors developed over the years seem to have been key to the preservation of the treasures of both the oral history and Cohen's unique set of papers. In 1994 Connors visited Cohen's home in Indiana and also met with the then-current head of AIT, Mike Sullivan. AIT was in the process of moving to a new facility. Connors writes of twenty-one boxes of materials including papers and early NET kinescopes, "These are important to document what NET did in school TV circa 1958–1961." Later in the memo he comments on the scope of material and writes, "I think that AIT is an important historical player in instructional programming." Connors closes the memo by suggesting bringing in someone named Chip Hixon on the NPBA payroll as a field staffer to go through the AIT files and, in essence, preprocess them. He suggests 150–200 hours paid by Foundation funds. This is a significant shift from just over a year earlier.[31]

By August 1996, during the second oral history trip to Bloomington (the first was October 1995), Connors closes the history with these words: "As far as I'm concerned, it's been my education into the real history of instructional television. It also gives me sort of a springboard to develop other interviews with people that you have designated. So I appreciate that, and I think this will be a great addition to the Archives, as well as the papers that I see around me here in this room. They will be processed as part of the collections available at the [National] Public Broadcasting Archives. So thank you so much, and we will talk again, I know." Connors and Cohen went on to collaborate on the editing of the oral history.[32] The shift in material of instructional television and radio was from internal assessments of "not a fit" to the printed and bound exclamation of "a great addition to the Archives."

Though I had reached out in 2022, I was sadly not able to discuss the oral history with Connors before his passing in 2023. Through reading Cohen's correspondence and documents and through conversations with those who worked with Cohen, such as David Gudaitis, Saul Rockman, and Bob Fox, I hypothesize that for those who spent time with Cohen talking about instructional television, Cohen's vast knowledge and passion must have been both obvious and inspiring. Perhaps Connors became likewise inspired to conduct the oral history, understanding that Cohen played a significant and unique role in instructional television.

While the archives at UMD play an essential role in preserving key ITV history in both paper and media formats, like most archives, they face resource constraints that limit scholarly access to programming. For example, in a small sampling of 16mm and videotape AIT programming available at the NAPB, these holdings are not currently mentioned in the finding guides. Viewing any of the fifteen- to twenty-minute productions must occur on campus and costs $100 per episode for transfer, with a waiting period for the transfer to occur. Also, copyright restrictions often limit the public's ability to view television collections in the United States and Canada. I refer to media housed at archives but largely inaccessible to either the public or most scholars, as "captive" media.

NAPB accepted that small sample of AIT programs from Ed Cohen. Would all the remaining AIT programming not preserved at the NAPB eventually become what is referred to as "orphan" media—media without a steward for preservation? And if so, how much of it would stand a chance of surviving? An answer to that question, and a new kind of solution to the captive media problem, would take another two decades to emerge.

THE STOELTJE-BLOOMINGTON CONFLUENCE: RESCUING THE REMAINING AIT LIBRARY

By 2013 producer David Gudaitis had been searching for a way to save the AIT material that remained.[33] There was no clear home for the AIT programs or records since Ed Cohen had not been able to launch a broad instructional radio and television archive collection at the NAPB in the 1990s. After a great deal of consternation wondering what would happen when AIT closed down, Gudaitis picked up the phone. He called someone just three miles away: Rachael Stoeltje, director of the Moving Image Archive at Indiana University Bloomington. He called the right person at the right time. Had it been just a few months earlier or perhaps just a few months later, the result could have been very different; there may be no AIT collection today. Stoeltje immediately wanted the AIT collection and understood both the value of the materials and their direct connection to the mission of the archive that she had worked to create just four years earlier.[34]

Stoeltje, once an undergraduate at Indiana University, trained in film preservation at Eastman House in Rochester, New York. She returned to IU to work on preservation of their film collections, including rescuing and preserving more than thirty-five thousand films that had been stored in a former bowling alley. She became the founding director of the Moving Image Archive in 2009.[35] Stoeltje started the new archive with a mission built on a foundation of the holdings already in IU's media collection: Bloomington held a premier collection of films, including works of Orson Welles, John Ford, Peter Bogdanovich, and the Kinsey Institute. It also held (and holds) one of the greatest collections of educational media in the world. This is because Indiana University Audio-Visual Center (AVC) had been a key distributor of A/V material dating back to World War I. Starting in 1955, the AVC was the exclusive distributor for NET, the predecessor of PBS in the 1950s.[36]

Stoeltje had heard about AIT and understood the connection to the educational aspect of her archive. AIT had essentially been born out of IU and connected to the leadership of university president Herman Wells, whose memoir offers details. In 1962 the Ford Foundation, funder of NET, wanted NET to divest from "school service broadcasting" to concentrate on public affairs and cultural programming (what would become PBS). The U.S. Office of Education made a grant to NET "to demonstrate the educational desirability and economic feasibility of a national agency providing recorded instructional television programs."[37] Ed Cohen led the grant project in New York as the National Instructional Television Library, then brought it to Bloomington in 1965 and became director of the renamed National Instructional Television. When the 1965 NET contract ended, it was the Indiana University Foundation, of whom Wells was the president, that

> advanced a substantial amount of money to keep the project going during the years 1968–70, after which it was believed the service could be supported entirely from earnings and over a period of six years could repay the advance made by the Foundation. In fact, the service was able to repay the Foundation ahead of schedule. The crux of NIT's achievement of self-support while continuing to strengthen its product was the recognition that it could not change immediately from entire economic dependence. Rather, a transition stage was necessary in which declining amounts of borrowed capital would complement increased earnings.[38]

By 1973 Cohen and his team had built the network of state and provincial agencies that formed their program consortia, which eventually, in combination with other distribution and networking with state chief school officers, led a pathway to economic stability and independence from Indiana University sponsorship under the new name of the Agency for Instructional Television.[39]

Additional synchronicities came into play. Gudaitis's 2013 call, two years before AIT closed its doors, also just happened to coincide with the launch of a massive university-wide digitization program. The program was funded with over $15 million from an initiative championed by the then-president of Indiana University, Michael McRobbie. It was called the Media Digitization Preservation Initiative (MDPI) and ran from 2013 to 2021. McRobbie held that preservation of knowledge was a fundamental mission of great universities.[40] By the early 2000s, many of the films held on campus were in danger of damage and loss. The goals of MDPI included the safeguarding and preservation of material across the IU campus and making that material more accessible to the public.

When Gudaitis reached out, by stroke of luck, there happened to still be room in the archive storage facility for the massive twenty-plus pallets of AIT material, so Stoeltje knew when she sent trucks to AIT over the course of two batches in 2013 and 2015, she could take in all the material. Eventually, the AIT collection would include more than twelve thousand audio and video items across twenty-three formats and 140 boxes of paper documents and images.

Most public television materials in major archives are not viewable by the public and also strictly limited for scholarly access: "captive" television. This captivity is due to a variety of factors including copyright, royalties, related legal entanglements, and digitization budgets or lack thereof. Unfortunately, the teaching and researching of television history and culture with limited viewing or screening access (or sometimes none) is challenging and attenuated. The way in which the AIT programs became accessible for viewing is a matter of precise timing, particular expertise, and philosophical archival approach. Access for the public to view archived television material is often quite rare. Stoeltje herself is an advocate of public access to archival material, citing the long-standing debates between the film archivists Henri Langlois, who was in favor of public screenings, and Ernest Lindgren, who did not permit archival prints to be screened. For Stoeltje, the films in the archives are cultural artifacts and part of our history. Stoeltje had learned over the first few years at the archive that she would need to make alterations to the deed of gift for the collection in order to allow for public viewing of the material. Important television holdings in the archive collection such as NET and later

WNET's groundbreaking *Black Journal* cannot currently be screened for the public. If the history of the material is to be shared, the way in which it was given to the archive had to change. Stoeltje brought aboard a copyright librarian and rewrote the archives' deed of gift so that the proper permissions could be granted and the public could view the AIT collection online. In so doing, Stoeltje facilitated the only access to these materials for the public outside of rare bootlegs by fans.[41] Canadian coproductions of many of the AIT series, some of which are held by TVO (formerly TVOntario) are not viewable by the public in Canada, and scholars must visit on site for limited viewing. Being able to view AIT materials online changes the way that television history cann be shared with and taught to the public. The AAPB (American Archives of Public Broadcasting), a collaboration of the Library of Congress and Boston's GBH (formerly WGBH), permits about 60 percent of their collection to be viewed by the public online.[42] The rest is limited due to copyright and other restrictions. GBH, with its own deep archives, does not provide open archival viewing for the public—only limited screenings for scholars over the web after an application process.[43] Had Gudaitis called a year or two earlier, there would have been no updated deed of gift and the public would not be able to view AIT programs as they can today.

Stoeltje recognized the value of the paper material for understanding the history of AIT. When she met with then-executive director of AIT, Chuck Wilson, Wilson at first did not expect Stoeltje to want the papers. Within those papers, now preserved in the archive and in the process of digitization, are not only teachers' guides and monthly newsletters preserving the history of AIT from the 1970s through the 2000s but also contracts with performers, scripts, stills, slides, budgets, catalogs, and board meeting notes. Most of these kinds of materials are not represented in Cohen's collection at the NPBA at the University of Maryland. Also crucial to the history: the paper collection includes a wide variety of research studies and papers conducted on and related to the programs, with only a handful reproduced in the Department of Education's ERIC (Educational Resources Information Center) database. Most ERIC entries, without attendant documents, often point back to AIT as the holder, which, of course, no longer exists. These materials allow for the history and context of the AIT collection to be told and the decades of research to be preserved and passed on. Because the programs did not have credits, these materials provide a path to find the filmmakers, designers, and educators behind the scores of AIT series.

And so, it is through this multistream confluence of events, each one happening at the right time at the right place, that all the potentials for this collection come to fruition. A founding director archivist was in Bloomington, one who immediately saw mission and institutional alignment and could send trucks to save nearby material. The archive happened to still have adequate space for such a sizable collection, a key issue for any archive and one that was raised as a problem by Tom Connors and Lauren Brown at UMD in 1993. Digitization on a massive scale happened to be prefinanced and could be planned. Stoeltje had recently learned from experience the need for a new kind of deed of gift that permits viewing of the materials for the public, and a copyright librarian had joined the staff. If any one of these elements had not occurred at the same time, we would not have the AIT collection and the elements of comprehensiveness and public access that make the collection so important for the preservation of the history of instructional broadcasting.

The archive staff at the Moving Image Archive at Indiana is still processing the paper collection to this day, more than ten years later. Despite gaps of entire series, such as the Emmy Award–winning *Matter of Fiction*, and a number of programs only remaining on faded or time-code burnt or center-captioned videotape, the AIT collection preserves a significant portion of instructional television from the late 1960s into the twenty-first century. Although entire ITV companies' catalogs seem to now be lost and destroyed, because AIT held such a significant part of the market share of instructional television, we can begin to reconstruct the history of this chronically understudied branch of television history.

Two decades after Ed Cohen's initial planning grant and vision for an industry-wide instructional TV and radio collection, and after Cohen's own papers preserved an important source of material at the National Public Broadcasting Archives, the AIT audio, visual, and paper collection had found a home in Bloomington. More than another ten years of digitization and organization are now making the collection accessible.

MISSION ALIGNMENT, BUT OVER TIME: INDIANA UNIVERSITY

Why did it take all these confluences and years for the AIT collection to find a home? At the end of Tom Connors's 1993 letter to Don McNeil regarding Ed Cohen's plans for an instructional TV and radio collection at the NPBA, Connors suggests, "And I think we could also consider other host institutions: Indiana University for example."[44] So why did Cohen not go directly to Bloomington with his plans in the early 1990s? Why would he launch a massive multiyear, dual-grant planning project for a new collection at the NPBA? After all, it was Indiana University president Herman Wells who provided the first major loan to NIT, which would eventually become AIT, independent from the university. AIT was geographically based in Bloomington, and the university had a large collection of instructional films dating back decades.

Perhaps it was Cohen's understanding of the differences between film rental and broadcast television and radio. Cohen knew Indiana University's background: in the 1950s his boss and mentor had been L. C. "Oly" Larson, who was then director of the IU Audiovisual Center.[45] Or perhaps it was Cohen's having worked at NET in New York, or that his AIT programs had played on PBS for over two decades. CPB had funded his AIT works, including *ThinkAbout*. Perhaps all these factors meant that Ed Cohen understood instructional television as squarely in the rubric of public broadcasting. But we also must remember that there was no Moving Image Archive at Indiana University until 2009, and had the Cohen collection or other instructional television and radio been placed at Bloomington in the 1990s, the AIT materials very well might have ended up in the former bowling alley from which Rachael Stoeltje retrieved 35,000 films. And even if the films survived that alley, could the tapes? Would any of the paper have survived? In the early 1990s there was not yet the institutional infrastructure at Indiana University to build a new broadcasting archive. But Don McNeil's National Public Broadcasting Archives, inaugurated in June 1990 at the University of Maryland, did have an infrastructure and staff. With the CPB imprimatur, perhaps it did seem to have the institutional force to oversee the archiving and history of the broader industries of instructional television and radio, and CPB did invest in both of Cohen's planning grants. Also, the distinct aspects of television and radio seem to be baked into the notion of a broadcasting archive as opposed to the film library that Bloomington held. Television programming had a different kind of distribution, and different methods of fundraising, production, and integration into daily TV schedules.

It seems, for Cohen in the 1990s, the NPBA could have been the right place at the right time, albeit with limited resources and mixed institutional support. While the video and film material from the Cohen collection remain not easily accessible, even to scholars, the Cohen *papers* are preserved. These include Cohen's handwritten meeting notes and correspondence with CPB, PBS, the Ford Foundation, Exxon, government officials, and hundreds of others, providing a view into the daily workings of the market leader, for decades, in instructional television. Despite NPBA's lack of space, staff, and funding to incorporate a broader ITV and radio collection, thankfully the Cohen papers are preserved. Without the NPBA, it is unlikely they would have survived.

ENTER THE RESEARCHER

I first wrote about instructional television as neglected and chronically understudied media in a paper for Thomas Streeter in 1997, while I was a graduate student at the University of Southern California.[46] Almost two decades later, I sought to better understand the relationship between ITV and contemporary approaches to interactive media in the classroom. By then, AIT had shuttered and I found myself without access to viewable programs and attendant paper materials. Then I discovered news of the archives at Indiana University. I had been resigned to the material having been lost, so the AIT collection at IU's Moving Image Archive was like lost treasures rescued from the bottom of the sea. Now I would be able to embark on the in-depth study I had long imagined. This began with a journey from New York to Indiana. With materials and contacts I found at the archives and in Bloomington, I began conducting dozens of interviews across the nation with producers, directors, executives, researchers, educators, some now in their eighties and nineties, some who, sadly, have recently passed. Over the last four years, I have been presenting my research at conferences. My discoveries in Bloomington then led me to the Edwin G. Cohen Papers at the University of Maryland. Along the way, I located a surviving, nearly complete 16mm print of "Travelin' Shoes" from the Emmy Award–winning *Inside/Out* with a collector in Australia. The print retained its original color nearly fifty years later. With Stoeltje's help it has now been added it to the collection at IU. Director John Allman, whom I have interviewed, has also recently contributed to the archive prints of many of the AIT shows he directed, copies of much better clarity than those previously held. All this material is crucial to the histories I am writing about: the relationship of late twentieth-century ITV to American and Canadian cultural, political, and educational media design history.

LESSONS AND LOOKING AHEAD

What can we take away from this winding path that led to saving the AIT collection, a collection that provides insights into decades of instructional television design, production, and contemporaneous research? Of the entire genre of instructional television, only a small percentage remains.

Some creators and distributors of the programs sometimes still hold material, and that material is degrading or in the process of being discarded. Can we change this trajectory to hold onto one of the more neglected parts of public television history?

How might we reduce the level of chance and synchronicity required to save key television collections? If we wish to hold onto our television cultural history, it is crucial for there to be more directed, long-term resourcing of television and broadcasting archives, so that archivists can be ready to act quickly when an unexpected and historic call, like David Gudaitis's, happens. These calls often require fast response to save materials from being interred in landfills. The importance of support for archiving and preservation from senior institutional leadership, such as university presidents, is crucial. Michael McRobbie's understanding that media preservation is a core function of universities is a position to be celebrated and encouraged. Ideally national archives would play a greater role. There is also a need for the sharing of best practices: for public access, for digitization, and to create new approaches to dealing with complex copyright issues. The Moving Image Archive's altered deed of gift is a good example of such a practice. Without such creative approaches, even television saved from destruction is destined to be held captive, unable to be viewed.

Enhancing and expanding networks of media historians and archivists could allow for easier identification of new at-risk collections and archives that have mission alignment and available space. How might we assist in promoting connections between the Association of Moving Image Archivists (AMIA) television committee and the broader communities of television scholars? The Library of Congress's Radio Preservation Task Force helps promote connections between researchers and archivists and identify and save endangered radio collections. Some of the work at its 2023 conference included scholarship on television under the broader rubric of broadcasting. Perhaps organizing under the broadcasting rubric can help expand this kind of work for television. In 2023 a new TV and radio history special interest group, or SIG, was launched through the Society for Cinema and Media Studies (SCMS). This suggests that there is growing potential for synergy across such groups for the preservation of television.

It is important to continue to expand our understanding of what counts as television. Scholars and archivists such as Caroline Frick, Laura Treat, Andrew Burke, and Axelle Demus have been bringing attention to local, community, and public access television as categories in need of study and preservation. Likewise, we need to understand ITV as an essential part of broadcast history and PBS history, with lessons for contemporary educators, designers, and media scholars. Educational and instructional media is now often studied under the rubric of "useful," "orphan," or "nontheatrical" media. Yet despite a wide variety of educational media, there does not appear to be a central gathering for those pursuing its many histories.[47] A gathering focused on learning and media could help advance preservation of instructional and educational programming.

The clock is ticking to preserve the remaining ITV television artifacts in private collections. We need to both simultaneously expand the archiving and public access options for these materials even as we convey those options proactively to key collection holders. We also need to arrest the trend of the discarding of this material. People with whom I conduct interviews often reveal that they had just recently cleared out what they had the year before, or six months earlier. I had a conversation in 2021 with a key distributor for ITV (to PBS stations) in North America in the 1970s and 1980s, by then in his eighties. He told me, "Had you reached out to me five years ago . . . I had a whole warehouse." I had been searching for teachers' guides for some of the Canadian ITV shows. Neither TVO nor the Archives of Ontario had any holdings. This distributor had had it all—five years earlier. But his paper material had been destroyed when the warehouse was emptied. This gentleman went on to tell me that he still had thousands of programs (from independent production companies long gone) on DVDs in boxes in his garage. I gently suggested he might consider, at some point down the line, planning a grant of the programs to an archive for eventual historical research. The last time we spoke, he was considering such a grant, but a potential archival home was not yet clear. I reached out again last year and this year, but have not heard back.

Sometimes our television heritage is searching for a place to call home with producers seeking out archives. And sometimes our archives miss out on television relegated to basements and garages, often languishing until those basements and garages are cleared—too often into dumpsters. Perhaps we can help strengthen the connections between us so that future generations can learn from and delight in the excavation of some of our television culture's most deeply sunken treasures.

NOTES I would like to acknowledge archivists important to this publication: Rachael Stoeltje, Michael Henry, Saul Kutnicki, Mike Mashon, Laura Beth Schnitker, Karen Cariani, Alan Gevinson, Andy Uhrich, and Madeline Webb-Michell. I would also like to thank a selection of the creators of the programs with whom I have been in conversation during my research and which conversations directly impacted this chapter: David Gudaitis, John Allman, Saul Rockman, Kay Sloan, and Bob and Doris Fox. Sadly, Bob and Doris have passed since our extensive conversation in 2019. I also acknowledge Research Computing at the Rochester Institute of Technology for providing computational resources and support that have contributed to the research reported in this publication.

1. ITV in this chapter refers exclusively to television intended for the classroom in the United States and Canada from roughly the 1950s to the 1990s, not to the British system established in 1994. It has sometimes been referred to as "classroom television" and sometimes referred to as "educational programming," although "educational television" typically is a broader category than television intended for classroom use.

2. David Gudaitis (producer, AIT), in discussion with the author, Bloomington, Indiana, July 8, 2019. Entire libraries of thousands of instructional television programs from the late 1960s through the 1980s have been lost or destroyed. For example, scant few programs seem to remain in existence from Great Plains National ITV Library, another major distributor of ITV. Based on my correspondence with Alexis Scargill, Media Archivist at Nebraska Public Media, in 2024 there appears to be no archive remaining of Great Plains material, only an occasional VHS tape listed in a public library online catalog which may or may not exist. According to the Edwin G. Cohen oral history discussed later in this chapter, the Great Plains collection had included key television works included in the MPATI collection. Likewise, the catalog of a small but significant production company, Ray Gladfelter's International Instructional Television Cooperative (later, Children's Television International), appears to be almost entirely lost or destroyed with the rare exception of an occasional off-air VHS bootleg episode posted on the Internet. TVO, formerly TVOntario, another significant producer of ITV, lacks a dedicated archive, though some material at the Archives of Ontario is currently viewable by scholars, only in person.

3. Allison Perlman, Victoria Cain, and Adam Laats have examined such earlier approaches and technologies, though their work had not yet explored ITV over PBS, which ran for more than twenty years. Allison Perlman, "Television Up in the Air: The Midwest Program on Airborne Television Instruction, 1959–1971," *Critical Studies in Media Communication* 27, no. 5 (2010): 477–97; Victoria E. M. Cain and Adam Laats, "A History of Technological Hype," *Phi Delta Kappan* 102, no. 6 (2021): 8–13; Victoria Cain, *Schools and Screens: A Watchful History* (Cambridge, Mass.: MIT Press, 2021).

4. Kay Robinson Sloan, *Thinking through Television: The First Six Years of the Skills Essential to Learning Project* (Bloomington, Ind.: Agency for Instructional Television, 1980). To trace Cohen's institutional lineage back through NET and earlier pre-PBS incarnations, see the online biography of Cohen in expanded notes in the finding aid for the Edwin G. Cohen Papers at the University of Maryland: https://archives.lib.umd.edu/repositories/2/resources/686#).

5. Sloan, *Thinking through Television*; Bob and Doris Fox, in discussion with the author, Bloomington, Indiana, July 10, 2019.
6. Edwin G. Cohen and Thomas Connors, "Edwin G. Cohen: An Oral History Interview Conducted by Thomas Connors," unpublished manuscript, vol. 2, August 19–20, 1996, 325, National Public Broadcasting Archives, University of Maryland at College Park Libraries (hereafter NPBA).
7. John Middleton, *Cooperative School Television and Educational Change: Consortium Development Process of the Agency for Instructional Television* (Bloomington, Ind.: AIT), 1979.
8. My forthcoming book-length study of instructional television examines the ITV genre from 1967 to 1987 for design precedents, in their pedagogical, historical, and political context, including civic and democratic education.
9. The reasons for the understudied nature of this material are multivalent: much of the research material until recently was held at the nonprofit agency level (with some exceptions in the ERIC educational research database); the programs themselves were out of parental view during school-day broadcast and usually omitted from TV listings in the newspaper or TV guide; the stigma of the "failed" classroom programs of the 1960s followed the genre despite radical changes in content, format, approach, and distribution. I explore this issue further in a forthcoming volume, *Useful Television*, edited by Kit Hughes, Marcus Stauff, and Anne-Katrin Weber.
10. List taken with minor edits from Edwin G. Cohen, "A Plan for Establishing and Perpetuating an Instructional Television and Radio Collection Within the National Public Broadcasting Archives," November 30, 1992, 6–8, Oral History Files, Administrative Files (unprocessed), "Activating an Instructional Television and Radio Collection" [1], Edwin G. Cohen Papers (unprocessed portion), National Public Broadcasting Archives, Special Collections, University of Maryland, College Park (hereafter Cohen Papers). A summarized version of this criteria is also included in the final 1995 report, "Activating an Instructional Television and Radio Collection within the National Public Broadcasting Archives: A CPB-supported Study," April 28, 1995, 3–4. Appendix A of "Activating" includes the entirety of the "Plan for Establishing" document.
11. Cohen, "Activating an Instructional Television and Radio Collection," 20.
12. Lauren R. Brown of Special Collections and University Archives is not to be confused with other Lauren Browns at the University of Maryland. See his bio at "Emerita and Emeritus Faculty," University of Maryland University Libraries, https://www.lib.umd.edu/about/org/emerita. He was curator of archives and manuscripts (1984–2011) and comanager of Special Collections and University Archives (2011–16).
13. Letter from Lauren Brown to Edwin G. Cohen, November 8, 1995, Oral History Files, Administrative Files 1 (unprocessed), "Activating an Instructional Television and Radio Collection" [2], Cohen Papers.
14. These programs are largely inaccessible or what I refer to as "captive" television and discuss later in this chapter.
15. Cohen and Connors, "Edwin G. Cohen: An Oral History Interview Conducted

by Thomas Connors," vol. 1, October 16–18, 1995, NPBA; Cohen and Connors, "Edwin G. Cohen," vol. 2.

16. I know of the papers because I interviewed Rockman and he sent me the manifests of materials donated. Saul Rockman, discussion with the author, January 1, 2020.

17. Lauren Brown to Ed Cohen, March 27, 1991, Archivist's Control Files, Edwin G. Cohen Collection, NPBA. According to these control files, Cohen had donated selected papers as of March 27, 1991, and had been referred to Lauren Brown by Don MacNeil. These transactions predate the initial proposal to CPB by Cohen. Perhaps in this early donation process, Cohen discovered the need for further archiving.

18. Tom Connors, "Memo to Don MacNeil re: Ed Cohen's Draft Proposal," August 25, 1993, Oral History Files Administrative Files 1 (unprocessed), "Cohen, Edwin: Instructional TV and Archive Proposal" [1].

19. Tom Connors, "Memo to Jo, Don, Lauren re: Ed Cohen and educational/instructional media archives," August 17, 1993, Oral History Files Administrative Files 1 (unprocessed), "Cohen, Edwin: Instructional TV and Archive Proposal."

20. The 14.5-hour oral history with Cohen is edited with Cohen, indexed, and bound in the NPBA. I believe I am the first scholar to find it, a quarter century later, thanks to the help of archivist Michael Henry.

21. Mashon would later become a curator at University of Maryland's Library of Broadcasting, and five years later, in 1998, a curator at the Moving Images Section of the Library of Congress. Despite my efforts, I was not able to reach Tom Connors for an interview and was saddened to learn of his passing in 2023. Though Mashon does not recollect the circumstances of the assignment, he is convinced that Connors would have wanted to better understand the history of ITV and its relation to CPB. Mike Mashon, in discussion with the author, September 13, 2023, Bloomington, Indiana.

22. Mike Mashon to Tom Connors, July 13, 1993, "re: Instructional Television Proposal from Edwin G. Cohen," Oral History, box 1 (unprocessed), "Cohen, Edwin: Instructional TV and Archive Proposal" [1], Cohen Papers.

23. Cohen and Connors, "Edwin G. Cohen," 1:181–82.

24. I explore these decades of ITV further in my other works, including Owen Gottlieb, "Turning Instructional Television Inside/Out: Reclaiming a Revolution from Erasure," Society for Cinema and Media Studies (SCMS), SCMS, Online, USA, March 19, 2021; Owen Gottlieb, "Trade-offs: Educational TV's Economics Literacies, Ideologies, and Narrative Designs, 1975–1985," Society for Cinema and Media Studies (SCMS), March 31, 2022; Owen Gottlieb, "Dispossessed Discriminations 1973: How a Salvaged ITV Co-production Preserves Canadian and American History," Film Studies Association of Canada (FSAC/ACÉC), (FSAC/ACÉC), May 12, 2022; Owen Gottlieb, "ThinkAbout It: Learning to Learn with ITV in the Long Seventies," Society for Cinema and Media Studies (SCMS), April 12, 2023; monograph on ITV in development.

25. Saul Rockman, "Instructional Television Is Alive and Well," in *The Future of Public Broadcasting*, ed. Cater Douglass and Nyhan Michael (New York: Praeger, 1976); Saul Rockman, "Realities of Change," in *Children and the Faces of Television:*

Teaching, Violence, Selling, ed. Edward Palmer and Dorr Aimeé (New York: Academic Press, 1980). In these two key chapters, Rockman outlines the long-standing sidelined status of instructional (classroom) television—despite the broad audience of children.

26. They were also shown throughout Canada, as AIT was a U.S./Canadian cooperative.
27. Mashon to Connors, July 13, 1993.
28. Sloan, *Thinking through Television*, 66–68. Cohen noted this funding and the series as a watershed moment for ITV in his oral history that Tom Connors would conduct just a few years later.
29. Laurie Ouellette, *Viewers Like You? How Public TV Failed the People* (New York: Columbia University Press, 2002); William Hoynes, *Public Television for Sale: Media, the Market, and the Public Sphere* (Boulder, Colo.: Westview, 1994).
30. Documents include box 97–16, box 5 (unprocessed), folder "Inside/Out," and box 16 (processed)—Budgets, Finances, and Funding, folder "Exxon 1972–1974," Cohen Papers; Paul Pillitteri, National Association of Television Arts and Sciences, correspondence with the author, 2021.
31. Tom [Connors], memo to Lauren [R. Brown], September 13, 1994, "Re: Ed Cohen, AIT," Oral History Files Administrative Files 1 (unprocessed), "Cohen, Edwin: Instructional TV and Archive Proposal [1]," Cohen Papers.
32. Cohen and Connors, "Edwin G. Cohen," 2:329.
33. In the intervening years, many series and documents from the AIT library were lost or destroyed, including the Emmy Award–winning John Robbins reading series *A Matter of Fiction* (1970), which AIT distributed for many years. Even the original producer, WETA (AIT was the distributor), only has a listing of one, possibly two quadruplex tapes in their own library, and two-inch quad tapes are increasingly challenging to transfer with few two-inch machines left in existence.
34. Rachel Stoeltje, video interview with the author, March 3, 2022.
35. The archive now holds more than 130,000 items spanning eighty years of film production. Indiana University Bloomington, "Moving Image Archive," 2024, https://libraries.indiana.edu/moving-image-archive.
36. Indiana University Bloomington, "About the IU Audio-Visual Center," Moving Image Archive, Indiana University Libraries, 2024, https://collections.libraries.indiana.edu/IULMIA/about-iuavc.
37. Herman B. Wells, *Being Lucky: Reminiscences and Reflections* (Bloomington: Indiana University Press, 2012), 390.
38. Wells, *Being Lucky*, 390–91.
39. For more detail on the formation of AIT, see Cohen and Connors, "Edwin G. Cohen," vol. 2, and related documents in the Cohen Papers.
40. "History," Media Digitization and Preservation Initiative, Indiana University, last updated 2021, https://mdpi.iu.edu/about/history.php.
41. While a limited number of bootlegs can currently be found online, those are controlled by private companies such as YouTube, who can simply delete programs at will and have no responsibility or mission to preserve television material. They most certainly have no fiduciary responsibility to preserve U.S. or Canadian (or

any other) television history or culture. That said, some material currently captive can only be viewed through such venues.
42. According to a personal conversation with Alan Gevinson at the Library of Congress and Karen Cariani at GBH, as of May 14, 2024, 60 percent of the AAPB collection is currently viewable to the public offsite. Out of 179,939 programs, 108,110 are available in the online reading room. A recent Mellon grant is funding more digitization, though each case must then be evaluated for availability in the online reading room for the public. WGBH rebranded to GBH in 2020. "WGBH Rebrands to GBH," GBH, last updated August 24, 2023, https://www.wgbh.org/foundation/press/press-releases/2020-08-31/wgbh-rebrands-to-gbh.
43. The online fiftieth-anniversary collection of GBH's *Zoom* program at AAPB (2022) may provide precedent for making other programs otherwise "captive" accessible to the public, though the particular *Zoom* episodes have their own specific attendant agreements that allowed for online screening to the public.
44. Tom Connors, memo to Don MacNeil, August 25, 1993, "re: Ed Cohen's Draft Proposal," Oral History Files Administrative Files 1 (unprocessed), folder "Cohen, Edwin: Instructional TV and Archive Proposal" [1], 2, Cohen Papers.
45. Cohen and Connors, "Edwin G. Cohen," 1:15–16.
46. Owen Gottlieb, "Excavating the Mimi: How Neglected ITV Collapses the Boundary between 'Educative' and 'Pleasurable,'" unpublished paper, TV 587, Prof. Thomas Streeter, University of Southern California, April 28, 1997.
47. While the Orphan Film Symposium has been the vanguard gathering for orphan/nontheatrical film (and in 2023, television with Mark Quigley's curation) in noncommercial or nonstewarded categories, its focus is not specifically on educational or instructional media. To my knowledge, it has not yet included instructional television. The Sound and Vision Conference 2021 (https://www.uantwerpen.be/en/projects/b-magic/events/events-archive/sound-and-vision-ex/) provides an example of bringing together scholars and researchers of the history of media for learning, though there are currently no plans for the event to occur again (personal correspondence with Pieter Verstraete).

CHAPTER 3

LAUREN BRATSLAVSKY

INVENTORYING, CLASSIFYING, AND NARROWLY INTERPRETING POST-BROADCAST VALUE

RESEARCH LEADING UP TO THE FORMATION OF THE MUSEUM OF BROADCASTING

Opening in 1976, the Museum of Broadcasting (MoB) was the first institution in the United States solely dedicated to television and radio history. Known today as the Paley Center for Media, it bears the name of its benefactor, William Paley, CBS chairman. Reflecting on why he founded the new institution, Paley said he knew "without such a repository, a precious body of broadcasting history could slip away, leaving only scattered collections and random holdings."[1]

It is more than coincidental that the institution opened after the latest wave of critical ire directed toward U.S. broadcasting. Discourses had long circulated about radio and then television as invading domestic spaces, bombarding people with crass commercialism, lowering cultural tastes, and manipulating public opinion, which led cultural critics, regulators, and social scientists to treat media as a source of society's ills.[2] Paley and the MoB's press kit pitched the new institution as an opportunity to "serve as a public resource" where scholars, students, and anyone can study and appreciate those programs that mattered for American cultural, political, social, and personal histories.[3] One *New York Times* reporter saw through the benevolent efforts of preservation in the public interest, noting the MoB was both "an attempt at legitimizing the medium most viewed with contempt in intellectual circles" and a monument to Paley's career.[4]

This institution is one of the many locations for broadcast history. Why focus on this one in particular? If communication history can be understood as the transmission and control of information,[5] the project of the Museum of Broadcasting signifies multiple levels of broadcasts and broadcasting as history: initial broadcasts as the management of mediated information, recorded broadcasts as a confluence of institutional, legal, financial, and personal logics to create recordings, and preserved broadcasts as the distillation of how technological capabilities and cultural discourses transfer the control of such recordings to archives. More simply, we may think of the preservation of post-broadcast records as which stories, words, and images were broadcast, which broadcasts were captured from the ephemeral and stored in a recorded form, and which recorded forms were—and potentially could be—transferred to contexts of memory. Understood as iterative levels of control over what has been known and what may be known in the future, the formation of the MoB foregrounds how legitimation occurs. However, this formation does not just point to strategies used by the industry in order to legitimate itself; it is also about how and why programs count as historical evidence, which parts count as evidence, and the requisite material infrastructures to re-mediate broadcast records as historical records. The institution's shape imprints how media can be interpreted. While this institution relies on archival logics—selection, acquisition, and preservation of records—the choice to call it a *museum* was a deliberate strategy to treat programs as discrete objects.

Critical historiographies and the archival turn approach traditional historiographies with skepticism and interrogate the forces that confer value on material as historical. Hence, the Museum of Broadcasting is framed as a barely cloaked public relations effort, as evidenced by narrow program selections as exemplars of broadcasting's public service (e.g., public affairs and monumental news events) and cultural contributions (e.g., drama anthologies).[6] Paley's remarks and the institution's initial collections match traditional historiographical approaches that present historical accounts as inevitable trajectories of technological advancements, momentous events, and unproblematic leadership. Media histories by the 1970s were typically celebratory accounts of "broadcasting as natural expression of American cultural values, economic practices, and political attitudes."[7] A critical perspective takes issue with the ideological assumptions in these historical accounts as well as the availability and use of certain primary sources, such as industry insiders, popular memories, and news articles, over other documentary traces.[8]

I contribute to existing scholarly skepticism; however, I argue there is more nuance to the Museum of Broadcasting's formation than Paley's vanity project to secure his legacy and elevate television's legitimacy. Little has been written about the research preceding the MoB's formation, which included studies to determine the feasibility to preserve television. I use the documentary traces of a four-year-long project referred to as the Bluem Report, which conveys several forces in promoting and inhibiting preservation, in order to examine how and why this institution became a museum.

CONSTRUCTING ARCHIVES AND CONSTRUCTING TELEVISION'S HISTORY

The archival turn in cultural studies refers to how scholars have increasingly critiqued the structures and processes in the production of social knowledge.[9] The archive becomes the object of study, whose "history and development speak to themes including memory, the exercise of power through knowledge, and the emergence of a distinctive, archivally based historiography."[10] How do institutions that collect, store, preserve, curate, and provide access shape the meanings and uses of what counts as historical evidence? Archives and related institutions containing and interpreting histories "come in to being in and as history as a result of specific political, cultural, and socioeconomic pressures—pressures which leave traces and which render archives themselves artifacts of history."[11] We can consider two sorts of traces: traces of the past collected as historical evidence within the archive, and traces on the archive itself. In the present study, the former refers to how broadcast's most visible products—the programs—become historical material. Traces on the archive can still refer to issues pertaining to media's physicality, such as technologies to record, transfer, and retrieve recorded content. The more complex traces on the archive stem from discursive constructions of value and structural features, such as the highly concentrated commercial broadcasting system. This framework motivates examinations about the MoB's origin and development by addressing the power to build the archive, select its holdings, and facilitate the contours of certain kinds of evidence.

Those who participate in the formation and maintenance of archives require technical and conceptual acumen to define how media, and which dimensions of media, constitute historical evidence. Archivist professionalization occurred in the late nineteenth century when historians and archivists had little expertise to evaluate modern, non-paper-based mass media as worthy for future preservation.[12] Media pose similar issues as other material considered for archival inclusions, namely, how content (or inscriptions) serve as records for historical memory. However, to capture the totality of media requires attention toward dimensions such as industries, technologies, representations, and so on. Media contain evidence representing time, place, and perspectives *and* technological, social, regulatory, and economic circumstances and practices.[13] But beyond the physical record being available, playback must also be possible. Still, people in positions to archive media must be able to articulate purposeful preservation. The medium did not necessarily contain its own preservation means because people viewed recordings for transmission purposes only and, more aptly, few people cared for preservation.[14] For instance, consider film preservation: despite technological capabilities to preserve film, a collective preservation effort required transformative scholarly and professional frameworks to construct film as heritage.[15] Heritage, or the designations of symbolic meanings such as national identities, social impact, cultural representations, and on, becomes a crucial means to motivate preservation plans.

SKEPTICISMS ABOUT PALEY'S MONUMENT

My skepticism about the origin of the MoB does not necessarily come from the institution's designation as a first, Paley's investments, or the crucial services the Paley Center continues to provide. The skepticism lies in the repetition of how and why the MoB emerged as an outgrowth of Paley's own stake in elevating television's cultural status, which manifests in two ways: Paley's story about the MoB's origin and the construction of television heritage.

Paley's autobiography and his opening-day remarks demonstrate a particular hubris to naturalize commercial broadcasting while dispersing preservation burdens. He claimed ownership of the idea that broadcasting deserved an institution dedicated to its own history. The mythologizing appears in Paley's autobiography and news reports about the opening. Paley explained: "I had an idea that the broadcasting industry should sponsor some sort of museum to preserve and make available the best of its output for students, scholars and any of the public."[16] He had been stewing on this idea since the early days of radio, talking with others, and waiting for the right time to dedicate his expertise and resources.[17] Paley's proclivity toward claiming ideas as his own is well documented.[18] His own opening-day remarks conflict with his autobiography when he said the idea came to him "some 10 years ago . . . that a concerted and organized preservation effort had to be made."[19]

Additionally, his ruminations do not align with industry reality. If he had the will, he could have committed resources to preservation in the same way he invested in talent, color television, and news. The MoB was presented as Paley's investment in broadcasting as a public service, but it was far more evident that networks demonstrated public service with cultural and public affairs programming. Thus, program stewardship was transferred to a nonprofit institution, funded by Paley. Public service rhetoric obscured the industry's primary objectives as commercial enterprises. The preservation of content was never a priority; indeed, the technologies and economics to transmit and receive broadcasts preceded content development.[20] Paley could control the interpretation of mass media. The commercial system was best because broadcasting "has remained independent—unintimidated by pressure from political forces, from government or from special interest groups." U.S. commercial broadcasting developed with an elaborate *individual station* licensee model that provided few regulatory prompts for long-term preservation and no apparent economic incentive for preservation until technologies and distribution structures could extract rebroadcast value. Conversely, public broadcasting systems (e.g., BBC) were extensions of the modern nation-state with centralized recordkeeping bureaucracies to serve internal needs as well as external accountability and cultural projects. Thus, the illusion of independence figures into archival formations by presenting U.S. broadcasting as a natural outgrowth of the country's economic and moral character. For example, Paley explained now that the "once-fledging industry has become a mature, responsible and important force in our national life ... it is time that we take stock of our past so that we can know and understand the heritage of the broadcast media in building our future."[21] The collective "we" was less an indictment of the industry for failing to care; it was the public's general failings to value broadcasting as cocreating American cultural heritage and history.

Broadcasting had reached a historicality, a point in time when it was feasible for a monument to a television history to come into being *and* to embrace television as a recorder of history.[22] That same year, copyright legislation directed the Library of Congress to form the American Television and Radio Archive, signifying broadcasts could be as historically and culturally worthy as the paper-based collections documenting American history. This occurred in a larger movement of "audiovisual consciousness" as some European nations formed national archives as well as an international community of moving image archivists.[23] Meanwhile, 1970s network television featured a slate of reruns, reunion specials, and retrospectives that codified sensibilities about golden-age programs, treasured performers and actors, significant milestones, and common tastes, all of which undoubtedly helped define a particular version of a television heritage as a collective cultural and social experience in the public's mind.[24]

It is in this context that the MoB was Paley's stake in defining a television heritage. The investment in essentially an archive-like institution meant control over how to interpret broadcasting as a positive force in society. Spigel, for example, explains the MoB as Paley's "brainchild": a mix of public relations to promote the television industry (and CBS), canonization of a television art form, and a tourist attraction that capitalized on nostalgia.[25] Kompare frames Paley's efforts as a series of strategies to connect certain parts of television to "capital-H 'History'" in the Museum and the Archive," meaning how programs could become privileged objects and "raw materials of historical knowledge" serving dominant narratives about how to know the world.[26] At face value, it is difficult to argue with radio and television content—and the experience of listening and viewing such content—as continuants of national heritage. But by addressing *who* is involved in defining *which* radio and television programs contribute to a notion of heritage, the formation of the MoB becomes one of the key defining moments for which audiovisual records constitute shared social and cultural experiences.

Two decades later, the Library of Congress's 1997 Television and Preservation Study was another milestone in broadcast preservation and articulations of television heritage. The MoB had been a prominent institution, as the report details about the MoB's origin: "From 1967 to 1971 the William Paley Foundation commissioned Dr. William B. Bluem to study the possibility of creating a master collection of broadcast programs."[27] This is curious on two accounts. First, although Paley was still the progenitor, the reference to a four-year-long study suggests there was more to the MoB's founding than one executive's mythologized desires. Second, in tracking down traces of Bluem's studies, I discovered the government document had a slight error. The professor's name was *A*. William Bluem. The error may be inconsequential, but the repetition of the slightly off name is a telling example about the life cycle of primary sources in that the library's report becomes a brisk record of a multiyear study.[28]

I approach the formation and the meanings of this institution by corroborating but also complicating the MoB's origin. While the public relations frame is crucial, it belies the richness of how this institution formed in terms of the processes to naturalize links between what was broadcast, why it matters as historical evidence, and how it becomes archival and/or museological objects. The documentation in the years prior to the MoB's opening day contributes to an accounting of the people, institutions, technologies, and discourses involved in the articulations of television's post-broadcast value. By post-broadcast value, I mean why a program was recorded and stored, even before long-term preservation or historical sensibility. The MoB's formation involved complex relations between academia and industry, motivations to semantically and symbolically articulate value, and procedures to build a centralized institution. I detail features of the Bluem Report to broadly address the following: What was the context of this research project? What were the methods, scope, and more detailed findings of this four-year study, particularly approaches to classifying value? What were the links and the gaps between Bluem's recommendations and the MoB's formation? More conceptually, how might the choice of museum for the new institution be significant in the retransmission of broadcasts as isolated objects?

THE BLUEM REPORT: ADMINISTRATIVE RESEARCH TO ASSESS TELEVISION MATERIALITY

Academic and industry contexts were not (and are not) sanctimoniously separate. Industry connections and research to advance industry outcomes could be conceptualized as projects to more broadly advance knowledge, but such relations have long sparked suspicion and raised questions about how academic labor benefits dominant power structure. In one sense, VanCour demonstrates how budding university mass communication programs relied on industry connections to build curriculum but then distanced themselves from industry management in order to cultivate a scholarly sensibility as opposed to a merely vocational practice and to establish boundaries from corporate influence. In another sense, administrative research was a means for mass communication scholars to legitimize themselves as social scientists by systematically studying media effects on behalf of industry, often with foundation support.[29]

In this context, Paley directed his philanthropic foundation to fund research about "the desirability and feasibility of establishing a master collection of documents representing the history of radio and television."[30] In 1967 the Paley Foundation commissioned A. William Bluem, a Syracuse University professor known for two key roles. First, he was a practitioner but also a scholar of television and the public interest, specifically documentaries. He possessed expertise to frame television's public service role and evaluate television shows as historical documents. Second, he was the editor of *Television Quarterly*, an academic-style journal sponsored by the Academy of Television Arts and Sciences, which Spigel describes as one of the industry's mechanisms to elevate television's status.[31] Bluem bridged academic and industry spheres. He utilized social scientific methods to survey people and develop selection criteria to balance subjective evaluations with practical considerations in the construction of a new institution. As evident throughout his research reports, he wrote with multiple constituencies in mind, including scholars, media makers, the general public, and, importantly, decision-makers who would take part in archival constructions.

The Bluem Report refers to a series of studies detailing the methods and findings for three phases between 1967 and 1971.[32] Project funders charged him with three main goals in evaluating the "state-of-the-art" of broadcast preservation: assess contemporary preservation efforts, survey the extent of "sight-and-sound" collection in various places (e.g., universities, cultural institutions, Library of Congress, and corporate inventories), and recommend what a "Library and History Center for Television and Radio" might look like.[33] The "library and history center" (LHC) label was a generic name for an imagined institution built to collect broadcast's past and serve various publics.

Phase one (1967–68) involved a series of surveys and site visits, mostly academic and cultural institutions. This yielded useful verification about preservation efforts, but in order to meet the project goals, more work was needed in the corporate archives. Phase two, or the 1969 CBS Study, extended foundation support to report on the CBS inventories. Bluem used this phase to develop inventorying and classifying methodologies to determine historical value. Phase three, or the NBC Holdings (1970–71), applied and refined inventory and classification schema. This phase received joint funding from the National Endowment for the Humanities. Bluem compiled his findings and concluded with suggesting goals and services of a hypothetical institution. Bluem's empirical data and recommendations served as talking points for conference attendees in March 1971 to develop the blueprint for what would become the Museum of Broadcasting.

Bluem and his colleagues drew on their academic training to define research questions and design methods of investigation.[34] Their research questions included: Was there interest in a centralized archive of broadcast history? Where, and to what extent, did recordings exist? How were they organized? And how would it be possible to aggregate the materials that existed into a preservation and access type of space? The research team visited and solicited data from universities, libraries, historical societies, museums, broadcast professionals, and others "engaged in broadcasting and/or motion picture collecting, storage, preservation, and service activities." They asked for accounts detailing the quantity and physical quality of recordings and invited various stakeholders to weigh in on the "the value of, and potential uses for, a 'master' collection of historical material."[35]

As evident by the scope of collected data from those who participated in the studies, the interest to preserve broadcast records did indeed exist. However, no one had a model for dealing with post-broadcast records, especially a means to assign priorities for preservation based on scholarly, historical, and pedagogical uses. Like the overall report, I focus mostly on the results pertaining to television. Among the four principal findings, Bluem concluded radio was of the highest priority for preservation because of the age and fragility of those records. Two of the principal findings summarized the need for a centralized institution. Television, as the fourth principal finding suggested, presently required more systematic retention and selection considerations. There were no prevailing methods to deal with television's post-broadcast material form.

INVENTORIES, PART 1: INSTITUTIONAL HOLDINGS

First, Bluem and his colleagues began their field studies with institutional holdings, meaning universities, libraries, museums, or archives. They interviewed over a hundred people at various universities with TV-radio departments as well as sent surveys to over four hundred colleges and universities, seeking input from interested departments and campus libraries.[36] Whereas there were many radio broadcasts in recorded form (estimated at 70,000), television in the institutional setting was in a much poorer state. Bluem remarked, "Although the television medium has been creating potentially valuable historical resource materials for over a quarter of a century, surprising few archival efforts of an institutional nature have been attempted. Indeed, fewer than 7,500 films, videotapes or kinescopes are presently retained by any institution and less than half that number are actually catalogued, indexed and available for use." The nature of these institutions conferred inherent cultural, historical, and/or other evidential value onto the broadcast records.[37] The majority of the institutional collections grew out of service-oriented uses such as pedagogical needs and emergent scholarly examination. None of the institutions had comprehensive catalogs or adequate funding. Various universities held an estimated 750 recordings in teaching collections, some of whom engaged in the new practice to record off-air. The two largest collections, each at around three thousand units, were the Peabody Collection at the University of Georgia and the Library of Congress Motion Picture Division.[38] The latter archive represented the beginnings of a formalized effort to preserve broadcast records via copyright mechanisms and library gifts, but the collection was of "dubious influence" because it was poorly cataloged and difficult to access, and it mostly contained contributions from those with financial and legal interests to do so. Another significant collection was the estimated six hundred recordings held at the *three* chapters of the "National Academy of TV Arts and Sciences 'Library and Museum.'" Paley surely knew of the Academy's efforts to build a national archival type of institution, but he was also probably aware of how "a general belt-tightening throughout the Academy operations" did not bode well to grow, let alone catalog, those holdings.[39] Thus, Bluem's research documents how competition leaves traces on industry-connected archives, as in the soon-to-be UCLA Film and Television Archive and the Museum of Broadcasting.

Without any systematic cataloging, selection methods, and means of access, such records could disappear. In sum, the first phase established the urgency to not only ensure the preservation of such records but also develop uniformity in the retention and selection of past and current broadcast recordings. Bluem turned to corporate holdings to ascertain a more complete picture of the state of preservation. Similar to the institutional inventories, the corporate holdings would reveal pragmatic issues about storage, cataloging, and retrieval, but had additional challenges associated to assigning value for the purposes of cultural, historical preservation.

INVENTORIES, PART 2: CORPORATE HOLDINGS

Bluem's ability to inventory CBS and NBC holdings was a function of who funded the research. Top CBS executives served on the Paley Foundation board, which helped Bluem initiate contact with various CBS divisions and stations. With the blessing of the NBC president, the VP of corporate information instructed departments involved in NBC's inventory management to oblige Bluem's inquiries.[40] The inventorying process for CBS and NBC involved identifying basic information such as titles, dates, source, whether the content aired, format (tape, film, kinescope), and technical condition.[41] Accounting for the CBS News Division, TV network, and one owned and operated station (WCBS), CBS held an estimated 52,000 recorded television programs. This number included kinescopes, films, and videotapes, or over 100,000 hours. NBC headquarters and storage facilities held an estimated 35,500 films, kinescopes, and tapes, or about 17,779 hours.[42]

These inventories demonstrated the idiosyncrasies about the management of post-broadcast records. As corporate assets, recordings existed for internal purposes, such as time-shifting, sponsor relations, legal protection, and news production. CBS and NBC haphazardly and minimally cataloged their holdings, a consequence of treating the films, tapes, and other recordings as "truly *operational inventories* [rather] than *archival collections*."[43] Each location had its own retention logics that dictated the availability and management of records, which were contingent on storage space, the reuse of tapes, and selling off assets.[44] For example, some videotape inventories were not completely trustworthy because tapes were actively in use, so some units were cut and reconfigured, or possibly erased.[45] Many of NBC's kinescopes had already gone through selection, leaving only those television records with conventionally inherent historical content—news, public affairs, and exemplars of the golden age. If there was a logic in the retention of more contemporary material, especially entertainment programs, that escaped Bluem's detection.

Using foundation mechanisms to assess corporate holdings was a revealing indicator about broadcast records' precarity between commercial assets and historical documents. NBC and CBS had internal, centralized bureaucracies for paper-based records management, but minimal formal retention policies or systematic inventories. Administrative research addressed the commercial broadcasters' gaps, providing a service to internal operations as much as (or perhaps even more so than) public service visions for broadcast records as vital documents for American history. Few people in these spaces thought it was their responsibility to be concerned about historical significance and long-term preservation.[46] This sentiment echoes Bluem's estimations about individual stations' retention practices; he estimated that about five hundred commercial and educational television stations held an average of ten recordings, and the three thousand radio stations averaged twenty recordings.[47]

Altogether, these institutional, corporate, and station inventories and surveys provided a more concrete picture than had previously been known. A substantial amount of broadcast records existed, despite inconsistencies in selection, acquisition, cataloging and description, preservation, and access. Excluding the limitations of technology, time, money, legal contracts, and labor, there was never any indication that all recordings merited inclusion in any space synonymous with history, memory, and future study. Bluem's recommended classificatory logics represent an attempt to balance academic and industrial desires for which post-broadcast records could easily and ideally be located in an archive.

THE SHAPE OF THE INSTITUTION

A centralized institution was vital for the systematic and strategic preservation of broadcast history. Bluem concluded, "Unless some concerted action is taken, the greatest part of the history of these media, together with the records of world and American history they have created, will be lost, hopelessly fragmented, and otherwise generally useless to posterity." As observed in both institutional and corporate settings, factors such as neglect, deterioration, financial constraints, legalities of ownership, and the overall lack of uniform retention policies precluded "efforts to attempt inclusive television preservation at this time."[48] Hence, the Paley Foundation directed Bluem to formulate recommendations for a hypothetical institution to be built from corporate holdings and other sources, which required him to tackle two related problems: the mission and services of such an institution, and the schema to guide selection for the institution's contents.

Archives, or really, any cultural institution, necessarily limit their contents and thus construct the contours of what enters into formalized spaces for historical memory. The generic "library and history center" connoted the vitality of broadcast records for academic, pedagogical, and, above all, public uses. In an era preceding home recording and concurrent to broadcast schedules containing repetitions of heritage-inflected programs, an LHC could serve an array of publics, regardless of academic, professional, or nostalgia tourist intentions. The vision for a *centralized* space for broadcast history was less a matter to metonymically enable CBS via the Paley Foundation to control memories of television. Rather, centralization was a means of codifying the professional care and management of both the materiality of broadcast's contents and its recorded form.[49]

All institutions related to the collection of historical material engage in selection and acquisition methods contingent on some notion of enduring value, usually based on valuations of utility for history, whether as evidence of how an organization functioned or the representation of a cultural, social, and/or political moment.[50] Some of the corporate inventories already demonstrated a level of control over memory by saving those records that serve history—the sight and sound recordings of inherently noteworthy events such as elections and news commentary. But the LHC label intended to capture the nascent attention toward television's role in popular culture. As Bluem put it, "We cannot ignore the significance of this material, and the need to preserve not only a printed 'paper-record' of what was said or done at a given time, but also those actual 'sight-and-sound' impressions of what has gone before. Perhaps we will only begin to understand in our time when we are afforded the opportunity to consider the impact of the new media in light of the complete sensory experience they convey."[51] Centralization could be a means of developing a representative collection containing the twentieth century's explosion of sensory records and made available for anyone to experience post-broadcast, enabling the kinds of history encounters ranging from nostalgia to critical scholarship. Furthermore, Bluem's research suggested that those outside of academia preferred a *new* institution; educators may have volunteered their departments as centers for broadcast history, but a space independent from a university could better "serve [media professionals and general public]'s information requirements."[52] Thus, he began to lay the groundwork for industry-defined ownership over the collection and interpretation of its own output as history.

It was neither logical nor possible to stage an all-encompassing archiving effort. Classification required layered approaches to deal with the relationship between new media as historical records, broadcast records as physical objects, and methods to ascertain historical worth. The questions about the physicality, legality, and costs of transferring corporate, private assets to a public-oriented institution would come after the more pressing issue: determining worthiness. As such, inventory and selection preceded acquisition and accession. Bluem approached the corporate archives as needing control. Classification at this stage was a crucial "intermediary" step because all the corporate holdings were "raw inventory control data." If the industry was to invest in its own historicality outside of the broadcast schedule, then it needed to account for its own failures to establish cataloging and preservation policies.[53] What can be known for a network's internal purposes is different than spaces of history. But if retention policies at the network level were to develop in relation to future-minded preservation, then this intervention could affect possibilities for what can be known for the projects of history. Still, the contours to prioritize preservation worthiness rested on discourses that naturalized commercial broadcasting as unproblematic and preeminent recorders of society and culture.

CLASSIFICATION OF VALUE

Bluem reasoned a classificatory logic that would later imprint on the new institution and, more broadly, echoed the ongoing conceptual problems of new and ubiquitous mass media in an archive setting. Reflecting on the state of corporate holdings, which were to be the primary sources for a "dominant national service institution," he noted, "one could not be at all certain of what was unique and what was duplication, what was complete and what was fragmentary, and—above all—what was worthy or [sic] retention and what could be abandoned in response to continuing operational demands for storage space and reduction of inventory costs."[54] If archives contain unique objects, what was unique about a recording that may be stored elsewhere? Which content merited automatic inclusion as a historical record and which could be more sparingly sampled? What was a complete, preservation-worthy record? And if his project was to recommend not only the criteria for a public-oriented broadcast archive but also strategy for the management of internal holdings, how might corporate archives acknowledge yet-to-be-determined historical value? Bluem's approach was not uncommon in archival and information sciences; the exponential growth of output by modern corporations, including audiovisual records, prompted various sampling and prioritization methods.[55] He chose to distill a schema by first establishing a rough estimation of the possible universe of recorded programs, then identifying preexisting conditions, and then creating tiered categories.

In the fifty years of American broadcasting, Bluem estimated the following: one billion hours of content had been broadcast, 10 percent or one hundred million hours had been recorded in some form, but of that, only 10 percent or one million hours were unique. The majority of broadcast content was "either never recorded at all or was recorded and subsequently destroyed," which was especially the case for locally originated radio and television content. The one-million-hour figure, then, was comprised mostly of network-originated programs. Roughly, Bluem posited 25 percent represented content inherently worth saving, as in 250,000 hours of programming conventionally understood as historical, specifically news, public affairs, and actualities. The remaining 750,000 hours of programming represented a swath of entertainment with "tangential historical value." A small fraction could be sparingly selected. The pressure to bring order and control to the preservation of broadcast history meant an asymmetrical focus to locate and save all 25 percent of total recordings and "eliminate all but one or two per cent of such general entertainment material from archival consideration." At that point, the field studies located about 150,000 hours with "potential historical value" held across institutional, corporate, and potentially private collections.[56]

The above estimates mapped the possible universe from which to then recommend sampling techniques. The patina of objectivity to limit the universe of possible programs privileged that which aired (in other words, that which already circulated in popular and critical memories) and that which was complete. In order to be useful for history, then, authenticity and fidelity translated as high-quality master or confirmed duplicate of a program as aired.[57] This criterion effectively eliminated hundreds of thousands of recorded programs, many of which were duplicate or overflow materials (e.g., B-roll footage).

A mechanism to tackle vast and scattered network holdings was the social scientific tiered sampling techniques. He developed a classification system to manage the corporate holdings, placing each program under a taxonomic structure that enabled rapid assessment for either definite preservation, possible preservation, or marginal interest. Classifying programs on a spectrum of significant to somewhat important to inconsequential was an efficient system of selection, which articulated both the scientific management of information and the political economic calculus to anticipate "time-consuming and expensive cataloging-and-indexing level of identification."[58] For example, a canister marked "Meet the Press" could be immediately assumed historically valuable while a canister without text description would require labor-intensive identification.

Class I programs mostly aligned with FCC classifications for public interest or serving programs, including news, public affairs, "serious" cultural content, educational material, and religious content. All programs that bore text-based indicators of news and public affairs content ought to be automatically considered worthy for inclusion in a prototypical history institution, while all other serious content could be evaluated on an item-to-item basis. Class II programs captured entertainment (or in other words, disposable), to be capped at a global 5 percent selection process, with an occasional larger ratio of sampling such as special sporting events (e.g., the Olympics). Class III content was a catchall for non-broadcast footage such as auditions, closed circuit, and production elements. Bluem, despite his background as a tele-documentary filmmaker, saw little need to classify such material for historical consideration. He acknowledged that while the three classifications were "quasi-subjective" assessments, these were useful in planning, including budget and staffing needs.[59] Additionally, the tiered system operationalized indexing and cataloging practices specific to Class I and Class II programs, which led to both internal retention policies and flows into spaces for historical preservation.

The clinical approach to classification reflected de facto articulations of value as an outgrowth of administrative research goals by deferring to "the operational realities" of a network or station archive, and by firmly anchoring material with conventional notions of historical utility (news, public affairs) and the networks' nostalgia narratives (e.g., critical and popular acclaimed programs already in circulation). Although he disclaimed that his classification system was just one possibility, the resulting taxonomic structure nevertheless reinforced the contemporary discursive construction of television as a significant carrier of certain kinds of documentary traces over others. The records held by corporate archives already contained versions of post-broadcast value, such as potential rerun value or protective legal value. Bluem's directive was to not only determine post-broadcast value in the service of history as a whole, popular culture histories specifically, or other forms of studying the art and craft of television but also bring order for the sake of daily and long-term internal operations. By deploying a tested system of classification, it would be a "quick way of cutting through to the heart of the contents of the broadcast holdings ... to provide some general estimates of the 'value' of such content."[60] Value would be operationalized according to classifications prioritizing post-broadcast records that could supplement conventional historiography as well as the industry's narratives of its own importance.

INTERPRETING THE MATERIAL: THE MUSEUM IS THE MESSAGE

As one newspaper headline proclaimed on the day of the MoB's opening, "The museum is the media," but it might as well have said the museum is the message.[61] The MoB's form and function reveal as much as its contents about why and how people cared about preservation. How did Bluem's recommendation for a library and history center become a museum? The Bluem Report contained the conceptual framework for an archival logic, as in collecting, cataloging, and preserving historical material as well as developing access procedures to support the study of such material. However, the choice to label the new institution *as a museum*, as opposed to a library, archive, or history center, inherently set a tone that obscured archival logics in favor of more publicity-driven logics.

The schema were vital early steps leading toward the formation of the MoB. But it is worth noting a dialectical tension embedded in Bluem's classificatory logics. While he directed some scorn toward the networks and studios for being more concerned with storage space and financial shortcuts than preservation (even of those records with unequivocal historic and public service value), he did not implicate the overall commercial structures. Yet he drew substantial inspiration from public broadcasting systems. In creating his classification and retention recommendations, he "makes eclectic use of principles of selection already adopted by the BBC, CBC and other[s]" and included the CBC's archival retention standards.[62] As extensions of the state, the infrastructures of these institutions had built-in features that supported preservation. The BBC and CBC were governed by a tradition of bureaucratic recordkeeping, such as documenting internal processes for public accountability or contributions to heritage. They were vested in their own preservation, tied to identities and collective experiences. Despite access issues and impositions on programming, these systems operated as a public service on par with other state agencies.[63] Conversely, the U.S. broadcasting system had no such overt structures. Notions of public service were predominantly funneled through commercial frameworks, such as building corporate goodwill or differentiation in the marketplace.[64] This tension would imprint on the new museum (and arguably, other archiving efforts) given ideological and structural influences that undercut visions for a centralized institution with representative collections. From the start, isolation of broadcast's products from its contexts and processes of production would already limit the enactment of archival principles.

The gulf between the 1971 conference to discuss Bluem's findings and the opening of the MoB is an indication of how priorities might have shifted to conform to the culture industry. The conference was an advisory council comprised of seventeen participants, mostly from intellectual contexts, including CBS VP and Paley Foundation VP Arthur Tourtellot, who was also a notable historian in his own right.[65] The initial blueprint called for an institution with "far ranging impact on historical studies."[66] Agenda items included presentations from the BBC and George Eastman House, which demonstrated an interest in policy and structural issues, and a concluding session for how to move forward. Bluem recommended a nonprofit institution led by a mix of experts from both the industry and the academy, with services to equally benefit academics (e.g., conferences, grants, etc.), industry members (e.g., program research, maintenance of master copies, etc.) and the public (e.g., exhibits, public lectures, etc.).

The initial collections and services skewed toward public engagement and popular memories. There was no mention of an advisory council to guide selection, as Bluem recommended; a curator selected programs based on popularity, prizes, and artistic merit. Despite the wealth of materials held by network and studio archives, the MoB started with a collection of about seven hundred television and radio shows.[67] These represented the early years in broadcasting, specifically those programs that were recorded *and* deemed worth preserving (the Class I designation). The initial rounds of selection and interpretative practices constructed a particular version of cultural heritage. The collection was neutered from the representative sample proposed by Bluem.

Granted, one source for institutional formations is the time to assess feasibility and costs.[68] Whatever consensus the conference participants reached, a multifaceted centralized institution had to be rooted in material realities. Bluem outlined obstacles such as acquisition (e.g., rights, industry cooperation, etc.), accession, cataloging standards, duplication, and financing. The sources to fund and the logistics to orchestrate legal contracts, technological infrastructure, and emergent computerized cataloging systems rendered the contours of the new institution.

A centralized institution was worthy to pursue, but the shape of the institution corroborates the framing of the Museum of Broadcasting as an industry-initiated legitimation project above all else. The new institution's board of trustees was a telling source. Unlike the conference with a group of professors, librarians, archivists, and historians, the board was entirely composed of industry executives. The time and talents of those with professional skills in informational and cultural management were largely cut.[69] However, one conference participant became the MoB's first director. Robert Saudek, a professor and producer of the critically acclaimed *Omnibus*, enhanced the institution's legitimacy. Reportedly, it was his idea to call the "history center" a museum so that broadcasting history could be "a living and engaging enterprise."[70]

Paper-based records were a part of the new institution but were rarely featured. When the MoB opened, it had a collection of scripts, books, periodicals, and "treasury of memorabilia." In this way, the MoB functioned in part as a library to support research and as a museum to support observations of artifacts. But the printed records were tangential to the novelty of viewing and/or listening to broadcasts in this new space. Thus, the MoB remediated the often-denigrated, banal medium as a celebrated source for history and culture. Ephemeral content became replayable objects containing what was typically a private, domestic, temporal experience. This was a museum without conventional material objects; instead it foregrounded a different kind of materiality: the modern marvels of computerized information management systems by way of catalogs and viewing carrels to facilitate the museumgoer's experience.[71]

Overall, the museum label materialized the substance to construct television heritage as American heritage. Ideally (or naively), an archive itself does not interpret the meanings and significance of its holdings for the archive users, whereas a museum is predicated on interpretation via the core mission to curate and exhibit its holdings. There are numerous gates between the broadcast moment and the rendering of that material content as containing post-broadcast value outside of the industry. The broadcast had to be captured on a recording medium in order to make the broadcast a discrete object. To render the post-broadcast record as valuable for the services of history, scholarship, and memory, people evaluated textual markers indicating possible broadcast contents. And after a series of selection criteria, acquisition procedures, and preservation efforts (including systems to transfer and maintain physical material), the form through which *museumgoers*, rather than archive or library visitors, interact with the museum's objects establishes the parameters for how to experience post-broadcast records. The amount of time, labor, expertise, finances, negotiations, and bureaucracy to acquire and catalog a broadcast record already signals a context for interpretation because the institution has already determined the worth and value of the holdings. Placing such objects in a cultural institution was another avenue to convince the public (and television's critics) of television's public contributions. These curated collections of objects reflected a distilled version of American cultural, social, and political life but nevertheless were collections that brought forth the visibility of "new" media (and new technologies to access that media) as historical material.

CONSTRUCTION OF INSTITUTIONS: LEGITIMACY, HERITAGE, PR

The Bluem Report and constitutive choices extend our historical inquiries into the construction of institutions devoted to interpreting post-broadcast value as well as the materiality involved in the preservation of broadcast content as objects. Undoubtedly, the MoB's formation was a project of legitimation to reorient television's reputation and articulate a particular view of American heritage. Parts of the formative study and the MoB's first press kit corroborates how this institution was a massively orchestrated public relations effort catalyzed and funded by Paley, but also on behalf of other mass media makers. The MoB was another outpost to signal a version of heritage where television could be appreciated post-broadcast and integrated into certain narratives supportive of dominant histories and experiences. Collecting complete programs as aired inscribed a major trace on the institution's formation. The MoB's contents mostly included recordings from CBS, NBC, ABC, and the Corporation for Public Broadcasting, thus diminishing contributions from forgotten networks and individual stations.

To pivot away from the narrative of the MoB as a monument to Paley's legacy, the labor and knowledge production involved in the formation of this institution represent the uses of administrative research to advance multiple frameworks for the care of broadcasting and its records, including professionalization of moving image archiving. Granted, the critical political economic lens stresses the use of tax-sheltered funds to engage in essentially competitive research (what is the state of television preservation) and consultation about the management of its own holdings.[72] As with most industry-funded research, Bluem carried out his tasks under a model of consensus, as in the acceptance of the networks' dominance and their participation in the "shared cultural and social values across American society."[73] But in a more generous or perhaps expansive view of administrative research, philanthropic-initiated research enabled a framework that otherwise might not have resulted in a cooperative project to initiate more concerted broadcast preservation efforts. The Bluem Report demonstrates that the MoB did not emerge overnight as a frivolous vanity project. After all, Paley did not open a Museum of CBS Broadcasting. Furthermore, the documentary traces of Bluem's systematic study validate how social scientific methods treated the problems television may pose for history rather than social ills.

The years preceding the Museum of Broadcasting's opening required multidimensional and emergent structures to transform television's past into a usable, meaningful collection of discrete objects. Buried in the institution's formation, or at least hidden from public and popular views, were archival and information management logics to treat post-broadcast records akin to conventional historical material. The archival logic was evident in the interest to preserve that which is unique and with historical value. The library logic was evident in the application of new computerized cataloging methods as well as the concept that anyone could enter this space and borrow a broadcast program. The MoB, though, remains the embodied articulation of how to value television from industry-defined optics. The lasting legacy on the production of knowledge may be more so on how to order such records rather than the available scope of records. Understood as a site in the legitimation of classification of broadcasts and its management through technological and professional infrastructures, the MoB was a node in a broader network to define and make use of post-broadcast value for what can be known and how it can be known.

NOTES

1. Kay Gardella, "The Museum Is the Media," *Daily News*, November 10, 1976, sec. Television, Museum of Broadcasting Publicity: 1976–1977, Paley Center for Media, New York.

2. For example, see Robert W. McChesney, *Telecommunications, Mass Media and Democracy: The Battle for the Control of U.S. Broadcasting, 1928–1935* (New York: Oxford University Press, 1998); William Boddy, *Fifties Television: The Industry and Its Critics* (Urbana: University of Illinois Press, 1990); Lynn Spigel, "Our TV Heritage: Television, the Archive, and the Reasons for Preservation," in *A Companion to Television*, ed. Janet Wasko (Malden, Mass.: Blackwell, 2005), 67–102; Horace Newcomb, "Studying Television: Same Questions, Different Contexts," *Cinema Journal* 45, no. 1 (2005): 107–11.

3. "Museum of Broadcasting Press Conference: Remarks of William S. Paley," November 9, 1976, 3, box 134, Daniel J. Boorstin Papers, Manuscript Division, Library of Congress, Washington, D.C. Paley's remarks were also printed in the MoB's first newsletter in fall 1977. See the Museum of Broadcasting file in the Library of Congress Motion Picture Room Files.

4. Judith Hennessee, "Tuning in the Past Is a Snap at the New Broadcasting Museum," *New York Times*, November 14, 1976.

5. John D. Stevens and Hazel Dicken Garcia, *Communication History* (Beverly Hills, Calif.: Sage, 1980).

6. Spigel, "Our TV Heritage"; Derek Kompare, *Rerun Nation: How Repeats Invented American Television* (New York: Routledge, 2005).

7. John Armstrong, "Applying Critical Theory to Electronic Media History," in *Methods of Historical Analysis in Electronic Media*, ed. Donald G. Godfrey (Mahwah, N.J.: Lawrence Erlbaum, 2006), 157.

8. Craig Allen, "Television Broadcast Records," in Godfrey, *Methods of Historical Analysis*, 207–32; Michele Hilmes, "Nailing Mercury: The Problem of Media Industry Historiography," in *Media Industries: History, Theory, and Method*, ed. Jennifer Holt and Alisa Perren (Malden, Mass.: Wiley-Blackwell, 2009), 21–33.

9. Broadly, critical interventions address the relationship between materials that become historical evidence and what can be known/becomes part of history. The archival process, including steps in acquiring, selecting, and describing collections and then providing access, "works *to create* information, to produce not only

social or historical understanding but the very elements of social and historical knowledge itself." Francis X. Blouin Jr. and William G. Rosenberg, eds., *Archives, Documentation, and Institutions of Social Memory* (Ann Arbor: University of Michigan Press, 2006), 86.
10. R. C. Head, "Preface: Historical Research on Archives and Knowledge Cultures: An Interdisciplinary Wave," *Archival Science* 10, no. 3 (2010): 191–94.
11. Antoinette M. Burton, *Archive Stories: Facts, Fictions, and the Writing of History* (Durham, N.C.: Duke University Press, 2005), 6.
12. Hugh Taylor, "Opening Address," in *Documents That Move and Speak: Audiovisual Archives in the New Information Age; Proceedings of a Symposium*, ed. Harold Naugler, National Archives of Canada, and International Council on Archives (Munich: K. G. Saur, 1992), 18–29.
13. Lisa Gitelman, *Always Already New: Media, History and the Data of Culture* (Cambridge, Mass.: MIT Press, 2006).
14. Jeff Martin, "The Dawn of Tape: Transmission Device as Preservation Medium," *Moving Image* 5, no. 1 (2005): 45–66; Fay Schreibman, "A Succinct History of American Television Archives," *Film and History* 21, nos. 2–3 (1991): 89–95.
15. Caroline Frick, *Saving Cinema: The Politics of Preservation* (New York: Oxford University Press, 2010); Ralph N. Sargent, *Preserving the Moving Image* (Washington, D.C.: Corporation for Public Broadcasting and the National Endowment for the Arts, 1974).
16. William S. Paley, *As It Happened: A Memoir* (Garden City, N.Y.: Doubleday, 1979), 368.
17. Perhaps Paley's participation on the Museum of Modern Art's board of trustees (1950s–60s) inspired such an idea. In the late 1950s Paley was on the Ad Hoc Committee for Films and Television, which advised MoMA's Film Library about television. See Lynn Spigel, *TV by Design: Modern Art and the Rise of Network Television* (Chicago: University of Chicago Press, 2008).
18. Sally Bedell Smith, *In All His Glory: The Life of William S. Paley, the Legendary Tycoon and His Brilliant Circle* (New York: Simon & Schuster, 1990); Douglas Gomery, *A History of Broadcasting in the United States* (Malden, Mass.: Blackwell, 2008).
19. "Museum of Broadcasting Press Conference," 2.
20. Raymond Williams, *Television: Technology and Cultural Form* (New York: Schocken, 1975).
21. "Museum of Broadcasting Press Conference," 1, 2.
22. Paddy Scannell, "Broadcasting Historiography and Historicality," *Screen* 45, no. 2 (2004): 130–41.
23. Jonathan Bignell and Andreas Fickers, *A European Television History* (Malden, Mass.: Wiley-Blackwell, 2009), 6; William T. Murphy, "Genesis of a Profession: Origins of the Film and Television Archives Advisory Committees," *Moving Image* 11, no. 1 (2011): 103–12.
24. Kompare, *Rerun Nation*.
25. Spigel, "Our TV Heritage," 82.
26. Kompare, *Rerun Nation*, 112.

27. William T. Murphy, *Television and Video Preservation 1997: A Report on the Current State of American Television and Video Preservation* (Washington, D.C.: Library of Congress, 1997), 7.

28. For example, Spigel references the Library of Congress report to indicate how Paley utilized academic contexts for legitimacy, thus repeating the minor error (Spigel, "Our TV Heritage").

29. Shawn VanCour, "Educating Tomorrow's Media Workers: Television Instruction at American Institutions of Higher Learning, 1945–1960," *Critical Studies in Media Communication* 33, no. 2 (2016): 195–209. For definitions and critiques of administrative research, see Hanno Hardt, "British Cultural Studies and the Return of the 'Critical' in American Mass Communication Research: Accommodation or Radical Change?," *Journal of Communication Inquiry* 10, no. 2 (June 1986): 117–24; David W. Park and Jefferson Pooley, *The History of Media and Communication Research: Contested Memories* (New York: Peter Lang, 2008).

30. A. William Bluem, "Preserving Broadcasting Materials of Historic Significance: Summary and Report of a Four-Year Study," January 1971, 1, Library Files, Paley Center for Media, New York.

31. Lynn Spigel, "The Making of a TV Literate Elite," in *The Television Studies Book*, ed. Christine Geraghty and David Lusted (New York: St. Martin's, 1998), 63–94.

32. The report itself was not called the Bluem Report; I follow the 1997 Television and Video Preservation, which referred to it as the Bluem report. I capitalize "Report."

33. Bluem, "Preserving Broadcasting Materials," 1.

34. The report indicates there were two staff investigators, three staff consultants, and an assortment of occasional consultants.

35. Bluem, "Preserving Broadcasting Materials," 2. These institutions were across the United States as well as Canada, England, Belgium, and East Germany. Also, he mentioned private collections (e.g., entrepreneurs and personal collections of writers, performers, advertising agencies) but focused on formal institutional and corporate collections.

36. Bluem, "Preserving Broadcasting Materials," 2. This occurred about three years before Ruth Schwartz, a professor at UCLA and early leader of their TV archive, did a similar survey. Ruth Schwartz, "Preserving TV Programs: Here Today—Gone Tomorrow," *Journal of Broadcasting* 17 (1972–73): 287).

37. Bluem, "Preserving Broadcasting Materials," 18, 21, 29.

38. The Peabody Collection is a reminder that collecting recorded programs does not imply preservation. The Peabody Collection was not secured until 1980 when the University of Georgia Library took in the collection and was able to ensure that tapes and films were properly preserved. See Schreibman, "Succinct History." Also see chapter 4 by Ruta Abolins in this book.

39. Bluem, "Preserving Broadcasting Materials," 24, 21.

40. A. William Bluem, "Preserving Broadcasting History: Final Report, Project No. H. 4660," 1971, 8, Section 5D, 749–827, Ford Foundation.

41. Bluem, "Preserving Broadcasting History," 6. The NBC inventory project also was an attempt to determine the technological and financial dimensions associated

with acquiring such programs. However, this part was never fully realized and tabled for later investigation and study.
42. Bluem, "Preserving Broadcasting Materials," 42–45.
43. Bluem, "Preserving Broadcasting Materials," 21 (emphasis in original). Bluem did not inventory ABC but made estimates based on the first phase's survey in conjunction with his findings from CBS and NBC.
44. Bluem, "Preserving Broadcasting Materials," 29.
45. A. William Bluem, "The Significance of Findings Reported Here to Future Development of a Library and History Center for Radio and Television," 1971, 10, Section 5D, 749–827, Ford Foundation.
46. Schreibman, "Succinct History."
47. Bluem, "Preserving Broadcasting Materials," 64.
48. Bluem, "Preserving Broadcasting Materials," 2.
49. Bluem, "Preserving Broadcasting Materials," 70–73.
50. Luke J. Gilliland-Swetland, "The Provenance of a Profession: The Permanence of the Public Archives and Historical Manuscripts Traditions in American Archival History," *American Archivist* 54, no. 2 (1991): 160–75.
51. A. William Bluem, "The NBC Holdings—A Summary of Research Findings," 1971, 19, Section 5D, 749–827, Ford Foundation.
52. Bluem, "Preserving Broadcasting Materials," 3.
53. Bluem, "NBC Holdings," 15, 11–12.
54. Bluem, "Preserving Broadcasting Materials," 29–30.
55. Terry Cook, "The Tyranny of the Medium: A Comment on 'Total Archives,'" *Archivaria* 9 (1979–80): 141–49; Helen Willa Samuels, "Who Controls the Past," *American Archivist* 49, no. 2 (1986): 109–24.
56. Bluem, "Preserving Broadcasting Materials," 12–13.
57. Bluem, "Preserving Broadcasting Materials," 35–36.
58. Bluem, "Preserving Broadcasting Materials," 32.
59. Bluem, "Preserving Broadcasting Materials," 2.
60. Bluem, "Preserving Broadcasting History," 16.
61. Gardella, "The Museum Is the Media."
62. Bluem, "Preserving Broadcasting Materials," 33, 76–78.
63. Paddy Scannell, "Television and History: Questioning the Archive," *Communication Review* 13, no. 1 (2010): 37–51; Ernest J. Dick, "An Archival Acquisition Strategy for the Broadcast Records of the Canadian Broadcasting Corporation," *Historical Journal of Film, Radio and Television* 11, no. 3 (October 1991): 253–68; Joyce Line, *Archival Collections of Non-Book Materials* (London: British Library, 1977).
64. Anna McCarthy, *The Citizen Machine: Governing by Television in 1950s America* (New York: New Press, 2010); Smith, *In All His Glory*.
65. Participants included library, history, or communication professors and leaders from PBS, BBC, George Eastman House, MoMA Film Department, *American Heritage*, Archives of American Art, and the Museum of Sciences.
66. Bluem, "Preserving Broadcasting Materials," 30.
67. Gardella, "The Museum Is the Media."

68. Bluem's research was initially funded through January 1971. The Paley Foundation extended the research project for another year in order to analyze costs for acquisition and services as well as a comparative competitive analysis of similar projects. Bluem, "Significance of Findings," 22.
69. Smith, *In All His Glory*; Kompare, *Rerun Nation*.
70. Spigel, "Our TV Heritage"; Douglas F. Gibbons, "The Museum of Broadcasting, New York," *Historical Journal of Film, Radio and Television* 1, no. 1 (March 1981): 67–70.
71. Lynn Spigel, "Housing Television: Architectures of the Archive," *Communication Review* 13, no. 1 (2010): 52–74; Amy Holdsworth, "'Television Resurrections': Television and Memory," *Cinema Journal* 47, no. 3 (2008): 137–44.
72. In addition to competing against the Television Academy's legitimation projects to partner with UCLA, it is possible that CBS's copyright battles with the Vanderbilt TV News Archive stemmed from Bluem's investigations or at the very least informed how Paley (and his surrogates) would proceed with the museum.
73. Hardt, "British Cultural Studies," 120.

PART II

THE ARCHIVE AS SOURCES OF AND INTERPRETERS FOR HERITAGE AND CULTURAL LEGITIMATION

CHAPTER 4

RUTA ABOLINS

HOW AN AWARD CREATED AN ARCHIVES

BROADCASTING HISTORY UNFOLDS
IN THE PEABODY AWARDS COLLECTION

"Since we would like to keep as complete a file of the entries from year to year as possible," wrote John E. Drewry, dean of the Henry Grady School of Journalism at the University of Georgia, to Fox Case, director of Public Relations at the Columbia Broadcasting System, "I wonder if it would be possible to let us have copies of these recordings. We have a feeling that in years to come they will undoubtedly have historical significance and should, therefore, be in the file of Peabody entries."[1]

If Drewry had not written those words, would there be a Peabody Awards Collection? The fact that the Peabody Awards Collection contains almost every entry since the awards began is noteworthy and due in large part to Drewry's recognition of the potential historical significance of the award. In another scenario, all the entries could have been returned. (In fact, some *have* been returned over the years, but only by request.) What did happen is genuinely remarkable. Almost everything has been retained, from the original analog media, artifacts, and papers to digital files. The letter from Dean Drewry to Fox Case signaled the intention to create a complete archive of all the entries and associated materials. Drewry saw that the then-new radio technology was essential to acknowledge, celebrating it with an award and saving the creative content entered. Without this foresight and the ability to store the collection in some manner, there would be no Peabody Awards Collection as it exists today.

This raises further questions. When does an assortment of stuff from an award become an archive? When was this collection of television and radio deemed important for the University of Georgia to save? And how did the Peabody Awards Collection become what it is today? To answer those questions, one must first understand how the Peabody Awards came to exist.

IN THE BEGINNING, 1940–1974

"We feel this is a unique collection," Peabody Awards director Worth McDougald wrote in 1974, "since the networks particularly are often calling us to locate their own materials which they no longer have. We are protecting it in every way possible and expect that it will form the nucleus for what may well be one of the most significant broadcasting collections in the nation."[2]

Nearly fifty years earlier, the idea for the award began in 1939 when John Drewry, the dean of the University of Georgia journalism school, met Lambdin Kay, the station director at WSB in Atlanta. They discussed how radio needed a public service award equivalent to Columbia University's Pulitzer Awards for print journalism. Within a year, university leadership approved and created the Peabody Award, named after George Foster Peabody, a life trustee of UGA.[3]

How entries would be received that first year was laid out by Dean Drewry in a letter to station managers in 1940. The entry criteria were broad, leaving the depth of the award justification up to the submitters. Drewry mentions this in his speech at the National Association of Broadcasters (NAB) and outlines some important information about the Awards:

> Write this office about your public service activities (non-commercial programs) of the year as you wish considered in this connection. You may enter as many such activities as you wish. You make your entry as simple or as elaborate as you choose. It may be a letter or an exhibit. Whatever the form, however, it should make perfectly clear to the judges the nature of the broadcast service you wish considered. In the words of the Regents' statute creating these awards, program subjects, program outlines, program transcripts, recordings, letters and other pertinent data should be presented as to comprise an exhibit that will be a faithful record of the station's particular contribution to public service offered for consideration in this connection.[4]

Under these guidelines, early entries did not always include recordings of the submitted programs, instead using scrapbooks and other items to make a case for the programs' worth. Nevertheless, many radio recordings on transcription discs were submitted and are still part of the collection today.

Memos about the first batch of entries to be judged by the panel of UGA faculty offer valuable documentation to trace the origins of today's collection. Three major chains and fifty-nine individual stations submitted a total of 153 recordings on transcription disc.[5] One entrant submitted fifty-seven recordings to be judged.[6] Some exhibits (i.e., entries) were incomplete. The main challenge was that UGA faculty did not have access to the equipment necessary to listen to the transcription discs; a memo mentions needing a turntable and parts and asking the Board of Regents for money to review content.[7] Of the 153 transcription discs mentioned in the memo, ninety-three still exist in the archives today. Where the other sixty recordings are, we can only wonder. They could have been returned or broken over the years, discarded, taken, or just misplaced and lost. For that first year, nine entries have associated scrapbooks or annual reports. Of those, three have no corresponding transcription discs at all, which aligns with the policy of accepting associated material to prove worth. Small stations in Washington, Missouri, Mississippi, and Ohio and one chain in New York supplied both transcription discs and associated paper documentation that we still have today. For example, a 1940 winner, KVOS out of Bellingham, Washington, sent in a transcription disc called *Peace Program* about Armistice Day that came in with a scrapbook on the Peace Arch, a monument at the border between Canada and the United States.

The first television award was created in 1948 (presented in 1949) for *The Actor's Studio: A Child Is Born*, which was submitted as a 16mm kinescope. The 1949 award program is still listed as an award for "Outstanding Meritorious Public Service."[8] By 1952 that had been changed to "Distinguished Achievement in Radio and Television."[9]

From the 1940s until 1969, the award grew by several hundred entries per year. Important to note here is that one entry does not necessarily equal one physical item. Longer programs were split over several reels or discs, or an entry might contain multiple episodes of a series. By 1969 there was a considerable amount of material to care for, with a total of 8,882 entries submitted, which translated into 9,411 physical media items. This does not include the associated papers or artifacts, which would have also been very significant in size. This content would have included scrapbooks as mentioned previously, but also the original entry forms, scripts, photos, press clippings, letters from viewers and listeners, press kits, flyers, and letters of recommendation. In later years when marketing became increasingly important for promoting programming, items such as T-shirts, hats, toys, stuffed animals, games, and so on were also submitted with award entries.

John Drewry stepped down as director of the Peabody Awards in 1963. In 1969 Dean Warren Agee sent a letter to Drewry asking him to consider working as the curator of the Peabody Awards. Agee states: "I have been struck by the immense treasure-house of materials which the Peabody Collection represents. Educationally and historically, they represent a most valuable collection. In their present form, however, uncatalogued and ill-preserved, the collections can be of little use to scholars or the public."[10] With that, Agee asked Drewry to consider working as a curator with administrative and student support to help him write something up for each entry that could become a catalog of the entire collection. In other words, they needed an archivist. Drewry did not take the position. What was mentioned as a possible "collection with historical significance" by Dean Drewry in 1941 was solidified by Agee in 1969 as a treasure trove of educationally and historically valuable material. This marks a significant increase in recognition of the value of the collection. Yet there was no formally assigned archivist for the collection until twenty-six years later, when the UGA Libraries created the position.

The Grady College of Journalism was originally housed in the Commerce Journalism Building, now known as Brooks Hall, and this is where the collection was initially stored. In 1969 the Grady College of Journalism moved to a newly built facility designed for journalism teaching,[11] and the collection moved to a second-floor space dubbed "the attic." This area, which had no climate control and was therefore a detrimental environment for audiovisual recordings, especially during hot and humid Georgia summers, was used to store the collection for several years. The move may have led to the realization that the growing collection was too much for the journalism school to continue to manage.

Drewry was succeeded by Worth McDougald, a journalism professor who would serve as director of the Peabody Awards until 1991. Dean Agee, no doubt with the help of McDougald, cemented the idea that the collection was intended for research. A 1971 draft message to Peabody Award entrants describes the "unique 32-year-old collection of outstanding tapes, films, and records comprising the Peabody Collection and made available for scholarly research and other educational purposes."[12] The collection was available to faculty for teaching at the journalism school, and letters with questions about the collection are found among McDougald's papers, along with his carbon-copied answers. Since the collection was housed at Grady, direct knowledge of who was using the collection for teaching was not documented in the remaining records.

A 1974 article from the UGA student newspaper *The Red and Black* mentions that the collection would be moving to the UGA Libraries.[13] Before the collection was moved to the library, a memo was released calling for everyone at Grady College to return any content "borrowed" from the Peabody Awards Collection. This information comes from a conversation with Andy Johnston, who worked at Grady at that time. He had taken many of the original 16mm kinescopes home for safekeeping, thereby saving them from the poor storage conditions in the attic.[14] In 2021 Mr. Johnston donated his own archives to Brown Media; in those materials was a missing Peabody entry, a 16mm kinescope of *Art Carney Meets Peter and the Wolf*. The kinescope has been repatriated into the archive and digitized, and is in excellent condition. Though most of the Peabody collection is present, there are still missing items. Whether they were never received, went missing, were broken or otherwise compromised, discarded, returned to the entrant on request, or lost is unknown. The same must be true for related papers and submitted artifacts. An instructor could have "borrowed" something and never returned it; again, there is no way of knowing.

A COLLECTION IN NEED OF AN ARCHIVE AT THE UGA LIBRARY, 1975–1990

"'The selections have been in such a horrible mess for so long that I almost think we won't get ourselves out of it. But when we do, they will be arranged and stored as an unparalleled archive of the broadcast industry.'"[15] So declared Vance Trussel, library media specialist for the collection, in a 1976 article in the UGA student newspaper. It was a hopeful vision. Most analog audiovisual collections are donated to archives when their creator runs out of space or when there is a change in ownership or rights. The same is true for the Peabody Awards Collection. At some point, the UGA Library and the Grady College of Journalism discussed the Peabody Awards Collection. This probably started in 1974 when the libraries added 200,000 square feet to the back of the original three-story library building.[16] Unfortunately, there is no official documentation about the collection transfer in the libraries. Worth McDougald from the Grady College of Journalism likely initiated the move in 1974.[17] This collection was a boon to the library because it held a large number of papers and artifacts in addition to the audiovisual content. The papers and the numerous types of artifacts went to the Hargrett Library, which was then housed in the Main Library at UGA. The audiovisual recordings went to a secure storage area dubbed "the cage."[18] That area was kept at the same temperature and humidity as the rest of the building. The addition of the collection to the libraries probably had more to do with the importance of the papers and artifacts as part of UGA history than a recognition of the potential value of the recordings. The Hargrett Library for Rare Books and Manuscripts already existed as a special collection within the UGA Libraries, and it houses the University Archives, to which the Peabody Awards Collection was an important addition. Bringing in 10,000+ analog media items was a daunting task, as mentioned in the quotation above, and there may have been a belief that it would be easier to work with than it actually was. Analog media is very challenging because of all the equipment needed to view and preserve it.

With no memo of understanding stating the relationship and responsibilities between the library and the journalism school, there was a natural setup for misunderstandings creating a strained relationship between the two departments. After the article about the library owning "a mess" appeared in *The Red and Black*, there were understandably some hard feelings from the journalism school about how the collection was portrayed. There was also a proposal attributed to Vance Trussell mentioned in correspondence by the dean of the journalism school that has not been located, which outlined how the collection should be handled. That proposal also did not help matters, as seen from a response letter dated April 1976 from Dean Scott Cutlip. Cutlip stated there was no transfer of ownership, that the library was overstepping boundaries, and that the libraries lacked the technical know-how to duplicate the content and the proper equipment to work with the collection; he also stated that the checkout parameters needed to be reworked. Cutlip's reservations signaled a fear that the collection's mishandling could taint the awards' reputation.[19] Cutlip's concerns were eventually assuaged before he died in 2000. He committed an endowment to the libraries to support the preservation of the Peabody Awards Collection specifically; those funds have been used to send fragile recordings, in particular the two-inch quad tapes, to specialty labs for preservation, and his donation continues to support the preservation of the collection.

A 1977 National Endowment for the Humanities (NEH) grant submitted by the Grady School of Journalism failed because there was no archival partnership to preserve the Peabody Awards.[20] Another grant application was submitted to the NEH in 1978 by the journalism school.[21] The NEH asked nine questions that the grant writer James Fletcher of the journalism school answered, giving an overview of what was happening with the collection at the time and what was intended with the grant. The grant agency asked how much use the collection was receiving per year. "The Peabody Collection is inaccessible. There are no playback facilities or study areas in the vicinity of the collection. The purpose of the proposed project is to make the collection accessible."[22] However, Fletcher did mention its use by scholars and some UGA undergraduates, noting that content was copied for use as needed by the Instructional Resource Center on campus. Clearly the journalism school and the libraries provided some mechanism for access, probably very limited and subject to appointment. The NEH asked what criteria would be used to determine which audiovisual content would be copied for researcher use. Fletcher answered "Everything" at first and then added, "Television material due to the relatively greater vulnerability of this material to the effects of time." For the budget, Fletcher stated that the project "requires the full-time expertise of a 'trained archivist.'" John Edwards is listed as the project archivist as he was the university archivist in the Hargrett Library during that time. Edwards was trained in working with paper archives, so there was still no expert for the audiovisual portion of the collection.

The grant was awarded for $125,000 over a three-year period to create a uniform finding aid for the content, rerecord three-quarter-inch tapes to VHS for research, rerecord audio for research, and preserve the papers.[23] A report on the first six months of the grant by Fletcher indicates that project staff focused on organizing the papers, that a hundred cubic feet of papers were processed, and that no work was done on the audiovisual portion of the collection.[24] This is not surprising, given that there were no audiovisual experts on staff and audiovisual archives were not as common or focused as they are today. For example, the Association of Moving Image Archivists, the world's leading professional organization focusing on audiovisual archives, was not founded until 1990.[25]

In a July 1979 letter to university archivist John Edwards, Wilson Page, one of the people working on the Peabody Awards grant, describes the journalism school as using entry numbers as unique identifiers for the audiovisual content. In contrast, the libraries organized the papers by year and location, which would be a common practice for a paper-only collection. As Page notes correctly, these approaches were incompatible. It meant that cross-referencing needed to be done to locate paper content with associated audiovisual content—not an ideal scenario for anyone wanting to do research in the collection.[26] These two separate identification methods remained in use until a project to reorganize the paper and artifact content was undertaken in 2012. That project involved creating a detailed folder-level finding aid for print materials and artifacts, using entry numbers as unique identifiers and titles for each entry, and providing a more detailed account of what is available in each entry folder, such as entry form, script, photographs, clippings, scrapbooks, and so on. The work was completed by student assistants hired by the Brown Media Archives and Peabody Awards Collection working in the Hargrett Library.

In 1980 the libraries began cataloging and rerecording content from the original audiovisual entry format to a "user" copy on audiocassette or VHS videotape for research purposes. The duplication work took place at a Peabody Recording Center, and about eight hours of content was transferred each week.[27] This rerecording project lasted through about 1991 when entry requirements were updated to require both a broadcast-quality copy and a review copy on VHS or audiocassette. As the technology evolved, review copies were submitted on DVD or CD. When each year's entries were transferred to the libraries, the review copies were then used as viewing or listening copies for researchers.[28] By 2013 all entries were submitted digitally, which continues today.

The Libraries Electromedia Center was opened in 1979; it contained purchased videotapes used for classroom instruction and the user copies of Peabody Awards audiovisual content. A 1986 article described a "videotape treasure trove," stating that there was no card catalog for the content, just a master printout at the front desk on the seventh floor of Libraries.[29] This was how access was provided for the Peabody Awards content until 1995.

In 1990, in honor of the fiftieth anniversary of the Peabody Awards, a temporary exhibit was created in downtown Athens, Georgia. This town-and-gown event was a collaboration between the Athens community, the Grady College of Journalism, and the UGA Libraries.[30] A commemorative hardbound version of the awards ceremony program was also published. The exhibit displayed the rich content of the Peabody Awards Collection and included elaborate scrapbooks, scripts, photographs, and promotional materials like dolls, games, and T-shirts. This exhibit also illustrates that exhibiting papers and artifacts is significantly easier than showcasing the original physical media or its contents.

THE ARCHIVES ARE CREATED, 1990–PRESENT

The National Archives and Records Administration defines an archive as "a place where people can go to gather first-hand facts, data, and evidence from letters, reports, notes, memos, photographs, and other primary sources."[31] Television scholar Derek Kompare describes the Peabody Awards Collection as an archive founded with an important vision to showcase particular strengths: "The Peabody Awards Collection is a model of how materials that stations, networks, and other producers were once particularly proud of but which otherwise would almost certainly be lost today can be preserved and made accessible to the public."[32] This foundation led to the collection's growth and renown.

By 1990 the Peabody Awards Collection had been at the libraries for fifteen years. It had grown to 18,941 total entries, which came to 22,722 physical media items held by the Media Department (also known as Media Services or Electromedia) in the libraries. Some cataloging had been done of about a hundred records of programs on 16mm film. These records were added to OCLC and the local online library catalog. However, that cataloging was still a small fraction of the total collection. The papers and artifacts had been organized by year and the submitting station's location and were accessible and managed by the Hargrett Library.

Big changes began when Dr. William Gray Potter joined the UGA Libraries as the library director in 1989, and a preservation assessment of the entire libraries' collections was done in 1990. These two events paved the way for the creation of the Media Archive.

The libraries' 1990 Preservation Plan makes it clear that effort was needed to preserve the analog media in the Peabody Awards Collection: "the Task Force recommends that master copies be made for use and the original pieces stored under strict security in a controlled environment preferably at a location outside the Libraries. This large and valuable collection deserves to receive a very high priority with the preservation effort because it is unique and important."[33] No specific recommendations were made because there was no expert on audiovisual archives on staff. By January 1991 Dr. Potter had outlined sixteen objectives for the libraries, including a site for a new library building, the implementation of a preservation program, and "control[led] access to the Media Collection."[34] By controlling access to the collection, Potter wanted to ensure that only duplicate copies of originally entered content were used for access and that there was a searchable catalog for the collection.

By April 1995 Potter saw the necessity for a new facility to house the libraries' three special collections, listing them as "the Hargrett Library, the Russell Library, and the Peabody Archives."[35] This acknowledgment of the Peabody Awards Collection helped change the collection's trajectory by putting it on par with the already long-established Special Collections within the UGA Libraries and legitimizing the creation of the Media Archives and Peabody Awards Collection.

Within several years, the libraries' archival media holdings had nearly doubled with the addition of the WSB Newsfilm Collection, formerly administered by UGA's Instructional Resource Center (now known as the Center for Teaching and Learning), in addition to several smaller audiovisual collections. A 1993 proposal for a media/Peabody librarian mentioned that such a librarian could also incorporate GPTV (Georgia Public Broadcasting) and Georgia Center (the UGA media production center) materials into the Media Archives.[36] Those collections are part of the archive today.

In 1995 Linda Tadic was hired as UGA's first audiovisual archivist. She took on the task of putting the Peabody Awards Collection in order, creating finding aids, and beginning to catalog the earliest television entries. Tadic was also tasked with managing the Media Department and its collection of purchased audiovisual materials.

With Tadic, a person with the expertise to take on the preservation and access of the collections, hired, the full creation of the archive began to take shape. Soon secure space was made available in the subbasement of the Main Library building to house the collection with specialized storage shelving. Spreadsheets were created to account for all the Peabody entries in the collection. Through Tadic, the Media Archive received an NEH grant in 1998 to preserve the African American history and culture television programming submitted to the Peabody Awards between 1949 and 1996. This was the first major step toward the concentrated effort of preserving the audiovisual portion of the collection versus providing just access alone. Additional staff was hired around this time to concentrate on the cataloging of the collection, with records being added to the libraries database and OCLC.

The University Archives contains an undated six-page document proposing the move of the Peabody Awards Collection and the Peabody Awards program office to the old Georgia Museum of Art (GMOA) building. It was probably written in 1995 or 1996 when an opportunity for space was made available near the UGA Library. The GMOA was moved to a newly built facility across campus in April 1996. The old GMOA building was initially constructed as the first UGA Library with funds from George Foster Peabody, so there was a beautiful symmetry in the proposal and the plan to use it in honor of the Peabody Awards. The collection is described as one of the top five in the country and second only to UCLA in size and scope, having over thirty thousand recordings as well as paper documentation and artifacts; it also mentions the Southeast Regional Emmys, another awards-based collection in the archive.[37] This plan never came to fruition.

In August 2000 I took over as director of the Media Archives. One of my first essential changes for the Peabody Awards Collection was working with the UGA Libraries Information and Technology Department on an online entry form created for Peabody entrants to fill out. This coordinated effort between the Peabody Awards Office and the archive meant no more data entry for paper-only entry forms. That information and the previously created spreadsheets were almost immediately uploaded into the newly created Peabody Awards Collection database. This was a game changer for the archive and for the use of the collection. Before this point, most of the collection was inaccessible for online searching. The Peabody database initially provided online access to the entire audiovisual content in the collection with minimal descriptive information including title, date, and originating station. Program descriptions and credits as well as a more defined description of the paper or artifacts associated with each entry would come later.

In 2002 the Media Archives was officially named the Walter J. Brown Media Archives and Peabody Awards Collection (BMA) in recognition of a generous monetary gift from the Watson-Brown Foundation in honor of Walter J. Brown (1903–95), a UGA graduate who knew and worked for Franklin Delano Roosevelt before founding the radio and television company Spartan Communications.[38] The archive became even more defined with the addition of a name.

In 2004 Brown Media received a $300,000 grant from Save America's Treasures to digitize local television content on three-quarter-inch U-matic videotape in the Peabody Awards Collection. This content is still some of the most unique in the collection. This grant started the archives on a path to the digitization of analog content that is still going on to this day. By 2008 the archives had also digitized content from the WSB Newsfilm Collection as a partner with the Digital Library of Georgia for inclusion in the Civil Rights Digital Library, funded by the National Historical Publications and Records Commission (NHPRC). This was followed by the more concentrated process of digitizing 16mm and smaller-gauge formats from the collection. After these grants, digitizing analog content in-house became the norm rather than the exception, with the archives continuing to use external specialty labs for large projects or fragile recordings. The department now digitizes analog content on demand. When a researcher finds an item of interest in the online catalog, if a digital copy is not already linked to the record, the researcher can request that a digital access copy be created. These files have a watermark and time code embedded. The watermark and time code prevent unauthorized usage while allowing scholars and researchers to use the collection without traveling to Athens, Georgia.

Over time, Brown Media's efforts to further preserve and provide access to the Peabody Awards Collection led to some exciting and important discoveries. In 2005 archivist Margaret Compton discovered a unique episode of *The Honeymooners* in the Peabody Awards Collection. It was broadcast on October 16, 1954, as a segment within an episode of *The Jackie Gleason Show* titled "The Love Letter." There are other unique items in the collection, but this one received widespread media attention when it was found.[39]

By 2010 ground was broken for the $46 million, 115,000 square foot building fulfilling the dream that Dr. Potter had in 1995 to create a space for the three special collections at UGA. At this time, Brown Media focused intensively on preparing the collection to be moved to the Special Collections Library by barcoding each item, creating a new website, and creating a specialized exhibit area with a large permanent gallery devoted to the Peabody Awards Collection. Brown Media archivists, myself included, recall that period between 2010 and 2012 as a blur, because so much happened to get the collections under even more control and to create a public exhibit while planning to move the entire operations to the new location.

In February 2012 the Special Collections Building opened. It houses the Hargrett Rare Book and Manuscript Library, the Richard B. Russell Library for Political Research and Studies, and the Walter J. Brown Media Archives and Peabody Awards Collection. There are exhibit spaces for all three entities, an auditorium, classrooms, research areas, and special event spaces. Most importantly, there is a secure high-density storage vault below ground that is temperature- and humidity-controlled to archival standards. Teaching using these collections is the norm rather than the exception. The UGA Special Collections Library hosts the Special Collections Faculty Teaching Fellows program, bringing faculty to the archive to help them create classes centered on UGA's special collections.

There are also students doing experiential learning projects and interns from high schools and library science programs working on the collections. UGA students and graduate assistants work in all three special collections, learning about the content while increasing the archives' ability to preserve and provide access to these rare materials. Most visibly and perhaps most significantly, there is an exhibition space that highlights the Peabody Awards Collection to anyone who comes into the building. Visitors include a yearly eighth-grade field trip for every student in Athens-Clarke County as well as UGA faculty, staff, and students; members of the Athens community; and tour groups from across the state of Georgia and beyond. The exhibits include artifacts sent in with entries and kiosks that show video content highlights and the award winners for each year.

By 2010 the Peabody Awards began receiving digital files on discs and drives for some entries. In 2013 the awards changed their submission requirements to an all-digital format. This necessitated adding a digital archivist to Brown Media's staff and a significant increase in digital storage capacity for the libraries.

In 2018 the archives received a National Historical Publications and Records Commission grant of $216,280 to digitize and preserve four thousand hours of public broadcasting content in the Peabody Awards Collection. This project was done in collaboration with the American Archive of Public Broadcasting (AAPB) and the Library of Congress. The AAPB hosts streaming copies of the content and searchable transcripts on their website, and preservation-quality copies of the digitized content are archived at the Library of Congress as well as Brown Media.

The effort to recatalog the print materials, artifacts, and photographs that were submitted along with Peabody entries began in 2012, and by 2022 all physical entries and artifacts have been processed so that now someone can search for a title or entry number and get an idea of what is there without stepping into the building. Beyond the entry form, there could be a script, photographs, clippings, scrapbooks, and so on. Remote researchers also have the option of getting scans of paper content. The collection is as searchable as it has ever been and the largest collection in the building if you consider all the audiovisual, digital files, papers, artifacts, and so forth that make up the entire collection, and it grows every year. It is also one of UGA's most highly used collections.

For the archives, the focus has never been on whether the program won a Peabody Award or not, though it is an important consideration. The fact that each year's entries constitute a slice of what creators consider their best programs makes the entire collection valuable. It has, for the archives, been more about trying to save as much content as possible, focusing on those programs not already being preserved by bigger entities or corporations. Preservation efforts also focus on programs that now exist in precarious analog carrier formats, though in truth, all our analog formats are in danger because of their age and equipment obsolescence. This reality led to the policy of digitization on demand by anyone who wants to see the content. Preservation of Peabody Awards entries, and indeed all of Brown Media Archives' collections, is equally shaped by archival considerations and researcher demand. If someone wants to see a particular program, that indicates the program is significant enough to warrant preservation. Historically, local television stations typically did not preserve their content, and early Peabody content can be rare—perhaps even the only existing copy. But beyond that, the smaller producers and documentarians, foreign entities, and nonprofit creators may lose content if the archive does not care for it. In sum, the priority is the entire collection, focusing primarily on the most at-risk content.

In today's world, what users expect of audiovisual content and, by association, audiovisual collections is that they are accessible online. The Brown Media Archives and Peabody Awards Collection does its best to make ease of use and accessibility its priority for those on the UGA campus and around the world. Most users do not enter the building; they view content online.

To support digital preservation activities, the UGA Libraries purchased one TB of storage in 2017. This storage is shared across the libraries for digital collections, but Brown Media Archives takes up most of the real estate. In 2022 this storage grew to two PB; the primary reason is the Brown Media Archives and Peabody Awards Collection. As of July 2022 BMA (including the Peabody Awards Collection) had 38,255 Archival Information Packages (AIPs) and 690 TB in its deep digital storage system called ARCHive. That is out of 125,580 AIPs and 752 TB for the libraries in total. Moving image digital files are large and take up much more space than audio, text, or image files, so even though BMA's AIPs account for only 30 percent of the total files, they total just over 90 percent of the storage space used. As of August 2022 the Peabody Awards Collection had 155,962 analog items and 58,155 digital files representing 76,947 programs.

This investment in digital stewardship is huge. It is a long-term commitment to the digitized analog content and to the born-digital files received for the award. Periodic investments in storage hardware using one-time funds that include a mix of privately raised gifts, media licensing revenue, and other library funding have enabled the purchase of the infrastructure. However, among the more challenging investments were establishing and sustaining recurring salaries for the people needed to manage and preserve the digitized media holding beyond Brown Media staff. There is now a head of digital stewardship as well as support and developer time from the Library Technology Department. Digital preservation is vital, but this work is never truly finished.[40]

Archives exist to preserve historical records within the context of their creation. At the University of Georgia, the history of the Peabody Awards program and the submitted materials are preserved side by side. Tracing the history of the awards in its archives, there is an early focus on print documentation—from entries that did not even include recordings of the programs in question to the processing of paper materials and artifacts before addressing the recorded media—gradually gave way to an understanding of and emphasis on the historical significance of the recordings themselves. A recognition of the archivability of the audiovisual recordings may have lagged, but it is now the driving purpose behind a dedicated staff and a department that stands alongside UGA's paper-based archives as an equal.

The intention from the beginning was to save the recordings and artifacts entered into the Peabody Awards. According to the records found in UGA's archives, the collection has always been important to the Grady College of Journalism and the University of Georgia Libraries; its retention was never in question. This is one of the amazing parts of this story: everyone thought it was essential to save. Getting it to the place where saving it and providing access to it were possible was the hard part, and that meant creating an archive that could take care of it, preserve it, provide access to it, and make it a priority. That finally happened fifty-five years after the award was conceived. Since 1995 the collection has become increasingly accessible, with much content preserved along the way. The Peabody Awards Collection is and will always be something that makes the University of Georgia distinct for being forward thinking in creating the award and the archive that preserves it.

NOTES   1. John E. Drewry to Fox Case, director of public relations at the Columbia Broadcasting System, April 5, 1941, George Foster Peabody Awards Records, ms 3000, Hargrett Library, University of Georgia, Athens, Georgia (hereafter cited as Peabody Awards Records).

2. Worth McDougald, Letter to Fred J. Gitner, "About the Peabody Awards Collection," July 30, 1974, Peabody Awards Records.
3. Pamphlet by John E. Drewry, "Bulletin of the University of Georgia," 1940, Peabody Awards Records.
4. Drewry pamphlet.
5. "Memo Re: Peabody Awards," January 24, 1941 Peabody Awards Records.
6. "Minutes of the First Meeting of the Faculty Committee for the Preliminary Selections for the George Foster Peabody Radio Awards," February 3, 1941, Peabody Awards Records.
7. "Memo Re: Peabody Awards," January 24, 1941.
8. *The George Foster Peabody Radio Awards for Outstanding Meritorious Public Service 1949*, Peabody Awards Records.
9. *The George Foster Peabody Awards for Distinguished Achievement in Radio and Television 1952*, Peabody Awards Records.
10. Warren K. Agee to Dean Emeritus John E. Drewry, "Peabody Collection Curator," July 29, 1969, Peabody Awards Records.
11. Zoe Maher, "#gradyhomeat50: Our Building through the Years," Grady College of Journalism and Mass Communication, November 6, 2019, https://grady.uga.edu/gradyhomeat50-our-building-through-the-years/.
12. Warren K. Agee, draft letter to Peabody entrants, "Our Thanks to You," 1971, Peabody Awards Records.
13. Randy Hughes, "Peabody Winners Stored in Library," *The Red and Black*, January 11, 1974, https://gahistoricnewspapers.galileo.usg.edu/lccn/gua1179162/1974-01-11/ed-1/seq-2/.
14. Ruta Abolins, conversation with Andy Johnston, October 11, 2021.
15. Pat Peeples, "Library Owns Mess," *The Red and Black*, January 20, 1976, https://gahistoricnewspapers.galileo.usg.edu/lccn/gua1179162/1976-01-20/ed-1/seq-2/.
16. "A Timeline of the University of Georgia Libraries," University Libraries, University of Georgia, accessed July 25, 2022, https://libs.uga.edu/history.
17. Hughes, "Peabody Winners Stored in Library"; Ruta Abolins, conversation with Bob Henneberger, head of the UGA Electromedia Department in 1974 and employee of the UGA Libraries from 1973 to 2000, about the Peabody Awards Collection, June 21, 2022. Henneberger also mentioned a meeting between the library and a representative from the Library of Congress to discuss the collection, likely an attempt to get advice or maybe place the collection with the LOC that did not move forward.
18. Henneberger conversation.
19. Scott Cutlip to Worth McDougald, "Proposal from Vance Trussell," April 26, 1976, Peabody Awards Records.
20. Robert Kingston to James E. Fletcher, "National Endowment for the Humanities Letter," Athens, Ga., May 23, 1977, Peabody Awards Records.
21. *Annual Report—School of Journalism, 1978–1979*, Henry W. Grady College of Journalism and Mass Communication Records, UA15-013, Hargrett Library, University of Georgia, Athens.

22. James E. Fletcher to Amy T. Lowitz, "Response to National Endowment for the Humanities," September 19, 1978, Peabody Awards Records. The entire account in this paragraph comes from this letter.
23. *Annual Report—School of Journalism, 1978–1979.*
24. James E. Fletcher to Amy Lowitz, "Semi-Annual Performance Report for NEH Grant," July 30, 1979, Peabody Awards Records.
25. "History," Association of Moving Image Archivists, accessed June 16, 2022, https://amianet.org/about/history/.
26. Wilson Page to James E. Fletcher, "Classification Schemes," July 10, 1979, Peabody Awards Records.
27. Ben Watson, "Radio-TV-Film Head to Direct Peabody Project," *The Red and Black*, June 26, 1980, https://gahistoricnewspapers.galileo.usg.edu/lccn/gua1179162/1980-06-26/ed-1/seq-2/.
28. Ruta Abolins, conversation with Mary Miller, July 21, 2022.
29. "Best Kept Secret: A Videotape Treasure Trove Exists at UGA Library," *Athens Observer*, February 6, 1986, sec. B, University of Georgia Libraries General Records, UA0010 newspaper clipping, University of Georgia Archives, Athens.
30. *Annual Report—School of Journalism, 1990–1991*, W. Henry Grady College of Journalism and Mass Communication Records, UA15-013.
31. "What's an Archives?" National Archives and Records Administration, last reviewed August 15, 2016, https://www.archives.gov/about/info/whats-an-archives.html.
32. Derek Kompare, "The Peabody Awards Collection and the Production of American Local Media History," in *Television History, the Peabody Archive, and Cultural Memory*, ed. Ethan Thompson, Jeffrey P. Jones, and Lucas Hatlen (Athens: University of Georgia Press, 2019), 44–45.
33. University of Georgia Libraries, Preservation Planning Program, Task Force on Condition of the Collections, *Final Report (*University of Georgia Libraries, December 1990), 13.
34. "Libraries Faculty Meeting," *Library Update*, January 17, 1991.
35. "Libraries Management Council," *Library Update*, April 12, 1995.
36. "Libraries Public Service/Collection Development," *Library Update*, September 30, 1993.
37. "Proposal for Space Reallocation," n.d., University of Georgia Libraries General Records, UA0010, University of Georgia Archives, Athens).
38. "Proposal for Space Reallocation."
39. "'Lost' Honeymooners," *UGA Today*, March 27, 2005, https://news.uga.edu/lost-honeymooners/.
40. Toby Graham, email to Ruta Abolins, November 4, 2022.

CHAPTER 5

HANNAH SPAULDING

LOCAL VALUE IN THE TELEVISION ARCHIVE

THE MEDIA ARCHIVE FOR CENTRAL ENGLAND

In 2010, *Critical Studies in Television* ran a special issue devoted to television archives. In this issue, scholars and archivists reflected on the relationship between archival practices, institutions, access initiatives, and television studies.[1] The role of television archives in shaping the field and writing television histories emerged prominently through these articles. Those that discuss British television archiving reflect thoughtfully on the media archives within the British Film Institute (BFI) and the archival operations of the BBC.[2] Yet one aspect of television archiving in the UK remains underexplored, namely, the role of regional media archives in collecting and preserving television history. These archives occupy an important place in the construction of British film and television heritage. Focusing on specific geographical regions in the UK and carrying television collections of factual and news programming, regional media archives preserve important and often overlooked aspects of television history.

In this chapter, I examine the regional media archive and argue for its importance as a collector and curator of historical television. Taking the Media Archive for Central England (MACE), whose remit concerns the moving image materials of the Midlands, as my key case study, I explore how the regional media archive articulates an alternative appraisal of televisual value, one in which locality is central. While regional television has included some of the UK's most notable series, it has also embodied programming that falls outside national and commercial canons. It is these more niche programs—the magazine series and local news broadcasts rooted in the counties, cities, and towns that created them—that find their home in regional media archives. By analyzing MACE's collection, archival logic, and access initiatives, I examine how place and local memory become central in the archive's presentation of these typically overlooked television programs. They emerge as key components of their collecting practices and public engagements, breaking down the often artificial boundaries of the broadcast region to excavate a granular sense of place within British television history. By removing television from its original broadcast context and repositioning it within the archive, I argue that MACE, and regional media archives more generally, elevates a system of televisual value rooted in geographic identities and memories of place that can recover "the local" in British television history.

I begin my chapter by situating MACE in relation to the British Film Institute (BFI), a central force in film and television archiving in the UK, and exploring how regional media archives define themselves in partnership with and distinction to the institute. I then turn more explicitly to regional media archives and British regional television, tracing the role of Independent Television (ITV) in the establishment of regional television franchises. I set up this context to clarify the sorts of television programs that end up in MACE—as well as other regional media archives—and the sometimes incongruous geographies of their remits. I conclude my chapter with an in-depth analysis of MACE. I examine the archive's collection, the role of television in this collection, the centrality of access to the archive, and the curation practices evident through its website and DVDs.

Regional media archives are critical to the preservation of television history often left out of national and commercial archives and for constructing an alternative system of television value rooted in the intimate experiences of the local. They enable scholars, artists, and members of the public to access regional television that, despite not having the reach of a national broadcast, defines the media landscape of individuals' everyday lives. These programs construct powerful representations of the places people lived and the spaces they occupied, building narratives and networks that shaped perceptions of local communities and experiences of belonging.[3] As such, while regional television, especially in its mundane, quotidian forms, might not appear to be as central to British television heritage as dramas like *The Wednesday Play* (BBC, 1964–70), such programs have value. They are vital not only to their audience of regional viewers but also to British television history and its cultural politics of place. Regional media archives collect, preserve, and organize this important but overlooked television material; they care for it, curate it, and make it accessible, giving it new life and new meanings through their community-driven archival practices.[4]

TELEVISION ARCHIVING IN THE UNITED KINGDOM

Television archiving in the UK has been shaped by the British Film Institute—an organization founded in 1933 to improve cinematic quality.[5] As part of its remit, the BFI established a film archive dedicated to preserving significant exemplars of the medium. In the late 1950s the institute expanded its archival efforts to include television, appointing a television officer in 1959 and a selection committee in 1962. Across both media, the institute's archival policies relied on efforts to determine the *value* of cinematic and television material. It concentrated on collecting only those moving image texts that would have "permanent national value"—notable for their artistic achievements, documentary relevance, educational quality, nationwide impact, and historical resonance.[6] These determinations of "value" were decided by committee, with members having to provide a clear rationale for their selections.

Yet archiving television produces its own distinct challenges. As a medium, television was often defined by ephemerality. In its early days, when programs were largely transmitted live, very few broadcast records were preserved.[7] In the 1960s, when videotape recording grew commonplace in the everyday production practices of the medium, it still did not guarantee that recordings would be kept. Stations would regularly record over their television tapes, video being seen less as a preservation medium than a flexible tool ideal not just for recording but for *rerecording*. Moreover, British copyright law made replaying television beyond its initial broadcast messy and expensive, involving negotiations with multiple rights holders.[8] These two factors led to a significant loss of historical television material, a condition that has shaped the BFI's current archival efforts (which involve the active recording of contemporary programs to create an ongoing television archive) and television history scholarship.[9]

This is not to say that *no* television was kept. Old programs, footage, and television segments were valuable resources for television producers. They could be plundered, retransmitted, or incorporated into new TV segments—as long as they fell within the boundaries of British copyright law. Since its inception, the BBC preserved archival records of both their programs and written documentation. Even as the BFI began to build their own television collection, the BBC elected to keep their archive themselves and did not formalize an archival relationship with the institute until much later, before which their collection remained relatively inaccessible.[10] Conversely, the commercial companies that made up ITV have a much longer relationship with the BFI. These companies had neither the permanence of the BBC nor the resources to archive material beyond what would be useful for their own production and financial interests. Thus the BFI and other archives, including regional media archives, served to assuage the danger of archival loss, preserving selections of ITV catalogs.[11]

In 1990 the Broadcasting Act formalized the maintenance and financial provision of a national television archive. The BFI codified its television "acquisition policy," which remained committed to creating "a collection containing all material of unique importance in areas such as drama, documentary, arts and news." More recently, the institute refined its policy, with a broader understanding of television's contribution to British cultural heritage: "The criterion for inclusion in the collection would be whether a program, or a section of broadcast time, stood as a significant exemplar of the art and practice of program making and television broadcasting, its history and its impact on and relationship to the people in the UK."[12] Therefore, despite changes in archival policy, the BFI remains committed to the collection and preservation of moving image material of permanent *national* and artistic value. Such criteria led to certain standards that determine what television enters the national archive, and what might find a home in other archival institutions who possess alternative definitions of value.

Since the 1970s British media collections have been kept by regional moving image archives. There are currently twelve regional media archives in the country: three national archives representing Scotland, Wales, and Northern Ireland, respectively, and nine English regional archives, covering London, East Anglia, the North East, the North West, the South East, the South West, Wessex, Yorkshire, and the Midlands. These archives cultivate film and television collections, acquiring, preserving, and rendering accessible media artifacts relevant to their geographic remits. The moving image materials they collect are kept for their *local* value. These archives collect media texts (films, television programs, and videos) that capture histories, cultures, geographies, and localities of the people and places in the region. In consequence, their collections contain moving image materials that would have been deemed too niche or locally specific to be of interest to a national archive. They provide a home for often overlooked films and television programs, providing alternative, regional records of British media history.

In addition, regional media archives are driven by a commitment to access.[13] Their aim is not only to collect and preserve moving image material but to make this material available to the public. Each archive does this in different ways, working to increase accessibility through digitization projects, opening their facilities to the public for onsite viewing, making the contents of their collection easily accessible through their website, holding public screenings, and releasing DVDs.[14] Thus, even as the BFI is a central force of film and television archiving in the UK, regional media archives provide their own distinct approaches to British film and television heritage, offering unique criteria of archival value rooted in the specificities of regional geography and the politics of public accessibility.

TELEVISION IN THE REGIONAL ARCHIVE

The place of television in regional media archives is shaped by the broader geographic contours of television in the UK. When television was first introduced to the British public in 1936, production was centered in London. The BBC's studios were based in the capital, as were the vast majority of its audience. In 1954 the launch of ITV helped establish regional television franchises, ushering in a wave of regional programming that would characterize British television in subsequent decades.[15] Regional television companies partnered with local theater groups to produce teleplays featuring stories, locations, and accents authentic to the region. Many of the programs produced by these partnerships became some of the most renowned television programming of the era, seen as ushering in a golden age of British television drama.[16] Though regional in their production, many of these programs were broadcast nationally, contributing to their cultural status and critical acclaim.

However, regional franchises also produced far more everyday kinds of television, shows often designed exclusively for a regional audience. They developed their own local news programs as alternatives or supplements to national broadcasts. And they created factual television programs, producing series that offered a regional spin on politics, culture, business, and domestic life. These programs told viewers about everyday events happening in their own communities. They featured familiar places and local accents, and tied national policies to regional concerns. Regional television thus represented a kind of "television from below," showcasing British culture, politics, and social life from within local communities.

It is these everyday, regionally specific forms of television that make up the majority of regional media archival collections. This material is typically given to regional archives by ITV or the BBC when it no longer seems financially beneficial to keep. The seemingly limited geographical relevance and lack of commercial viability of these programs means that their value lies in the representation of local places, communities, and histories. These qualities are further pronounced by the format of these texts in regional media archives. Much of their television holdings, especially their news collections, are not whole episodes but segments (and sometimes B-roll footage) designed to be incorporated into a live broadcast.[17] Most nightly local news broadcasts were transmitted live and often generated no physical copy. What was kept and eventually acquired by regional media archives were program segments recorded on film or videotape, which would be incorporated into a live broadcast.[18] These items thus entered the archive as stand-alone media texts that could be organized by date, topic, and location. By storing the segments that made up a news broadcast rather than keeping a record of the broadcast itself, television companies created the conditions that would shape the prominence of local value in the television archive. Cataloged as unique entries, representations of specific places and individual stories can now be experienced, collected, and viewed on their own, not as part of a television episode featuring content from across the region.

When television is removed from its original broadcast context, taken out of the TV flow, and deposited and reorganized within the regional media archive, locality and identity emerge as central organizing principals. Place, and the experiences and histories of different communities within these places, become a way into local history and television history. The remit of regional media archives is explicitly about place—about cultivating a collection of moving image materials that capture the nuances of the spaces, lives, communities, and landscapes that make up their region. Locality and identity (and the connections between locality and identity) thus emerge as central vectors of value; they steer the logics, curatorial practices, and user interactions of the archive. As Frank Gray, director of Screen Archive South East, contends: "Archivists have been developing collections that reflect the diversity and variety of film history, and it is because of their representations of and multiple connections to communities and everyday lives that these archives and their collections have built such strong and powerful bonds with individuals and communities and their memories."[19] The texts selected for regional archives not only tell us something about the places where they were made and the audiences they were trying to reach; they also hold a powerful and intimate meaning for the people and communities to which they are tied. Their value is rooted in this local specificity—their ability to represent the diverse, complex, and sometime incongruous spaces that make up these regions.

THE MEDIA ARCHIVE FOR CENTRAL ENGLAND

To fully unpack the complexities of local value in the regional media archive, I now turn to the central case study in this chapter: the Media Archive for Central England. MACE is a relatively new archival institution. A registered charity operating since 2000 and housed at the University of Lincoln at the time of writing, the archive's mission is to collect, preserve, and provide access to moving image materials from the Midlands. The MACE collection contains over 65,000 individual items, descriptions of which can all be accessed through the archive's website. While the archive includes amateur film, home movies, industrial film, and documentaries, the bulk of MACE's collection is television material. It holds a wide array of television texts produced by the longest-running ITV franchise holders in the Midlands, Associated Television (ATV) and Central Television—the company that emerged out of ATV's restructuring in the early 1980s.

Local news in particular is prominently represented in MACE's collection. The archive includes 59,670 items listed as "television news" from a variety of programs produced in the region. There are segments from *Midlands News* (ATV, 1956–69), *ATV Today* (ATV, 1964–81), *Central News* (Central Television, 1982–94), and *Central News East* (Central Television, 1984–94).[20] The dominance of television news in the archive stems from a few reasons. First, compared to other forms of media collected in regional archives, there is just more television news to begin with. Unlike home movies or industrial films, news is not a one-off event but a consistent and recurring media broadcast. It is transmitted weekly if not daily, and unlike many other television series and serials, it does not have a clear end date. Consequently, television news generates a vast body of media objects to be collected and preserved. In addition, MACE's television news collection consists largely of individual segments and filmed features, rather than records of entire broadcast episodes. As such, for every day of news represented in the archive, MACE holds several individual items—those one- to ten-minute on-location stories that together make up a full episode of television.

Alongside news, factual television dominates the archive. MACE holds dozens of magazine and documentary programs, covering a wide range of topics, from business (*Venture*, Central Television, 1982–89) to politics (*Left Right and Centre*, ATV, 1978–82) to homemaking (*Woman Today*, ATV, 1970–73) to diasporic culture and experiences (*Here and Now*, Central Television, 1980–90). MACE collects both full episodes of these programs and filmed segments designed to be inserted into a broadcast. Both episodes and segments are tagged and cataloged; where possible they are digitized and put on the website, although full episodes are often clipped due to copyright limits.[21] As part of the archive, these episodes and inserts stand outside of broadcast flow, searchable by program, topic, year, and location. They are thus severed to a certain extent from their original exhibition contexts and framed instead as significant representatives of cultural practices, personal experiences, places, and historical periods.

The ITV regional programming of MACE's collection presents news, politics, culture, and industry from an explicitly local perspective. They focus on events that occur throughout the East and West Midlands, profiling community members and showcasing spaces throughout the cities, towns, and countryside that make up these regions. Even when reporting on events affecting the entire country, the regional focus of this programing is felt in the ways in which the subject matter is approached. For instance, a fourteen-minute segment from *Here and Now*, one of Central Television's only programs produced by and aimed at people of color in the UK, focused on discrimination in education and employment faced by Black youth.[22] While the segment discusses racism and educational inequalities experienced by Black and Asian people across the UK, the story's focus is on the Midlands. Reporter Vera Gilbert interviews school administrators, parents, students, teachers, and city officials in Nottingham and Coventry. She asks their perspectives on why Black youth in particular are being steered toward lower qualifications and facing fewer opportunities on the job market, as well as how they believe they can rectify these inequities.

The diversity of the places and stories encompassed by the regional television programming held at MACE reflects the sometimes incongruous and uneven nature of regional television in the Midlands. While the region was divided between West and East, the same companies held the franchise for both regions, which received many of the same television programs—regional boundaries determined less by some distinct unifying culture than by transmitter technology and the efficiency of regional production centers. The Midlands included Birmingham, the second-largest city in the UK; the former industrial towns of the Potteries and the Black Country; textile centers like Leicester and Nottingham; and many small rural communities. These distinct localities have their own identities, cultures, accents, industries, immigration patterns, politics, and social concerns.[23] Regional television programs have not always accounted for the full richness and diversity of their regions, often concentrating production within larger cities. These issues were exacerbated in the era immediately after the establishment of ITV by the fact that television companies held franchises for multiple regions at once, and thus their attention was often divided, with Midlands and Northern regions receiving less attention from franchise holders than those in the South.[24]

A regional media archive like MACE can not only expose the biases within regional television representation but also emphasize the local, by isolating specific television segments from particular programs and making them searchable by geographic location. The attention to locality has been discussed at length by Julie E. Robinson in her analysis of regional television representations of the Black Country. Robinson examines a range of television documentaries, series, and reports made about the community from the 1960s to the 1980s, all of which present a very distinct vision of its culture, people, and approach to life. The Black Country has a long history both as a center of British industry marked by mining and metalworks and as an area with distinct traditions, cultural forms, and modes of performance. Robinson explores interest in the Black Country by television producers. While this interest stemmed at least in part from the area's unique dialect, history, and cultural practices, and thus its exoticness, which presumably made stories about it of interest to audiences both inside and outside the Black Country, the way the area was depicted also emerged out of the connection between television producers and community members already involved in preserving and promoting local history. Many of these television spots aired when industries that had long been the financial heart of the area were declining, as were many of the cultural practices and forms of performance present in these communities. These programs, often working directly with local historians and performers, comment on the history of the region and embrace folk cultural practices, using Black Country dialect and integrating poetry, folk songs, and comedy as a form of commentary.[25] They produced an audiovisual representation of the community aligned with broader local cultural movements at the time, reinforcing, preserving, and celebrating local identity—a local identity now accessible through MACE's archives.

While MACE can provide access to a television history of place often absent from or obscured within national and commercial archives, regional television should not be examined uncritically. The preservation of these television texts also allows scholars to uncover more troubling aspects of their coverage. Using MACE's collection, Rachel Yemm's study "Immigration, Race, and Local Media in the Midlands: 1960–1985" examines how regional television operated predominantly from a white perspective, projecting a white gaze into local news and magazine programs. Yemm argues that despite the waves of immigration from former British colonies experienced in the UK following the Second World War, which established many Black and Brown communities throughout the Midlands, television programs within the region typically directed their coverage toward an imagined white, working-class audience. The fact that many of these immigrant communities living throughout the Midlands were also working class did not matter. Their concerns and experiences were still largely ignored by regional television programs.[26]

Yemm argues that immigrant communities were underrepresented in local television news. Black and Brown journalists were largely absent both behind and in front of the camera.[27] When stories were reported on immigrant communities, they often adopted a white perspective, if not an explicitly racist one. In fact, ATV's failure to express perspectives and experiences of Black and Brown residents was an issue in their attempt to renew their franchise bid.[28] As part of their efforts to secure a Midlands contract in 1980, the restructured Central Television promised to improve coverage of immigrant communities, including launching *Here and Now*. Yemm concludes her study by looking at *Here and Now*, which she argues represents an important alternative to Midlands regional television's centering of whiteness. By having a program that not only focused on the stories and experiences of Britain's immigrant communities but hired journalists of color to tell these stories, Yemm demonstrates how the program represented an important counterpoint to most television in the region. *Here and Now* offered far more nuanced and critical accounts of current events, including the Handsworth uprisings, which many mainstream programs condemned as riots.[29] The collection and preservation of regional television in archives like MACE thus not only allows for scholars to study the ways in which specific locations are represented on screen but also enables broader studies about the connection between region and the politics of representation.

Like other regional media archives, MACE is access driven. This aim is clearly articulated on its website, which explicitly lays out the archive's mission and charitable status: "To make film, video and digital materials of the region as accessible as possible... so we can better understand, appreciate, and enjoy the history and culture of the midlands."[30] This centrality of public access is not merely expressed by the archive's stated aims but is the central organization principle of the archive as a whole. Their daily operations center on what Dr. Clare Watson (director of MACE) describes as "access-led preservation."[31] Whenever they acquire new material, they preserve it, catalog it, and make it accessible to the public as quickly as possible. Public demand is a key aspect driving such efforts—if someone is interested in certain materials, they are often prioritized for cataloging and digitization. As an archive they work with researchers, artists, and members of the public. They have assisted with a variety of community screenings, licensed materials for creative productions, and opened up their doors to anyone wishing to view their holdings.[32] Significantly, MACE's catalog is not secret but entirely open and available on their website, which was designed to facilitate user interaction.[33] The archive's home page consists almost entirely of a search bar that takes up the entire width of the screen.[34] This website design invites users to type in anything—their hometown, a particular event, the name of a program—and see the resulting relevant titles from the archive's collection. Accessing archival materials does not involve picking through finding aids or advanced knowledge of MACE's collections. Instead, anyone can see the available archival holdings, catalog entries, and relevant metadata, organized and arranged according to search protocols rather than the archive's own internal organizing structure.[35]

The centrality of access to MACE is further underscored by what you see after you enter a term in the search bar. MACE emphasizes the capacity for digitization and online viewing, with a selection of titles available to watch immediately. Items that do not have digital video available are still organized in a way that emphasizes their potential future as digital objects. They appear on screen as small thumbnails, the same size and shape as items that can be watched online. When you click on them, you are taken to a page with more detail about the object, an explanation that the "video clip is not available online *yet*" (emphasis added) and a link to make an inquiry to facilitate accessing the desired archival material. The choice of the word "yet" and the emphasis on making an inquiry invite the user to both imagine a future of expanded virtual engagement with the archive and position in-person viewing as a potential faster alternative until this day arrives.

In addition to access, the organization of MACE's collection available through its website emphasizes transmedia connections. The general search function does not automatically group results according to format or genre. Amateur films, sponsored films, television news, and magazine programs all appear side by side, creating a continuity between different types of media texts. For instance, a basic search for the city of Lincoln included local news footage, industrial films, documentaries, and home movies. These results were organized by relevance, although this can be changed to sort results by date, title, or availability of digital video. While this way of organizing database searching is very common, in the context of the media archive it also functions to forge connections and deemphasize the separation of individual collections.

MACE's access and transmedial approach is further underscored in the Themes section of their website.[36] This section is actively curated, largely by MACE's senior curator Phil Leach, and framed as a means of giving users a structured inroad to the archive. It is described as a "screening room" and consists entirely of digitized media texts that can be viewed immediately. There are ten themes currently listed on the website, ranging in topic from "Happy Christmas!" to "The Right to Protest." Underscoring the archive's commitment to access and public service, the website also offers users the opportunity to suggest topics themselves that MACE could "explore as we continue to bring this ever-expanding archive to life." Television material is prominent in the vast majority of these themes (only excluded from two compilations, one dedicated to home movies and amateur films, and the other focused on British life during World War II). In fact, some themes, including "The Right to Protest," are made up entirely of television programming. The television content available in these themed selections is made up not of entire episodes but broadcast segments. Split off from their original exhibition contexts, these texts are repurposed and reintegrated, becoming a part of a thematic archival digital exhibition, meant to be seen in conjunction with other television segments or film texts. Theme thus bridges this material together, forging new organizing principles for television content, displacing the dominance of time so central to broadcast television exhibition. Even as television materials make up the majority of MACE's collection, their position in the archive and their place within thematic curation transform these texts, inspiring transmedial connections and intimate engagements. They turn from segments of a factual television broadcast into distinct media texts that can be read as evidence of history and important parts of British heritage in their own right.

The final way MACE organizes and renders accessible their media archival objects is through the sale of DVDs. The MACE DVDs, like the curated themes, are organized around a variety of different topics, often combining media formats and genres: television programs are regularly positioned alongside industrial films, home movies, and documentaries.[37] The DVDs are organized into three subcategories: thematic compilations, TV nostalgia, and Midlands. The thematic compilations resemble those available for online viewing and cover a range of topics. A few of them focus on specific industries tied to distinct places, for example, the Birmingham motorcycle industry and the East Midlands textile industry, while others explore different forms of transportation and leisure activities.[38] TV nostalgia includes some of the most media-specific curation of the entire archive. The two titles in this section are both documentaries about ATV that consist of moving image texts from the MACE archives, interviews, and other newly produced segments.[39]

Finally, there are those DVDs grouped under the Midlands category. Here we see local value operating at its most pronounced. The compilations in these categories each concentrate on a specific place, emphasizing the diverse histories, cultures, communities, and industries that make up the rather nebulous region of the Midlands. Topics include *Rebuilding Coventry, Derbyshire on Film: The Peak District, Shropshire Lives,* and *Made in Leicester*.[40] By compiling moving image material belonging to a single location, these DVDs promise viewers an intimate exploration of place. They are, according to the archive's description, "perfect for those wanting to see places that they knew in the past," aimed at an imagined local audience whose nostalgic longings can be met in the afterlives of regional film and television.[41] Thus, while theme remains one of the central curation principles of MACE's collection, place is never far from its heart. Not only is its remit bound by geography, but much of its organization, collection, and curation works to further emphasize the specific histories and intimate views of the many local places and communities within its regional boundaries.

In a film and television archival field defined by the BFI, the regional media archives of the UK are not always given adequate attention. Yet these small, access-oriented archives, with their geographically specific remits, slimmer operating budgets, and collection of everyday, perhaps even mundane media texts, offer vital resources for television scholars and media historians. Their holdings include revealing collections of regional television and local news. They offer an important glimpse into the kinds of television that British viewers watched every day to tell them about the places they live and the communities of which they are a part. As such, I argue that the regional media archive elevates a kind of television not always considered prestigious or worthy of preservation in national archives and commercial institutions. By collecting and rendering accessible local news and regional factual programming, these archives articulate an alternative conception of television value, one not determined by national importance or profitability but rooted in locality and community. When regional television texts are experienced as part of regional media archives, they emerge as representations of specific places, microhistories, and local communities.

Focusing on the Media Archive for Central England illuminates how one specific regional media archive functions to reinforce this localism through their collection, organization, and access initiatives. MACE's collection deconstructs the sometimes incongruous nature of the broadcast region, allowing for stories documenting specific spaces and exploring particular topics to be seen and experienced as stand-alone texts. The website's search protocols, thematic curations, and DVD sales further reconfigure regional television programming, turning it into a thoroughly local experience, one that encourages transmedial connections, cultural memory, and political commentary. These archives transform television texts in important and revealing ways. While the lack of many full television episodes in these archival collections can represent a loss of the television record, the segments preserved, cataloged, and curated by MACE can also work to emphasize granular textures of place, community, and identity found within regional television. They can forge novel connections and increasingly local television experiences. Thus, while economic and national value are key ways in which television archives have made their collection decisions, regional media archives position local value as an important alternative matrix of television appraisal. In collecting, curating, and organizing regional television according to this value, the regional media archive can encourage new approaches to British cultural heritage and television history.

NOTES

1. Robin Nelson and Lez Cooke, "Television Archives: Accessing TV History," *Critical Studies in Television* 5, no. 2 (September 1, 2010): xvii–xix, https://doi.org/10.7227/CST.5.2.2.

2. Jacquie Kavanagh and Adam Lee, "Accessing TV History: Accessing BBC Archives," *Critical Studies in Television* 5, no. 2 (September 1, 2010): 68–72, https://doi.org/10.7227/CST.5.2.8; Lisa Kerrigan, "Stories That Never End: Television Fiction in the BFI National Archive," *Critical Studies in Television* 5, no. 2 (September 1, 2010): 73–76, https://doi.org/10.7227/CST.5.2.9; Steve Bryant, "National Television Archives and Their Role," *Critical Studies in Tele-*

vision 5, no. 2 (September 1, 2010): 60–67, https://doi.org/10.7227/CST.5.2.7; Heather Sutherland, "'It Ought to Be a Dream': Archives and Establishing the History of BBC Light Entertainment Production, 1975–87," *Critical Studies in Television* 5, no. 2 (September 1, 2010): 154–70, https://doi.org/10.7227/CST.5.2.18.

3. Recent studies of local and regional media are part of what Iueun Franklin calls a "spatial turn" in media studies, which works to attend to the geographic contours of media practices, aesthetics, and politics—and to unpack media outside of the terrain of the national. Examples of such work include Hugh Chignell, Ieuan Franklin, and Kristin Skoog's edited collection *Regional Aesthetics: Mapping UK Media Cultures* (London: Palgrave Macmillan, 2015), Christopher Ali's *Media Localism: The Policies of Place* (Urbana: University of Illinois Press, 2017), and Annie Laurie Sullivan's article "WGPR-TV Detroit: Building Black Media Infrastructure in the Postrebellion City," *Velvet Light Trap* 83 (March 22, 2019): 32, https://doi.org/10.7560/VLT8304.

4. Thank you to Clare Watson, Phil Leach, and the rest of the team at MACE who were invaluable to this chapter.

5. The history of the BFI, their archive, and the nuances of their remit are explored in depth by Penelope Houston in *Keepers of the Frame: The Film Archives* (London: British Film Institute, 1994).

6. Houston, *Keepers of the Frame*, 142, 26.

7. Steve Bryant, *The Television Heritage*, The Broadcasting Debate 4 (London: British Film Institute, 1989), 9–11.

8. Kavanagh and Lee, "Accessing TV History," 70, 69.

9. Bryant, "National Television Archives and Their Role," 60–67; Bryant, *Television Heritage*; Jason Jacobs, *The Intimate Screen: Early British Television Drama*, Oxford Television Studies (Oxford: Oxford University Press, 2000).

10. Today the BBC archives are divided by type of material. Television programs are available through the BFI, radio broadcasts are stored in the British Library Sound Archive, and the BBC has a collection of written materials in a separate archive in Caversham. The issue of access and Public Service Broadcast (PSB) archives has become increasingly important today, as digitalization efforts offer the potential to truly turn media archives into public resources. Karl Knapskog explores how PSB archives, who, as broadcasters funded by the public through license fees, are negotiating the desire to make their collections accessible (not merely to watch but also to use in creative practice), the demand for increasing profitability, and the copyright law. He outlines the different issues at stake as archives confront the possibilities afforded by digital media and explores several European case studies, offering different approaches to and engagements with digital accessibility. Knapskog, "Archives in Public Service," *Critical Studies in Television* 5, no. 2 (September 1, 2010): 20–33.

11. This relationship was established in 1968 when Associated-Rediffusion Television lost its London franchise and was subsequently dissolved, putting their television catalog in jeopardy. In response, the BFI stepped in, picking up a large portion of

their archive. Bryant, "National Television Archives and Their Role," 61; Houston, *Keepers of the Frame*, 147.
12. Bryant, "National Television Archives and Their Role," 62–63, 65.
13. This commitment further distinguishes these institutions from the BFI, whose access initiatives are secondary to their preservation practices. Houston, *Keepers of the Frame*, 108–10.
14. These initiatives are discussed by regional media archive staff in articles published in the *Journal of Film Preservation*: Maryann Gomes, "Value and Role of Regional Film Archives in Great Britain," *Journal of Film Preservation* 50 (1995): 61; Frank Gray, "Regional Archives—Negotiating the Actual and the Virtual in Changing Times," *Journal of Film Preservation* 95 (2016): 65–70.
15. While by the 1950s the BBC also had regional offices, the centrality of regionality to ITV encouraged a broader shift toward local production in the industry writ large. Lez Cooke, *A Sense of Place: Regional British Television Drama, 1956–82* (Manchester: Manchester University Press, 2012), 24.
16. It is these dramas that Cooke analyzes at length in his book.
17. This is not only true for MACE's television collection (which I analyze in the following section) but is also evident in collections of other regional media archives, including the East Anglian Film Archive, the Yorkshire Film Archive, and the Screen Archive South East.
18. Thank you to Phil Leach, MACE's senior curator, for breaking down this process for me.
19. Gray, "Regional Archives," 66–67.
20. The timelines of these different news broadcasts reflect structural changes in regional television. ATV, which held the ITV franchise in the East and West Midlands, had repeatedly been criticized for failing to provide sufficiently rich regional coverage. As part of their new bid to maintain broadcast rights to the Midlands, the company was restructured. Changing their name to Central Television, they opened an additional production studio in Nottingham and replaced *ATV Today* with *Central News* (based in Birmingham) and *Central News East* (based in Nottingham). In 1994 Carlton, another ITV company, purchased Central Television, then a decade later merged with Grenada to form ITV. *ITV Central News* still broadcasts television in the Midlands today. For more on ATV's restructuring, see Julie E. Robinson, "Gi' It Some 'Ommer: ITV Regional Programming and the Performance of the Black Country," in Chignell et al., *Regional Aesthetics*, 143–45.
21. The MACE website makes clear whether an item is a clip of a full episode (of which only a portion is accessible online) or a filmed insert. Sometimes if only an insert is available, it is because the original episode does not exist in its complete form.
22. *Here and Now*, "Education," June 6, 1982, https://www.macearchive.org/films/here-and-now-06061982-education.
23. Rachel Yemm, "Immigration, Race, and Local Media in the Midlands: 1960–1985" (PhD diss., Lincoln, University of Lincoln, 2018), 28–29.
24. Robinson, "Gi' It Some 'Ommer," 144–45.

25. Robinson, 142, 148–52.
26. Yemm, "Immigration, Race, and Local Media," 17–18.
27. This is not to say that ATV had no Black journalists. In 1969 ATV hired Barbara Blake, who had been working as one of the only Black television reporters since the early 1960s. However, Yemm notes that the work environment at ATV was particularly hostile to Blake, something even evident onscreen. In one notable example, Blake was asked to swim in a pool as part of a story that profiled a lecturer involved in race science research into swimming, who argued that Black people were naturally poor swimmers. In her report, Blake not only had to confront this lecturer's racism, but her swimming was even framed as evidence supporting the racist research. *ATV Today*, "Swimming Research," May 12, 1970, https://www.macearchive.org/films/atv-today-12051970-swimming-research.
28. Yemm, "Immigration, Race, and Local Media," 55.
29. Yemm, 249–94.
30. "About MACE," MACE Archive, September 5, 2016, https://www.macearchive.org/about-mace. It is worth noting that access is key to MACE's definition as a charity, driving its work and institutional identity.
31. Clare Watson, video conversation with author, November 11, 2022.
32. Examples of MACE's involvement with a variety of different community, research, and educational initiatives are described by Kat Pearson in her blog post on the International Association for Media and History's website, "A Day at the Archives . . . Media Archive for Central England (MACE)," *IAMHIST Blog*, April 7, 2021, http://iamhist.net/2021/04/media-archive-central-england-mace/.
33. In our conversation, Clare Watson confirmed that this web design was intentional and came out of extensive research into user journeys.
34. "Homepage," MACE Archive, July 28, 2016, https://www.macearchive.org/homepage.
35. While the BFI archive also has a public search function through its website, the size and scope of its collection make navigation more complicated. For instance, users have to select what types of materials they want to be included in their results (e.g., films and television works, scripts, press cuttings), and their results can also include items not held by the archive directly. "Collections Search," British Film Institute, accessed July 31, 2022, http://collections-search.bfi.org.uk/web/search/simple.
36. "Themes," MACE Archive, September 5, 2016, https://www.macearchive.org/mace-themes.
37. "MACE DVDs," MACE Archive, October 12, 2016, https://www.macearchive.org/resources/mace-dvds.
38. On industry: *Bits Stuck Anywhere: The Decline of BSA and the Birmingham Motorcycle Industry*, 2016, https://www.macearchive.org/bits-stuck-anywhere-decline-bsa-and-birmingham-motorcycle-industry; *Clothing the Nation: The East Midlands Textile Industry*, 2016, https://www.macearchive.org/clothing-nation-east-midlands-textile-industry. On sport and leisure: *Life on the Cut*, 2016, https://www.macearchive.org/life-cut; *The Sporting Midlands*, 2016, https://www.macearchive.org/sporting-midlands.

39. *From ATVLand in Colour*, 2016, https://www.macearchive.org/atvland-colour; *From Headlines to Tight-Lines: The Story of ATV Today*, 2016, https://www.macearchive.org/headlines-tight-lines-story-atv-today.

40. *Rebuilding Coventry*, 2016, https://www.macearchive.org/rebuilding-coventry; *Derbyshire on Film: The Peak District*, 2016, https://www.macearchive.org/derbyshire-film-peak-district; *Shropshire Lives*, 2016, https://www.macearchive.org/shropshire-lives; *Made in Leicester*, 2016, https://www.macearchive.org/made-leicester.

41. "MACE DVDs."

CHAPTER 6

WALTER PODRAZIK

WRITING TOMORROW'S HISTORY TODAY

LESSONS LEARNED FROM PIECES OF THE PAST FOR TOMORROW'S ARCHIVING AND EXHIBITORY

"This history should be preserved."[1] That declaration to the Chicago chapter of the National Academy of Television in 1982 by member Bruce DuMont led to the founding of Chicago's Museum of Broadcast Communications (MBC) five years later. It was dedicated to preserving "valuable recordings that were already in danger of being lost" and, further, "to celebrat[ing] the contributions of Chicago broadcasters to television history." By the twenty-first century the MBC was one of more than a dozen institutions in the United States dedicated to the mission of capturing a medium that has permeated all aspects of culture.[2] Nonetheless, broadcasting has consistently defied full capture within brick-and-mortar walls.

In both television and radio there are gaps in the stacks of created material. Broadcasting is a medium whose content too often literally vanishes into thin air. Not even the Library of Congress, while executing copyright registrations, has collected and stored recordings of every episode of every series, news program, or entertainment special. For some live broadcasts, there may never have been a "fixed form" copy to store.

The task of collecting programming has been further complicated by the business of ownership. U.S. television and radio products have been consistently created chiefly for profit. Support for educational and historical use has been either an incidental by-product or pursued with underwriting and an eye for more return. Online purveyors have disrupted the models further in two directions. Some have established paywall access to content. Others such as YouTube and Google effectively created expectations by the public that everything is online, what is online should be free, and ultimately a few short clips are all that is needed for understanding history. Behind the paywalls, such services as Netflix, Disney+, and Amazon Prime Video have successfully adapted the model of charging admission, like cable television and movie theaters. At the same time, the ubiquitous presence of YouTube has fed the public's perception that somehow "everything is out there." "Check YouTube" has become as common an assumption as "Google it."

Nonetheless, some recent public projects illustrate how to draw on institutional archival resources in order to transform broadcast history into accessible and informative narratives. In the end, these institutions also demonstrate how they are able to adapt so that the business-side issues are less in conflict with commercial interests and more a part of a mutually beneficial relationship.

This chapter looks at offerings from the Library of American Broadcasting Foundation (LABF) with its collection housed at the University of Maryland, the Museum of Broadcast Communications in Chicago (MBC), and a consortium in Chicago from the MBC, the Newberry Library, and the Chicago History Museum (CHM). These respective institutions have deftly used their assets while dealing with issues of rights, access, and display. They have demonstrated the power of hands-on presentations of broadcast history, from the beginning to today. They have further shown that inspired specialized research can flow from such presentations.

SERVING A PUBLIC'S INTEREST AND DEVELOPED EXPERTISE

Institutions curating broadcast/media history do so in the context of audiences that have been immersed in radio and television for more than a century. In that time, media consumption has evolved from the ephemeral live and in-person event to a myriad of entertainment, business, and political events captured electronically and intended for remote and asynchronous experience.

Virtually everyone in the general public wishing to tune in ended up possessing the necessary equipment to do so.[3] Such equipment effectively brought the equivalent to the content of movie theaters and sports stadiums into their homes. In that process, broadcasters and characters entered the country's collective personal space, creating a sense of intimacy and familiarity. Yet until the emergence and embracing of home video recording beginning in the late 1970s, this was a one-way relationship. Audiences still could not gain access to the specific media moments they cared about when they wished to. In general, they could only click the on/off switch between stations offering the ABC, CBS, and NBC networks, as well as a limited number of unaffiliated independents.

While some material during the 1950s–60s era was captured in cut-down/adapted form as educational "multimedia" film and audio offerings, the technical requirements for playback limited ease of access on the general consumer level to those investing in the playback equipment, chiefly community centers, schools, and libraries.[4] Larger institutions, mostly education related, launched initiatives to gather recorded media, but even they faced the practical issue of the sheer volume of created media, most privately owned. Recognizing the impossibility of capturing everything, institutions chose to focus on particulars.

For example, the Vanderbilt Television News Archive began in August 1968 with a mission of "recording, preserving, and providing access to television news broadcasts of the national networks."[5] Its website notes a core collection including evening news from ABC, CBS, and NBC (since 1968), and broadcasts from CNN (since 1995) and Fox News (since 2004). These finite collecting parameters were accompanied by rules spelling out procedures to accessing the recordings, primarily through associated sponsoring institutions such as colleges and universities.

In 1965–68 the Academy of Television Arts and Sciences "joined forces with the UCLA Theater Arts Department" to create a television library.[6] That project began significantly adding material in 1972 starting with the Jack Benny Television Collection and donations of specific programs from Capital Cities/ABC, and growth continued from there. The material was housed in California and primarily available for on-site appointment viewing, over time including extensive user guides on subjects ranging from understanding copyright rules to techniques for off-site access.[7]

In 1975 CBS industry pioneer William S. Paley founded the Paley Center (originally named the Museum of Broadcasting). This curated collection drew from a wide spectrum of sources (not just CBS) and covered television and radio to that point in the twentieth century. From the beginning the Paley Center was designed to be a general public walk-in resource, located in central Manhattan. There were consoles set up for individual or small group viewing. To clearly establish parameters, the Paley Center stated up front the realities affecting its collection.[8] They did not have everything ever broadcast and noted, "We do not own the rights to the individual programs that are here." Nonetheless, the collection was sufficiently wide ranging to satisfy typical visitors, for whom the alternative to that point had been chiefly random reruns on local broadcast stations. They also chose not to collect and display the physical objects, props, papers, and assorted ephemera.

Other institutions looking at broadcast history departed at the start from a primary focus on collecting video and audio and instead incorporated those elements as part of an approach that included narrative panels, personal papers, photos, and historical objects.

The Texas Broadcast Museum in Kilgore, Texas, touted an eclectic mix of local event space, broadcast equipment, and memorabilia including the Lee Harvey Oswald camera, described as "being present at Oswald's assassination."[9] In Bowie, Maryland, the National Capital Radio and Television Museum displayed (and offered for institutional loan) vintage equipment while also serving as a hub for active hobbyists.

The Library of American Broadcasting Foundation (LABF) collection at the University of Maryland, the Museum of Broadcast Communications in Chicago (MBC), and the Chicago History Museum (CHM) were among the institutions mixing collected recorded media along with physical papers and objects.[10]

All the institutions devoted to video had to recalibrate when home audiences at last had their opportunities to access video directly. This began in earnest following the 1984 Supreme Court ruling in the so-called Betamax case (*Sony Corp. of America v. Universal City Studios, Inc.*) affirming that over-the-air video recording was legal for personal use.[11] Consequently, members of the general public were assured that they could continue to build their own personal viewing libraries from material they recorded off the air, including television airings of major feature films.

When YouTube (beginning in 2005) and other streaming services entered as computer access sites, that accelerated the process of bringing portions of historical TV video libraries to any computer.[12] By 2006 there were already 65,000 uploads to YouTube per day, and in that same year, Google acquired the service for $1.65 billion. Some of the daily postings inevitably included unauthorized uploads of copyrighted content, raising legal objections by their owners, including a suit by Viacom in March 2007.[13] While attempting to stem that flow, some content owners coupled the objections with action on another front: formally entering the streaming market themselves, striking licensing deals, and developing their own individual competing sites. These took form as paid subscriptions such as Paramount+ (from CBS) and Peacock (from NBCUniversal) and ad-supported platforms such as Tubi (an existing service acquired by Fox).[14]

Every show was not out there, but there were plenty of touchstones reaching as far back as the 1940s and skipping through the decades. The existence of such alternative sources meant that the desire to embrace nostalgic memories of past eras could be broadly satisfied through streaming. Typically, services (such as Tubi) organized their offerings not only by title but also by other tags such as genre and season. These could be accessed in any order, quickly viewed, replayed, and freeze-framed. This was the structure of a video library, set up for casual browsing. Yet all of these businesses treated their offerings essentially as a warehouse of widgets, irrespective of the condition (sometimes less than pristine) and content of the video. Episodes of a screwball sitcom were interchangeable with episodes of a drama anthology because at heart they were all part of a continuous content flow meant to occupy a user's time.

These online services dramatically reframed how potential casual visitors might regard the institutions dedicated to formally collecting and archiving media history. Those institutions were no longer seen as the only place for video access. The institutions had to offer and embrace a more expansive public persona. For their own branding, this meant that the institutions had to effectively tout their mission of treating media and the media audience with knowledgeable respect, offering curated quality over sheer quantity.

This was an incentive to stress finely tuned event programming and to pursue other opportunities to define their collecting mission, with a special emphasis on capturing the impact of local broadcasting. For example, at the passing of *Soul Train* creator Don Cornelius in 2012, there was a packed memorial gathering at Chicago's Museum of Broadcast Communications celebrating his life. Connecting institution back to media, that night's event was also broadcast live on Chicago radio station WVON, where Cornelius worked before launching that music and dance show.[15] In a retrospective exhibit marking its thirty-fifth anniversary, the Museum of Broadcast Communications reflected on such local connections, noting, "The preservation and appreciation of the world of broadcasting touched everyday life, with an education mission that treated with respect material that was too often dismissed as frivolous, ephemeral, and unimportant." Appropriately, in conjunction with the presence of "media everywhere," that exhibition panel concluded with an observation that could apply to every collecting institution: "For members of the general public, the museum was doing more than preserving broadcast history. It was celebrating their own."[16] This instance is among the reasons why collecting institutions offer the added value of a curated experience, as explained in the subsequent sections about the Library of American Broadcasting at the University of Maryland, the Museum of Broadcast Communications, and a collaborative exhibit about *Kukla, Fran and Ollie*.

THE (VIRTUAL) TELEVISION ANNIVERSARY IN A CENTURY OF BROADCASTING

The 2020 centennial of broadcasting provided an appropriate hook for media institutions to embrace and articulate the historical role of radio and television, connecting the past and present on multiple levels to a signature event.

For the Library of American Broadcasting (LAB), embracing a century of the medium perfectly fit its description as "the nation's preeminent collection of historical broadcast materials in one location." After all, it had begun in 1972 "in a basement" at the National Association of Broadcasters building in downtown Washington, D.C., "by a dedicated band of radio and TV pioneers" to assure that "the record of the industry's accomplishments and service would not be lost to history."[17] That setting shifted when the LAB began an association with the University of Maryland in College Park in 1994.[18] Going into 2020, that association had been in place for a quarter century, with the LAB materials occupying some 25,000 square feet housed within the Hornbake Library building on campus. The massive, multiform collection truly covered a century's worth of broadcast history material that encompassed audio tapes, recorded discs, video, photos, magazines, manuscripts, and more, along with the space for curation activities and individual research.

To maintain this enterprise, the Library of American Broadcasting Foundation (LABF) successfully nurtured financial support from throughout the industry, converging each year in its annual Giants of Broadcasting and Electronic Arts awards luncheon in Manhattan.[19] That event included personal appearances by the award recipients (industry leaders and creative performers), along with introductory remarks, video background pieces, and spirited attendee table talk. In the face of COVID-19, however, the 2020 Giants event was canceled and not available for an anniversary acknowledgment of that 1920 presidential coverage moment. Similarly, COVID-19 restrictions limited any physical public exhibit, including at the College Park site. Nonetheless, members of the LABF board felt that it was important for the organization to publicly mark the birth of broadcasting, as part of the library's mission. LABF cochair Ginny Morris stated in a press release, "Broadcasting has a storied past that needs to be commemorated and celebrated."[20]

In response to COVID-19 restrictions, an LABF subcommittee planned a virtual alternative, arranging with the National Association of Broadcasters (NAB) to coproduce a one-hour prerecorded streaming event titled *100 Years of Broadcast News: Challenges Met, Challenges Anew*. The production first aired as part of the October 2020 NAB Show New York—normally an in-person event, itself moved online due to COVID-19. Thereafter the video was available at the LABF website.[21]

The first twelve-minute portion of the one-hour program provided the historical context that also allowed a smooth pivot to the role of television. A self-contained video piece from KDKA News in Pittsburgh featured anchor Larry Richert, who walked viewers through a recreation of the 1920 technical transmission studio shack site, describing in detail the broadcast of that first election night. In a conversational exchange between LABF cochairs Ginny Morris (CEO of Hubbard Radio) and Heidi Raphael (chief communications officer of Beasley Media), the two shared insights into the personal and corporate backgrounds that were part of that first radio venture. Former U.S. senator Gordon Smith (NAB president) provided further context, setting the story of that first transmitted news event as part of an ongoing commitment by broadcasters to serve their communities. The balance of the one-hour program was devoted to individual interviews with four respected broadcast journalists who represented wide-ranging professional backgrounds over the decades: Ted Koppel, Soledad O'Brien, Carol Marin, and Robert Siegel. Award-winning journalist and LABF board member Marci Burdick conducted the interviews, pressing each to analyze the past and look at the industry challenges going forward.[22]

At the time, staging such conversations virtually was not yet routine, so this production itself marked a moment of shared broadcast history for those involved. All of the elements were tied together through a virtual production process by the LABF (led by Chandra Clark at the University of Alabama) and the NAB (led by Tobi Hall in Washington, D.C.). Library site curator Michael Henry (at the University of Maryland) gathered images for montages to be incorporated into the finished product.

The *100 Years* production served as an invigorating reminder of an often underappreciated strength of a collecting institution dedicated to chronicling and preserving the media: connections throughout multiple circles of business, government, and academia. Within its own board membership, for example, the LABF included leaders in the business of production, sales, station ownership, and programming, as well as disciplines that applied academic research principles to historical narrative and documentary news projects.[23] Interest in a collecting institution was not an ancillary indulgence; such appreciation embodied respect for their chosen profession and their own individual careers. On a personal level, these collecting institutions captured the best of the industry's best and were a source of pride.

Such positive acknowledgments had long been a part of the successful fundraising in support of the library, especially through its Giants event. They all came together again in order to tell a story that was woven together in spite of an environment of restricted shared space and limited travel due to COVID-19. This was not simply COVID-19 accelerating a project previously planned. Instead, *100 Years* reflected an inspired and innovative view of the library's assets, demonstrating how they could be used to further raise the profile of the institution. By conducting its own interviews and set-up pieces, the LABF avoided having to rely on the copyrighted materials of others. Instead, it created and owned its own finished work, while touting the archival materials that made it possible.

Further new collaborations with the NAB followed. At the once-again-in-person NAB convention in Las Vegas in April 2022, the LABF presented a newly instituted award on stage to LeVar Burton.[24] The actor, director, and educator received the first-ever Insight Award from the LABF, attracting industry and popular press coverage. These opened opportunities for offering additional news coverage story hooks, pointing back to the collection. When the library reopened to in-person access at the University of Maryland in August 2021, there were new threads to chronicle. These included guides to Black history from the audio news collection and research into memorable commercial theme music.[25]

Such opportunities continued to grow. At the April 2023 NAB convention, the LABF presented its second Insight Award to *60 Minutes*. For the October 2023 NAB show in New York, the LABF presented its new Excellence in Broadcast Preservation award to industry veteran David Gleason for his two-decade project, the World Radio History Archive.[26] Building further in 2023, the LABF set up the "Radio and Podcasting Power Session" in partnership with the University of Maryland, Benztown, and the Broadcast Education Association (BEA) to guide college radio and podcasting producers on how to make use of the audio archives and other library resources.[27] There was a podcast in association with the NAB on "Preserving Broadcast History" in August 2023, followed on October 26 by a session on site at the NAB convention in New York.[28]

Continuing proactively, during 2023 the LAB increased its regular social media postings, drawing from its historical collection in Maryland of still photos and associated documents. Rather than being limited to just the "famous" anniversaries, these cumulatively and collectively offered a locally focused picture of broadcasting that recognized the importance of local milestones and leaders. For instance, using LinkedIn, the LABF noted in November 2023 that Harry Nigocia, host of the "Mid-day Serenade" program on WJBW in New Orleans, celebrated twenty years with the station in 1952.[29]

All of these public profiles and successful collaborations enhanced the overall LAB institution, the use of the Library of American Broadcasting collection at the University of Maryland, and its viability as a resource in education, research, and entertainment, while building a better understanding of media.

THE RADIO ANNIVERSARY IN A CENTURY OF BROADCASTING

For the Museum of Broadcast Communications in Chicago, fully embracing the *radio* aspect of the hundred-year anniversary of the KDKA broadcast was an ideal launching point for a new in-person exhibit on the history of radio, planned for the MBC's downtown location. From its beginning in 1982, the MBC saw both radio and television as part of its curatorial mission, drawing both financial and archival contributions such as early *Kukla, Fran and Ollie* TV episode films from Burr Tillstrom and some fifty thousand broadcasts from radio historian Chuck Schaden.[30] The MBC had become the home of the Radio Hall of Fame (RHOF) in 1991, which provided a built-in support setting for the *Century of Radio* exhibit. There were selected plaques of many of its 310 inductees already on display, with others in storage available to supplement the history woven into their stories. The initial plan was to time that new exhibit to move in after the departure in mid-2020 of a traveling exhibition from the Rock and Roll Hall of Fame (*Rock on TV*).

The first year of COVID-19 restrictions in 2020 put those plans on hold. As a stand-alone institution, the MBC was particularly affected by imposed requirements limiting admission, as well as the public's hesitancy to go out at all. As a result, moving forward on new exhibit design and installation was delayed through 2020 into 2021. Because such constraints were national, affecting any other site for setup, the MBC was allowed to extend the *Rock on TV* exhibit until September 2020, for those times it could open its doors as the pandemic requirements repeatedly shifted.

One of the key assets of the MBC was having its established exhibition space in downtown Chicago. Using the time created by the COVID-19 delays, provisional planning moved forward with scripting and design, in the process tapping academic and business experts and advisors, including those from its own board (Carol Summerfield, Jim Carlton, and David Plier) as well the University of Illinois at Chicago (Rebecca Lind) and the University of Michigan (Susan Douglas). MBC deputy director Aileen Bishop provided production supervision. The images came through Creative Commons and the museum's own archives.

The exhibit, *A Century of Radio*, opened in October 2021, nearly a year after the KDKA anniversary. That hook remained relevant, though, as the starting point for the hundred-year radio narrative. Appropriately, in that same month the Radio Hall of Fame held its in-person 2021 honoree induction event, which had been staged remotely in 2020. Taking advantage of some eight thousand square feet of exhibition space, the MBC created a self-guided walking tour through images, sounds, and artifacts. Existing MBC materials dovetailed with the new exhibit and included wall shelves holding thirty-four radios of the past, three of the actual puppets from the Edgar Bergen–Charlie McCarthy radio programs, and the display of RHOF plaques.

The overall design was low-key and welcoming, epitomized by a pair of comfortable chairs and a couch placed in the center of the main exhibit room. These were adjacent to a radio console cabinet with shelves holding ten-inch 78 rpm records, accompanied by piped-in sounds of vintage radio programs and music. Evocative of the pre-television age, this faux living room invited visitors to sit, relax, and listen, while also taking in the exhibit panels on the surrounding walls. The narrative panels were arranged chronologically and used large, easy-to-read text and similarly large photo images. A pair of video screens offered TV commercials about radio stations, news stories about radio (including BBC reports about 1960s UK pirate radio stations), and radio news reports set to video images (including the assassination of John Lennon and the *Challenger* explosion). Three sixty-five-inch-tall touch screens along the opening corridor replicated the familiar world of contemporary online searching. These panels each offered separate access to an MBC-curated time line from 1835 to the present so that with a simple swipe, visitors could choose a year, a subject essay, links to further information, and selected audio clips. Nesting such detailed information in a digital format allowed the printed panels to be clear and unencumbered. This digital content also recognized the expectations of audiences for internet access by allowing portions of the storytelling for *A Century of Radio* to be accessed online outside the MBC physical space. (In-person visitors also received a QR code to continue the experience at home with access to the time line.)[31]

Carrying through the hundred-year history of broadcasting as a radio story allowed the MBC to reinforce a key branding specialty. In conjunction with the Radio Hall of Fame, this emphasis carved out a clear identity of institutional expertise, a contemporary continuation of *A Century of Radio*. This was further embraced when, in 2023, the MBC found it necessary to refocus resources away from maintaining an exhibition setting year-round and closed the doors of its building. The museum carefully packed its institutional resources for storage and limited access. In November 2023 MBC CEO David Plier wrote: "For the next 18–20 months, we will focus on online exhibitory including 'The Great Debates' and '8 Decades of Television Commercials.' We plan on creating an exhibit on 'The Story of Late Night Television' in honor of Johnny Carson's Centennial in late 2025."[32]

ANOTHER ANNIVERSARY: A LEGACY OF PUPPETRY

Only a quarter century after the birth of commercial radio, in the 1940s, television was beginning its ascent within American popular culture, bonding with a new generation of audiences. In 2022 three Chicago cultural institutions jointly planned and executed an event to celebrate a pair of anniversaries from those early TV days. "Back with You Again: Celebrating 75 Years of Kukla, Fran, Ollie, and Chicago Children's TV" would mark the birth of creator Burr Tillstrom as well as the seventy-fifth anniversary of his most famous work, the programs featuring his puppet characters Kukla and Ollie and their human friend Fran Allison, which launched in Chicago. Spearheaded by Paul Durica (as director of exhibitions at the Chicago History Museum), "Back with You Again" brought together representatives from the Chicago History Museum, the Newberry Library, and the Museum of Broadcasting to celebrate the broadcast kickoff of *Kukla, Fran and Ollie*.[33] CHM and the MBC had the greatest concentration of assets for the project, with their respective collections of objects, documents, and media files. The Burr Tillstrom collection was housed at CHM, including the Kukla and Ollie puppets.

Children's television was a core focus at the Chicago Museum of Broadcasting, with signature artifacts from key Chicago-based programs prominently displayed as part of its permanent collection. MBC deputy director Aileen Bishop could point visitors to costumes, puppets, and sets from *Bozo's Circus*, *Garfield Goose*, and Bill Jackson's *Cartoon Town*.

As a centerpiece, the consortium decided to present an original TV program in the style of the original series as a streaming event featuring a contemporary cast, new puppets, and a new story—all pointing back with appreciation to the original *Kukla, Fran and Ollie*.

The "Back with You Again" project was done with the approval and cooperation of the Tillstrom estate. The actual artifacts were already in hand and housed at the CHM. "Back with You Again" also coincided with an already ongoing program by the estate to digitize and post online archival episodes of *Kukla, Fran and Ollie* for the public to view at no charge. Access to the original episodes removed many of the potential business barriers to the event. Nonetheless, there were still two details to finesse.

First, as part of the terms of the donation agreement between Tillstrom and CHM, none of the original puppets themselves could be animated by others.[34] Second, from a programming perspective, the release of original *Kukla, Fran and Ollie* episodes for free online viewing meant that merely screening these same episodes would in a way only confirm that "everything is already online" and potentially add little that was new to the scholarship and understanding of the era. Instead, Durica drew on a team (actors, director, technical support) for a clever hybrid: staging a nearly eighty-minute special as back-to-back-to-back "episodes" of a Kukla, Fran and Ollie–type program: *Rita, Fran and Dragon*. Each of the three segments specially called out one of the three consortium members. Rather than staging *Rita, Fran and Dragon* at any one of the institutions, the event was executed at a production facility outside downtown Chicago, at the Co-Prosperity Sphere southwest of downtown in the Bridgeport neighborhood. There, a limited invited audience attended in person while additional public viewing display gatherings were set up at the MBC and CHM (in combination with the Newberry). A selection from the available digitized episodes of *Kukla, Fran and Ollie* did make an appearance, serving as scene-setting warm-up trailers running before the new production.

Rita, Fran and Dragon aired via live streaming October 15, 2022, the Saturday nearest the seventy-fifth anniversary of the October 13, 1947, premiere of *Kukla, Fran and Ollie*; it was also recorded and archived for later access. The production embraced the gentle but spirited style of *Kukla, Fran and Ollie* as the marquee puppet characters of Rita and Dragon (voiced by Dana Kroop and Kevin Hogan) engaged in conversation with their human cohosts, starting with Fran (Laura Mackenzie), friend Brandon (Brandon Cloyd), and The Announcer (Chris Rathjen).

Deliberately transmitted in black and white, the episodes used the same basic staging techniques as the 1950s TV world by focusing the action on a puppet proscenium stage made from a simple scenery flat. The unifying story thread was the quest by Rita and Dragon to fill in their own genealogy and to understand the legacy of TV puppetry. To that end, the puppets were visited by a succession of cast members who each stepped up to the cut-out stage window. Some were part of a tight acting company that had carefully studied the craft of 1950s live television in order to improvise through original new skits such as reading fan mail and baking an anniversary cake. Equally important to the authenticity of the production, there were also guests who were not formally rehearsed but who also improvised as they delivered information to the puppets in their areas of expertise. These guests included Dassia Posner (Northwestern University), Justin Snyder (Opera in Focus), musician Lily Emerson, Walter Podrazik (Museum of Broadcast Communications), and producer Paul Durica (from the Chicago History Museum). They provided historical background on not only the original *Kukla, Fran and Ollie* TV series but also the general development of children's television and the centuries-old art of puppetry itself.[35]

There was joint promotion of the event by the institutions on their respective websites. Most prominent, there was an appreciative feature at the *Chicago Tribune* by Rick Kogan, a writer familiar with all the players and with respect for popular culture milestones, especially those with Chicago roots.[36]

The "Back with You Again" project once again illustrated how archival collections could serve as catalysts for new, original work that would showcase the importance of the respective institutions. Previously, producer Paul Durica had used similar techniques in telling the story of television pioneer Dave Garroway (original host of *The Today Show*), casting actors as historical figures.[37] For 2024, a similar approach was planned for the centennial anniversary of the Chicago-based *National Barn Dance* radio program.

TOMORROW'S SUCCESS TODAY

The COVID-19 pandemic has been described as "the great accelerant" for changes that were already looming.[38] These archival institutions demonstrated that the COVID-19 disruption did that, and more, as it allowed for taking different approaches to their missions in dealing with a significantly altered cultural landscape. In that light, all these projects illustrated how the contemporary commercial retail notion of "pop-up" stores could also be applied to institutional exhibitory projects.[39] A singular public event (whether a live performance, an award presentation, or a finished video premiere) would have its moment and then "live on" as a reference point, repeatedly garnering attention and pointing potential users to the resources of the institution.

Overall, for exhibitory considerations, the dead-stop departure from business as usual allowed for reassessing assets—especially recognizing the assets of peer respect and credibility. Responding to the challenges of the time, archiving institutions put together programs and events on tighter-than-ever budgets, measuring success in part by the resulting total engagement, confirming the power of hands-on curated presentations of broadcast history.

Part of the altered landscape also was to acknowledge that institutions could no longer assume a primary gateway status for historical media content. Consumer online access via streaming had opened wide those gates. Yet that could also be regarded as an opportunity to reach out to and engage a more media-savvy audience.

For archiving considerations, judicious choice looms as more important than ever. There is little need for an archival institution to position itself as just another nostalgic video store because there is one around every corner of the digital world. Curator Michael Henry pointedly noted that the archives in Maryland did not need to pursue items that were already well covered elsewhere, commercially in stores, on the air, and via streaming.[40]

Looking ahead, then, additions to each collecting institution should reflect its defined vision, building on strengths that can invite further research, engagement, scholarship, and funding. Through all this, institutions can enhance their visibility and viability by continuing to create their own original work such as documentaries, public events, and specialty subject guides. They can also be the knowledgeable education advisors in honing such areas as podcast production by offering not only the how but also the why. The institutions in this report have confirmed the power of hands-on curated presentations of broadcast history in making the assets of their institutions relevant to researchers, historians, producers, writers, and the general public.

In a culture awash with video detail, there are publics ripe for discovering more through imaginative offerings by such archival institutions. Nostalgia will always be an easy initial lure, but true curated engagement teaches more. It is like the difference between fast-food casual dining and lingering over a meal at a chef-owned restaurant where the offerings have themes and stories behind them. Those savored moments inevitably leave the strongest impression.

NOTES

1. Walter Podrazik, from "Before There Were Walls," the opening panel to the 2017 exhibition marking the thirty-fifth anniversary of the Museum of Broadcast Communications.
2. List of thirteen U.S. institutions dedicated to capturing portions of video history, included in the author's November 2018 report *Peer Institutions* for the Library of American Broadcasting Foundation, of which he is a member of the board: Library of American Broadcasting at University of Maryland; Library of Congress; Museum of Broadcast Communications in Chicago; Museum of the Moving Image; National Capital Radio and Television Museum; National Comedy Center; Paley Center for Media (New York, Los Angeles); Texas Museum of Broadcasting and Communications; Wisconsin Center for Film and Theater Research; Syracuse University (Bleier Center for Television and Popular Culture); UCLA Film and Television Archive; Vanderbilt Television News Archive.
3. Over just ten years of measurement of ownership of radio receivers, the percentage jumped from less than 1 percent in 1922 to 60 percent in 1932. Christopher H. Sterling and John Michael Kittross, *Stay Tuned: A History of American Broadcasting*, 3rd ed. (Mahwah, N.J.: Routledge, 2002), 862. For the first ten years of measurement for television, the percentages went from 9 percent in 1950 to 87 percent in 1960 (864).
4. Paul Ivester traces the educational film industry from the 1930s to the 1980s, including such content distributors as Coronet Films and Encyclopedia Britannica, in "Simplified History of Educational Film Producers," 2002, www.paulvester.com/schoolfilm/history.htm. In addition, there were such studio film shorts as the 1956 RCA educational documentary "The Story of Television" (https://www.youtube.com/watch?v=XUk3NX9YTu0) and Disney's 1959 "Donald in Mathmagic Land" (following its theatrical and TV releases; https://www.youtube.com/watch?v=8BqnN72OlqA).
5. Vanderbilt Television News Archive, https://tvnews.vanderbilt.edu, accessed January 31, 2023.
6. "Our History," UCLA and Television Archive, https://www.cinema.ucla.edu/our-history, accessed January 31, 2023.

7. A list of links to services at the UCLA site can be found at "Services and Resources," UCLA Library, https://www.library.ucla.edu/help/services-resources, accessed January 31, 2023.
8. "FAQs," Paley Center for Media, https://www.paleycenter.org/about/about-faq/, accessed January 31, 2023.
9. Descriptions of the Texas Broadcast Museum taken from the FAQs at the institution's website at https://texasbroadcastmuseum.com.
10. Library of American Broadcasting Foundation, http://www.tvradiolibrary.org; Museum of Broadcast Communications, http://museum.tv; Chicago History Museum, http://chicagohistory.org.
11. "Sony Corp. of Am. v. Universal City Studios, Inc., 464 U.S. 417 (1984)," https://www.copyright.gov/fair-use/summaries/sonycorp-universal-1984.pdf; "U.S. Copyright Office Fair Use Index," last updated November 2023, https://copyright.gov/fair-use/index.html.
12. "History of YouTube," Wikipedia, last updated July 26, 2024, https://en.wikipedia.org/wiki/History_of_YouTube.
13. Jeremy W. Peters, "Viacom Sues Google over YouTube Video Clips," *New York Times*, March 14, 2007, https://www.nytimes.com/2007/03/14/business/14viacom.web.html.
14. *Editors' note:* see the work of Derek Kompare for histories and analyses of investments in over-the-air channels and streaming services with substantial libraries of rerun, for example, "MeTV: Old-Time TV's Last Stand?" in *From Networks to Netflix: A Guide to Changing Channels*, ed. Derek Johnson (New York: Routledge, 2022).
15. Ivanna Hampton and Lauren Jiggetts, "Friends, Fans Honor Don Cornelius," NBC 5 Chicago, last updated February 8, 2012, https://www.nbcchicago.com/news/local/public-memorial-for-don-cornelius/1948738/.
16. Podrazik, "Before There Were Walls" panel.
17. Narrative details from the "About the Library" history of the LAB on p. 8 of the Giants 2022 program book for the Giants of Broadcasting and Electronic Arts event held November 15, 2022.
18. *Editors' note:* at the time, the LAB was known as the Broadcast Pioneers Library.
19. The Library of American Broadcasting Foundation's Annual Giants of Broadcasting and Electronic Arts, produced by the International Radio and Television Society Foundation (Giants 2022 program book, p. 3).
20. "NAB, LABF to Feature '100 Years of Broadcast News' Celebration at NAB Show New York," press release, October 16, 2020, https://www.nab.org/documents/newsroom/pressRelease.asp?id=5848.
21. Christina Clapp, "100 Years of Broadcast News: Challenges Met, Challenges Anew," NABAmplify, November 25, 2020, https://amplify.nabshow.com/articles/100-years-of-broadcast-news-challenges-met-challenges-anew/.
22. Among the associations cited in the October 16, 2020, for the interviewer and each of the interviewed journalists: Ted Koppel, *CBS Sunday Morning* and ABC's *Nightline*; Soledad O'Brien, CNN's *Matter of Fact with Soledad O'Brien*; Carol Marin, political editor at WTTW-TV Chicago; Robert Siegel, host of NPR's

All Things Considered; interviewer Marci Burdick, former head of Schurz Communications and 2017 Missouri Broadcasters Association Broadcaster of the Year (https://www.missouribroadcasters.org/hall-of-fame/marci-burdick/).

23. As of 2023, examples of the Library of American Broadcasting Foundation board professional membership association included (among others) such businesses and institutions as Beasley Broadcast Group, LG Electronics, Benztown, the University of Alabama, and the Broadcast Education Association.
24. "LeVar Burton to Receive Inaugural Insight Award from Library of American Broadcasting Foundation at 2022 NAB Show," press release, March 24, 2022, NABSHOW, https://nabshow.com/2022/news-releases/levar-burton-to-receive-inaugural-insight-award/.
25. Laura Schnitker and Jim Baxter, "From Amos 'n' Andy to Civil Rights: The Inclusion of Blackness in Commercial Radio Broadcasts," University of Maryland Libraries, https://exhibitions.lib.umd.edu/libraryofamericanbroadcasting/featured/blackness-in-commercial-radio-broadcasts, accessed August 8, 2024; Juan Manuel Hernandez Chico, "'Have You Tried Wheaties?' The Lost Art of Jingle Writing," https://exhibitions.lib.umd.edu/libraryofamericanbroadcasting/featured/jingles, accessed August 8, 2024.
26. "Radio Archivist David Gleason to Be Honored by LABF at NAB Show New York," Inside Radio, October 17, 2023, https://www.insideradio.com/free/radio-archivist-david-gleason-to-be-honored-by-labf-at-nab-show-new-york/article_189340a6-6d10-11ee-88f9-e3c6b7e1ce1a.html.
27. "Benztown Partners with LABF for Radio and Podcast Power Session," Benztown, November 9, 2022, https://benztown.com/press/radio-power-session/.
28. For links to the podcasts and associated events, see "Preserving Broadcast History," NAB, August 23, 2023, https://www.nab.org/events/082323Webinar/watch.asp, and "Help the NAB and LABF Preserve Your Broadcast History," Radio Ink, August 16, 2023, https://radioink.com/2023/08/16/help-the-nab-and-labf-preserve-your-broadcast-history/.
29. Library of American Broadcasting, LinkedIn, December 2023, https://www.linkedin.com/company/the-library-of-american-broadcasting/.
30. Podrazik, Burr Tillstrom donation in "Kick Off" section of the "Before There Were Walls" exhibition panel; Chuck Schaden donation in "Origins" section of the "National Radio Hall of Fame" 2017 exhibition panel.
31. Aileen Bishop (MBC deputy director), email and text correspondence with author, 2022–23.
32. David Plier, email correspondence with author, November 14, 2023.
33. Bishop and Paul Durica (CHM director of exhibitions), email and text correspondence with author, 2022–23.
34. Durica, in discussion with the author, confirmed the parameters of the arrangement between CHM and Tillstrom from consulted paperwork.
35. All descriptions in the text concerning "Rita, Fran, and Dragon" taken from Lumpen's nearly eighty-minute program at https://vimeo.com/767812738. There is a long period at the beginning of the video focused on a test pattern. Moving images and audio commence at 3:34.

36. Rick Kogan, "Kukla, Fran, Ollie and You: Some Chicago Puppets Charmed a Generation and Helped 'Invent' TV," *Chicago Tribune*, October 16, 2022, https://www.chicagotribune.com/entertainment/ct-ent-kukla-fran-ollie-puppets-anniversary-kogan-20221013-eqsxzkd4vbbpdbo244jtoexiui-story.html.
37. Lumpen, "Pocket Guide to Hell Presents Garroway at Large," December 2021, https://vimeo.com/649248708.
38. Sam Lessin, "How Covid Accelerated Changes Already in the Making," The Information, December 22, 2020, https://www.theinformation.com/articles/how-covid-accelerated-changes-already-in-the-making.
39. "A pop-up shop is a temporary retail space that is typically used to introduce a new product line, test a new market or generate awareness for a product or cause" (https://www.techtarget.com/whatis/definition/pop-up-shop). In a direct conversation with the author prior to the November 13, 2023, board meeting, LABF cochairs Jack Goodman and Heidi Raphael concurred with that characterization.
40. Michael Henry, discussion with the author, November 8, 2022, University of Maryland Hornbake Library.

CHAPTER 7

LYNNE CARMICHAEL

TELEVISION ARCHIVES IN AUSTRALIA
"THE PASSING DOWN OF MEMORY..."

"Despite what the beginners sometimes seem to imagine," wrote historian Marc Bloch in the 1940s, "documents do not suddenly materialize, in one place or another, as if by some mysterious decree of the gods. Their presence or absence in the depths of this archive or that library are due to human causes which by no means elude analysis. The problems posed by their transmission, far from having importance only for technical experts, are most intimately connected with the life of the past, for what is here at stake is nothing less than the passing down of memory from one generation to another."[1] While Bloch was describing documentary archives, his comments are equally applicable to archival preservation of audiovisual records. Indeed, the "problems posed by their transmission" are even more pertinent. Paper documents are relatively stable, but audiovisual media must be kept in appropriate conditions to avoid deterioration. Researchers require obsolete playback equipment or software—and even when digitized, preservation may require ongoing checking and reformatting as data standards and software become obsolete.

Archivability in this context is regarded as the answer to the fundamental questions of what's kept in television archives and why. There are four dimensions to archivability for the audiovisual record: technology, production, curation, and access—in this context, access for researchers. First, the technological dimension asks: What can be recorded and stored? What standards ensure compatibility between formats and equipment? How do we deal with obsolete technologies and formats? What is lost in the process of digitizing formats? The production domain raises questions about what kind of content is recorded. What kinds of programs are produced by the agency or department? What is the brief for a particular program that determines factors such as the intended audience, scope, and budget? The curatorial dimension of archivability addresses questions of what is selected for inclusion in a curated collection. What versions of recordings are kept? Is it only the final product, or are component recordings retained? Are raw camera tapes and tapes of interviews retained after they have been edited for a news story? How are collected recordings preserved for ongoing use? What metadata standards are employed? Finally, the access dimension is of particular importance in this chapter. Are the collections accessible to researchers or for in-house use only? How can researchers interrogate the collections, analyze content, and inform their scholarship via archived material? Are there options to study visual content that has not been retained via scripts or transcripts, for example?

In answering these questions this chapter is based on a combination of experience in locating and documenting music collections in the Australian Broadcasting Commission/Corporation (ABC), which, since my retirement, informed work toward my PhD thesis.[2] My thesis investigated the importance of the ABC in the development and support of classical music in Australia. This research relied heavily on the ABC's archival resources for classical music conceptualized as Howard Becker's "exhibition spaces"—curated spaces constrained in terms of space, money, or other resources.[3] Conceptualizing collections as "exhibition spaces" enables their use as sources of implicit evidence about the collecting organization's values—essentially "reverse engineering" an understanding of collection policies that were never formally articulated from the evidence of what is included in the space. This concept, then, is particularly helpful in archival research where collections lack an explicit policy—not least because it reflects the way in which archives are created. In 2004 I interviewed eighteen ABC music producers in relation to collections of recorded music that they retained outside of the formal ABC archival collections. None had a formal collection policy, although all of the producers were easily able to verbalize what they retained in their working collections. For example, the producer/presenter of a world music radio program indicated that he kept everything recorded from concerts, music festivals, and studio recordings except "poor" performances. In fact, therefore, his collection reflected his programming brief and his selection of performers and events for recording and use in broadcasts. Analysis of his collection could establish his programming priorities and emphases that he did not articulate directly.

This chapter investigates the way in which collections and curation systems may evolve within a public service broadcaster and then examines archival research in an Australian context, providing a basic overview of the ABC as both public service broadcaster and "archive creator." This is followed by an outline of the context of archives in Australia and a case study of research conducted in the ABC archives investigating telecasts of Australian ballets in the 1950s and 1960s. Finally, it applies the Australian case to a broader understanding of archivability.

EVOLUTION OF COLLECTION AND CURATION IN A BROADCASTING ENVIRONMENT

In both radio and television, commercial forms of audiovisual content (for example, film and gramophone records) preceded the development of broadcasting. While these were significant in providing content for the new media, live performance remained the norm for some time, and methods of recording this live-to-air content evolved as a means of capturing performances for later use. For television these recording technologies included telerecording (also known as kinescope) and later video recording. The need for content capture was particularly evident where a single broadcaster might cover wide areas with different time zones or where content needed to be physically transported from one area to another.

Once content was created it needed to be stored until its planned use was complete. This raised the question of when it might be deemed no longer needed. The first methodology for this decision-making that I have identified involved sending lists of recordings to the producers/creators of the content and asking them what they thought should be retained or culled. As with the producer of the world music program mentioned above, this might be based on quality of performance criteria as well as reflect the creators' basic decisions about what was recorded for their programming and occasional commercial releases of CDs (that is to say, both broadcasting and commercial criteria were considered).

Once the decision to retain some recordings for "permanent" use was made, the "store" became a "collection" and inevitably required a more formal level of curation—some means of identifying, labeling, and retaining recordings. This might also entail a card catalog or computer listing of recordings. As my investigations showed, producers preferred to keep these collections themselves rather than entrusting them to the organizational archive. This was for physical convenience (having them close by) and to avoid the need to deal with the more formal retrieval and access systems that the archive might require.

Eventually, however, shortage of space, the ending of the program, or the obsolescence of the format in which it was preserved would make the retention of a production collection unviable or inconvenient, at which point it might well be turned over to the organizational archive and thus subject to the archive's collection policy and processes. Regardless of policy requirements, in many cases it may be assumed that the selection processes already applied by the producers (from "working" copy to "store" and then to "production collection") are sufficient to justify retention in the archive. Indeed, this has parallels with "records management" archiving processes where a "disposal policy" determines the time frame for the retention of specific classes of material and those items designated as "permanent retention," once no longer in active use by the area where they are created, that are retained in an "archive."

Having examined in general how archival collections of audiovisual items reach an "archival" collection, the next section of this chapter examines the particular case of the ABC and its context of Australian national collections of audiovisual content.

AUSTRALIAN BROADCASTING CORPORATION

A knowledge of the organization to be studied is an essential first step in archival research because, unlike "classified" collections in libraries, which locate items by systems such as Dewey or Library of Congress classification schedules, archival records are retained in the "order" or "series" in which they are created. Where the archive deals with a number of organizations, for example, it will identify an "agency" (the organization that created the item) and the "series" (detailing the department within the organization and the function of the archival records, such as the program name and dates). Finally, the item will comprise the particular episode with metadata showing dates of recording/broadcast and a description of creators and content along with technical information about format.

In my research, for example, to access information about music production and its archives, it was essential to know that classical music was created in the Music Department until 1985. After that date the situation became more complicated as the ABC underwent a number of departmental restructures so that responsibility for music was dealt with in different areas of the organization. Finding documents for my research thus required tracking music production areas via sources such as organization charts in annual reports, newspaper articles, and books. This structural knowledge in itself, however, was evidence that the role of classical music was less central to the organization's agenda.

Understanding the structure of the ABC is important as it is now a large and complex organization that has undergone a number of changes that inevitably affect where collections are created and maintained. The Australian Broadcasting Commission was founded in 1932 via an Act of Parliament by which the Australian government took control of an earlier commercial broadcaster (the Australian Broadcasting Company) to create a national, public service broadcaster.[4] The foundational statute stressed the importance of music as a role of the new broadcaster, which led to the formation of six symphony orchestras, dance bands, choirs, and other music ensembles. In 1983 the commission became a corporation with a reduced mandate for musical involvement, and by the end of the twentieth century, all of these musical ensembles had been disbanded or, in the case of the orchestras, divested to the control of Symphony Australia. Nowadays, the ABC is regarded (and promotes itself) as primarily a news-gathering organization. Having started as a single radio network, the ABC of 2022 comprised four national radio networks, including two music networks, ABC Classic and Triple J (alternative music), as well as an international channel (Radio Australia), eight Metro channels (in state capitals plus the Northern Territory and Australian Capital Territory), and more than forty local channels in regional and rural areas around the country. There are seven digital audio channels available online or via digital television. Television, from a single channel in two capital cities in 1956, now comprises six digital channels and a streaming service (iView). Inevitably, tracking archived content is therefore more complex than it was with a single network of radio stations.

As a public service broadcaster, the ABC shares with organizations such as the BBC characteristic cultural and national goals—but it should not be seen as a clone of its predecessor. First, while the BBC enjoyed many years as a monopoly broadcaster, the ABC has existed since its inception among commercial broadcasters in the same market. Furthermore, since 1948 the ABC has been funded by government allocation rather than license fees. This makes the very existence of the ABC considerably less secure than the BBC's Royal Charter.

Geographically, the ABC serves a very large area.[5] Australia is governed by six state governments as well as a "federal government." The eastern states (Tasmania, Victoria, New South Wales, and Queensland) are some three hours ahead of the time zone of Western Australia.[6] This makes broadcasting national programs complicated—for example, the ABC Classic music network relies on an automated recording and rebroadcast system so that all states hear the program at the same time according to the time zone in their area. The ABC shares this federal/state organizational structure with state and regional programs as well as national ones. While essential to ensure that local interests are considered, this structure is inherently hierarchical and bureaucratic.

ABC ARCHIVES

The ABC archives of documents, radio, and television were formally established in 1971. This follows the pattern of the evolution of archives outlined above, coming rather later than the actual collections of content. Documents and images are available from the 1930s, while music recordings created by the ABC include discs from the 1940s and tape from the 1950s. Television broadcasting began in 1956, and until the advent of videotape in the 1960s, telerecordings were made for programs scheduled in other locations.[7] In 2000 the ABC began digitizing earlier formats of material into its digital repository.

The development of suitable technology is an essential component of the archivability of television content. In both radio and television, early performances relied heavily on "live-to-air" content until suitable recording technology became available. Adding the significant cost of recording (equipment, additional skilled staff, and ongoing costs of storage) had to be justified. Preservation for future researchers was certainly not a high priority, so the cost of recording needed to satisfy practical requirements—particularly the need to avoid repeating expensive live performances. An equally important element of archivability is the question of how material is preserved—that is to say, how it is curated to minimize deterioration and how ongoing access to it can be assured. Retention in an archive is an expense borne by the broadcaster in terms of specialist staff, storage media, and space—for audio and visual media, space with temperature and humidity control.

How, then, did the ABC make decisions about what to retain? The need to preserve live content for future use is, as noted above, a primary justification for this expenditure, and in most cases with musical content, this is a decision made at a relatively early stage by the creators of the content. At times this might be decided relatively simply on anticipated reuse, but sometimes the longer view was evident. In 1942 the ABC's federal director of music, responsible for all of the classical music activities within the ABC from 1936 until his retirement in 1963, clearly outlined his rationale for the inauguration of the ABC's in-house music recordings activities as "very valuable propaganda to send to England or America—as illustrating Australian composition—besides being valuable to us for future programming."[8]

James's use of the term "propaganda" here simply meant that recordings would be useful in promoting Australian composition abroad, and ABC recordings were, indeed, widely used for international exchange via prestigious events such as the *Prix Italia* and the Paris Rostrum. Furthermore, recording contracts were components of competition prizes, widely used as program resources, and often as masters for commercial releases. Perhaps their most important function, however, has been the preservation of an archive of Australian musical compositions and performances.

By 1971, however, the role of the ABC was increasingly seen as news gathering, and the archives developed a special relationship with that area (especially television). As news became an increasingly visual medium (eschewing the earlier "talking head" format), "fast turnaround" for reuse of audio and visual content in news bulletins was essential. Footage from news bulletins was captured and cataloged daily. Camera tapes including footage of interviews and background shots were assessed for usefulness in future stories or for "overlays" to be used behind presenters to represent the nature of the story (for instance, bank notes for financial stories). These selected items were added to the collection and cataloged. This copyrighted visual material created by the ABC for its own use became a valuable commercial resource made available to other broadcasters via Library Sales. Such material is therefore available to researchers, but at considerable cost.

In other areas (music, for example) it was more common for material to be retained in production collections within work areas. My 2004 survey of interviews identified small working collections, including personal collections, with an idiosyncratic shelving order (if any). In the area of classical music, however, resources were routinely shared between the various states. This encouraged the Music Department and its successors to form their own managed collections with their own numbering/shelving systems and catalogs. Production collections tended to come to the Archives section of the ABC once a producer left (so-called abandoned collections) or when shortage of space forced a reassessment of what was stored within the department. As the music collections coordinator, it would then be my role to assess the collection, and items might be integrated into the ABC archive or discarded, especially where the condition of the recording was irredeemable or the content could not be identified. Ultimately, recordings retained might be consigned to the National Archives of Australia (NAA) in accordance with the Records Disposal Schedule negotiated between the ABC and the NAA. The reasons for this arrangement are outlined below.

AUSTRALIAN ARCHIVAL ORGANIZATION

In addition to understanding the organizational structure of the institution to be investigated, archival researchers benefit from understanding the range of potential archival resources (essentially, where to look for what). This section of the chapter therefore outlines Australian archives at the national level. Individual states have archives under different names, such as the Public Record Office, Victoria (PROV), and are beyond the scope of this chapter.

The collaboration between the ABC and the NAA is a legislative arrangement because the ABC is a government agency. Like the ABC, the NAA is a federal organization; indeed, its precursor was formed in 1901 at the same time as the six autonomous colonial states became federated into the Commonwealth of Australia. At that time, national archival and bibliographic resources both resided in the Commonwealth Parliamentary Library, and in 1923 two concurrent names reflected its dual functions: Commonwealth Parliamentary Library and Commonwealth National Library. In 1961 the collections were split into three functional areas: the Parliamentary Library, the National Library of Australia, and the Commonwealth Archives Office. The Parliamentary Library has continued under that name, while the Commonwealth Archives Office became the Australian Archives in 1975 and then the National Archives of Australia in 1983.[9] While the National Library of Australia (NLA) also retains that name to the present day, in 1984 part of the NLA collection was transferred to the National Film and Sound Archive (NFSA, between 1999 and 2004 known as Screensound).[10] For researchers interested in commercial broadcasting in Australia, then, the NFSA would be the first point of call. As NAA collections are sourced essentially from government agencies, in terms of broadcasting this means it is the primary archive for both the ABC and the Special Broadcasting Service (SBS)—a multilingual hybrid (funded by both government and advertising) broadcasting service established in 1978.[11]

A consequence of this history is difficulty in determining where media history resources are actually held. Indeed, ABC materials can be found in the NLA and the NFSA as well as the NAA. How, then, can researchers locate archival media resources?

ACCESS TO AUSTRALIAN ARCHIVAL COLLECTIONS

Most of the research sources in Australia have online databases to provide access to their collections. Indeed, the National Library of Australia has an online source called Trove, which includes digitized newspapers, magazines, journals, and annual reports of immense value to media researchers interested in Australian topics.[12] The NLA, while not specifically an archive, does include collections of manuscripts of interest to media scholars, for example, the Musica Australis collection comprising musical scores, diaries, and correspondence gathered during the creation of a landmark ABC program on pre-Federation music broadcast between 1969 and 1971—that is, prior to the formation of the NFSA.[13]

While the NFSA is primarily the source for archival resources for commercial broadcasters, there are ABC materials in the collection and, given restricted access to the ABC itself, it is a useful source for research into the ABC—especially as it has a very well-designed search engine and a significant collection of oral histories. The NAA has a somewhat more complex online search engine, and not all contents of this collection can be found in online searches. Archival content that appears in the online search tool has been assessed by archival staff as open access; resources may be assessed as restricted if deemed confidential. Material held in NAA storage but not yet assessed is only reviewed when it is requested, and NAA specialists assist researchers to locate material not yet displayed online. As the NAA is seriously underfunded, it is advisable to give its researchers plenty of notice before visiting the reading room. Despite general underfunding, the preservation of Australian historical footage was significantly enhanced when the NAA and other archival collections were, in December 2021, awarded AU$41.9m to digitize at-risk materials.[14]

CASE STUDY: TELEVISED BALLETS, 1956–1966

This case is of particular interest to archivability of television resources in identifying technological, production, curatorial, and access dimensions of a specific area of the ABC archival collections. Identifying the recordings of televised ballets involved privileged access to the ABC archives, including film, video and still images, and documentary sources.[15] The items in the collections analyzed were produced and recorded on technology that was obsolete in the archival collections of the 2000s (film from telerecordings and videotape that was being replaced by digital formats) and, indeed, some of the ballets had already been digitized. The main reason that they had been telerecorded or, later, videotaped was because in the 1950s and 1960s the ABC could not easily relay live-to-air broadcasts around the country and so a recording was needed to present the program in another state. As they existed in production collections, they had been accepted into the organizational archives as having already been identified by the producers as valuable. The catalogs (part of the curatorial process of archives) did not, however, include genre information and so ballets could only be located by title. Fortunately, the ABC's Document Archives had lists of operas and ballets created by John Widdicombe (a former ABC producer in the early days of television) as part of the process of evaluating content for permanent retention within the production area.[16] With these lists (comprising titles and dates of recordings/broadcasts) the works could be traced in various catalogs to identify composers and choreographers. Most importantly, they provided "identifiers" to locate archival recordings for additional information from "idents" and credits (especially dancers and synopses). And, of course, I could view the ballets themselves.

Where no vision survived, it was occasionally possible to find additional information from the photo database, especially for set designs—sets themselves are rarely retained due to the space requirements and the need to recycle materials. Color television arrived in Australia in 1975, so photographs of the sets were the only way to see the colors used in costumes and sets telecast (and recorded) in black and white. Color photographs of sets and costumes sometimes also appeared in popular magazines such as the *Australian Women's Weekly*, which also proved a valuable source for understanding the way in which opera and ballet on television was promoted to potentially new audiences. At times contemporaneous reviews in the press provided useful additional material or comment. Of course, the broader context of the ballets and the companies that produced them was found in books, theses, and articles in journals and online as well as in archival documents and the occasional documentary[17] or televised interviews with dancers[18] or choreographers. These supplementary resources were valuable in providing information about the recordings beyond the metadata in catalogs and at times were necessarily surrogates for recordings that were lost.

What began as an exercise to "locate and document" became an analysis of the ballets exploring two particular questions: What proportion of the ballets had an Australian composer or choreographer? What were the "themes" of the Australian ballets? As my research progressed it became evident that the ABC had fortuitously captured a very interesting period in the history of Australian ballet in the 1950s and 1960s when a number of small companies flourished but did not long survive the inauguration of the government sponsored Australian Ballet (company) in 1962.

As there is considerable scholarly literature investigating ballet developments at this time, what did my study of the archives add to our knowledge? In planning for the advent of television the then-Federal Director of Music, William James, reported on overseas experience broadcasting "serious" music on television and identified "visual" forms of music (opera and ballet in particular) as the most promising: "But even in this form of music there are problems in presentation and drastic editing is often necessary to make it suitable for T.V. requirements."[19]

The recordings of televised ballets allow us to see and evaluate how the ballets were adapted to the new media to enable the ABC as a public service broadcaster acting in its national/cultural role—that is to say providing a broad and general audience with access to cultural activity not otherwise available to them. By having a detailed record of the ballets' broadcast it was, furthermore, possible to deduce the ABC's "preferred" composers, choreographers, and themes. A study of the actual vision might have been useful for other analysis (e.g., an examination of changing body type and dance styles between the 1950s and later periods).[20]

Research in the ABC archival collections revealed the ABC's innovative role in the new medium of television as it encouraged the small ballet companies of the 1950s and 1960s—including works by a number of Australian composers in an era when they had relatively few alternative sources of income. Furthermore, the national broadcaster fostered an image of Australia via ballets that dealt with, among other things, drought (*Snowy!*), beach culture (*The Beach Inspector and the Mermaid*), machismo and Australian Rules Football (*The Display*), and indigenous mythology (*The First Boomerang*, *The Waratah*, and *Brolga*). These televised ballets, then, fulfilled the ABC's national objectives enunciated in 1947: "Since its inception in 1932, the Commission has felt it has a responsibility to stimulate and foster creative musical art in Australia. In doing so, it has hoped to lay the foundation of an essentially national musical literature, which will reflect worthily the spirit and aspirations of the people.[21]

Once the technology for recording ABC productions became available, the recordings themselves became a vital component in preserving Australia's "national musical literature." Through curated collections, music recordings, as James predicted in 1942, became available not only for re-use within the ABC but for international exchange to enhance the reputation of Australian composers and performers on the international scene. Furthermore, the conceptualization of collections as Beckerian "exhibition spaces" allows us to establish which Australian composers and performers were accorded the prestige of exposure within the national broadcaster's programs—in essence, to divine, after the event, the ABC's collection policies and inherent values. In the absence of specific collection policies, this allows us to "reverse engineer" policies that were rarely documented.

ARCHIVABILITY

Archives have selection policies, even if they are not clearly articulated. What can we learn from the case study of televised ballet about the nature of archival selection? Firstly, there was an immediate need to record the live performances of ballets in order to transport the film/videotape to another location for rebroadcast. This was deemed preferable to a repeated live performance. Secondly, ballets were retained because, with their highly trained performers and payment for commissions or rights to existing ballets, they were extremely expensive productions. In 1968, for example, a ballet cost AU$20,000 to produce.[22] In comparison, at that time this was the budget for ten weeks of a weeknight current affairs program, about fifteen weekly current affairs shows, or a little over four weeks of an ongoing soap opera.[23] Thirdly, despite the high production costs, ballet productions were high prestige cultural events and therefore valuable not only for national broadcasts but for international exchange. *Snowy!* was, for example, an entry in the prestigious *Prix Italia* competition as a documentary.[24] Such broadcasts are especially appropriate in the context of the cultural aims of public service broadcasting. Finally, while the ballets in the ABC Archives may be too dated for rebroadcast, they are "unique" in a way that variety programs, following a fairly standardized format with unremarkable repertoire, were not.

Although this chapter deals with ballet telecasts in Australia, there are significant lessons about what constitutes archivability of television programs. Initially it is important to establish whether it is likely that the research resources exist—key factors being the history of recording technology for media in use at the time as well as the nature of the television content for investigation. The case of the televised ballets indicates that "event" television is more likely to survive due to the costs of production, the prestige for the broadcaster, and the potential for reuse in commercial form or for exposure in prestigious international fora such as the *Prix Italia*. Music programs that are less costly to produce and are produced more frequently, unless they have unique features such as a very important guest artist, may be "sampled" in archives—to demonstrate the style and content of the programs. This was certainly evident in the ABC archives in the era of the televised ballets. The program "lay outs" (schedules) of the 1950s and 1960s, for example, demonstrate that variety programs were much more frequently broadcast but usually only the first and last program of the series were retained.[25]

Of equal importance to the researcher is an understanding of the archival environment in which television content is curated. This paper has outlined in some detail the situation in Australia as an example of the kinds of archives (broadcasting, national, state, and "special" archives[26]) that can be expected to retain audio-visual broadcasts. The kinds of archives and the way that they function are not unique to Australia and similar means of access will exist in other countries (via online searches, in person, researcher assisted, and via "finding aids," for example). While broadcasting archives and production collections may not be easily accessible to the majority of researchers, broadcasting research is possible in other kinds of archives.

If researchers and technological and production workers understand the nature and scope and, indeed, the organizational limits, of archives, they can become informed lobbyists to support national archives to engage with political/legal processes to ensure that as many archives as possible are open to researchers or made available more widely online and that inactive collections of recordings in the production areas of our broadcasters are regularly consigned to appropriate collections for preservation rather than actively destroyed or rendered unusable by decay and obsolescence.

NOTES

1. Marc Bloch, *The Historian's Craft* (Manchester: Manchester University Press, 1954), 71.
2. The ABC was formed in 1932 as the Australian Broadcasting Commission and became the Australian Broadcasting Corporation in 1983. "ABC" applies to the organization in general. The corporation's website is https://www.abc.net.au/.

3. Howard S. Becker "'Art Worlds' Revisited," *Sociological Forum* 5, no. 3 (1990): 500–501, http://www.jstor.org/stable/684401.
4. The complex origins of radio in Australia are beyond the scope of this chapter. For further information see, for example, Bridget Griffen-Foley, *Changing Stations: The Story of Australian Commercial Radio* (Sydney: UNSW Press, 2009).
5. Australia is the 6th largest country—larger than India but with a population of approximately 26 million in comparison with India's population of more than 1.3 billion.
6. This becomes somewhat complicated during summertime when Queensland remains on "Eastern Standard Time."
7. Films from monitors of live broadcasts-also called "kinescope" or "kine" recordings.
8. William James, Memo, Guild of Australian Composers, January 22, 1942, in Guild of Australian Composers General 1942, NAA: ST1607/1, 7/7/1 (hereafter cited as Guild of Australian Composers, NAA: Item 2230 7316). Emphasis added.
9. The website of the National Archives of Australia is at https://www.naa.gov.au/.
10. The website of the National Film and Sound Archive is at https://www.nfsa.gov.au/.
11. The website of the Special Broadcasting Service is at https://www.sbs.com.au/.
12. The website of Trove is at https://trove.nla.gov.au/.
13. Lynne Carmichael, "*Musica Australis*," 2016, https://doi.org/10.26180/5EC31F266B5BF.
14. https://www.abc.net.au/news/2021-12-03/federal-funding-to-save-historical-records-of-australian-past/100671398.
15. My research arose from my role as the ABC's Coordinator of Music Collections, which involved, among other things, collating musical resources previously scattered by "format" into the Consolidated Legacy Music Recordings database which eventually, in 2018 contained 40,000 entries for musical recordings from 1942 until the early 2000s.
16. List of early TV ballets 1957–1963 Compiled by John Widdicombe, ABC: D13/5231; List of early TV ballets c1962–1966 Compiled by John Widdicombe, ABC: D13/5232; Opera on ABC Television researched and compiled by John Widdicombe, Assembled by Glenda Helman and Carol Lee, ABC: D12/15209.
17. Mandy Chang, "*A Thousand Encores: The Ballets Russes in Australia.*" Australia: ABC TV, November 3, 2009.
18. *Interview with former Ballet Russe Dancers. 7:30.* Broadcast: 28/06/2006
19. W. G. James [Federal Director of Music], Serious music in T.V. 11 October 1956, ABC Music 1 [Finding Aid].
20. Robin Grove, "Balancing Acts: Ballet in Australia, 1930–55," *Voices: The Quarterly Journal of the National Library of Australia* 6, no. 2 (Winter 1996): 21–34.
21. William James, Memo to Charles Moses (General Manager), November 27, 1947, in ABC: Music 1. (hereafter cited as ABC: Music 1.).
22. Approximately AU$160,000 in 2021—about U.S.$116,000.
23. T. S. Duckmanton (General Manager, ABC) Music Programme Policy, April 10, 1968, ABC Music 1 [Finding Aid]

24. It is, of course, unusual for a ballet to take the form of a documentary of an engineering project and the balletic form is supplemented by narration by a well-known Australian actor of the day, Leonard Teale. Its avant-garde choreography by Margaret Barr is very abstract and it may, indeed, be the only ballet in existence with a role for a dancer representing a theodolite!
25. Programme Lay-out Books, Victoria, 1956–1967. ABC: B09/90–B09/98.
26. Special archives are those related to themes or individuals, e.g., the archives devoted to the life and work of the dancer and choreographer, Laurel Martyn, in Melbourne, Victoria.

PART III

TRANSFORMING THE EPHEMERAL INTO MORE VISIBLE AND LEGIBLE HISTORICAL MATERIAL

CHAPTER 8

ERIC HOYT, MARY HUELSBECK,
AMANDA SMITH, MAUREEN MAUK,
OLIVIA JOHNSTON RILEY, MATT ST. JOHN,
PAULINE LAMPERT, AND LESLEY STEVENSON

REVIVING NEGLECTED GIANTS

DIGITALLY PRESERVING AND SHARING
TWO EARLY TELEVISION COLLECTIONS

Stories of television and the archive are often framed in terms of failure and absence: limited access, lack of foresight, partial or complete loss. While there have been plenty of such cases in our field, some of them heartbreaking, we would like to share something different—a story of recovery, preservation, and access. This is a success story, rooted in collaborations, curiosity, and a willingness to explore the boundaries of what was possible. The result is that all of the WCFTR's episodes of *The Faye Emerson Show* (1949–1951) and *World of Giants* (1958) have been digitized, and many of them can be freely viewed online.

Over the past several years, the Wisconsin Center for Film and Theater Research (WCFTR) has collaborated with enterprising UW-Madison graduate students to revive television programs within the WCFTR collections. We have chosen the verb "revive" to signal the wide range of work and interests involved, encompassing the archival work of cataloging, rehousing, and digitizing film, as well as the research-oriented work of producing scholarship and outreach activities of sharing the collections with a broad public. A revival necessitates both the preservation of these materials and the multifaceted efforts to make these programs as accessible as possible. Enabling accessibility involves not only making materials readily available to scholars but also facilitating a nonhierarchical approach to scholarship wherein all who are interested have some means of experiencing and studying this content. With this in mind, we have also chosen to approach this chapter with coauthorship in mind. We are writing this as a mix of university faculty (Hoyt), archivists (Huelsbeck and Smith), graduate student archival project assistants (Lampert, St. John, and Stevenson), and graduate students pursuing research into *The Faye Emerson Show* (Mauk) and *World of Giants* (Riley). All of us played parts, some unexpected, in this revival work.

In what follows, we present our work together through the sequence in which it unfolded: first the WCFTR acquired the collections, then curious graduate students came to them with exciting research questions, then we fully processed and digitized the 16mm film prints, then we investigated the copyright status, and now we are curating and sharing the programs online using the knowledge we gained along the way. We hope that organizing the chapter this way makes it more accessible—both in terms of readability and humility (as it will become clear, we moved forward incrementally, not with some sort of master plan). We also hope that this chapter has generalizable takeaways and that it can serve as more than a mere chronicle of our work. By focusing on two specific television programs, it allows for a useful format comparison. Whereas *The Faye Emerson Show* was a live series that was kinescoped and syndicated, *World of Giants* was a filmed program that was produced for syndication but only lasted thirteen episodes. Both shows had been largely neglected by television scholars, audiences, and distributors until researchers came to them with new questions. But before that was possible, before there was any possibility of digitization and copyright searches, the programs needed to enter the archive.

BACKGROUND:
THE WCFTR AND COLLECTING TELEVISION PROGRAMS

Founded in 1960 as a partnership between the University of Wisconsin–Madison and the Wisconsin Historical Society, the WCFTR initially focused its collecting efforts on the world of the American theater. However, since many writers also wrote for film, and increasingly television, material for all three areas was accepted. From the beginning, the WCFTR has collected both audiovisual materials and paper materials that document film, television, and theater productions. Notable television-related collections donated in the first five years of the WCFTR's existence included those from Paddy Chayefsky (1962), David Davidson (1962), John Frankenheimer (1963), E. Jack Neuman (1963), Jerome Ross (1963), and Rod Serling (1965). With these collections and others, the WCFTR began to develop the core of its television holdings, which comprise productions from the 1940s to the 1960s. Genres represented in the collections include anthology dramas, television documentaries, comedies, action/adventure series, and variety shows. Although they are connected by our efforts in digitizing early television, the two series discussed in this chapter are in different collections and arrived at the WCFTR decades apart, with *World of Giants* in the United Artists collection and *The Faye Emerson Show* in Emerson's personal collection donated by her son.

The United Artists and Faye Emerson collections at the WCFTR represent two kinds of collections, with United Artists as a collection donated by an organization and Emerson by an individual. This distinction frequently affects the range and type of material. Collections donated by organizations or corporations are typically much larger than those from individuals, and they are often more complete in their paper documentation and audiovisual materials. Individual collections like Emerson's do not typically include viewing copies, although her materials include kinescopes for many episodes. Collections from individuals are more often composed of documents such as correspondence or scripts. The WCFTR has historically focused on individual collections, so the United Artists collection, with its extensive corporate records and correspondence, was an unusual acquisition for the Center.

The donation of the United Artists collection in 1969 was a transformative moment for the WCFTR. Under the leadership of Tino Balio, the WCFTR sought out and accepted the studio's collection, which remains our largest. The collection contains hundreds of boxes of corporate records and correspondence, beginning with the founding of United Artists in 1919 as a film distributor for the work of film artists and independent producers.[1] However, the collection also contains the work of entities and subsidiary companies that United Artists had acquired. This includes the film libraries of Warner Bros. (1923–48), Monogram Pictures (1931–46), and RKO (1929–55), all of which were heavily exploited through television distribution agreements during the mid- to late 1950s.[2]

While the companies listed above are best known as motion picture companies, the collection also includes holdings from television producers. Among the work from subsidiary companies included in this immense collection were the production documents and audiovisual materials from Ziv-TV Productions (1948–65). The company's founder, Frederick Ziv, was an early pioneer of syndicated programming for television. With more than 2,300 episodes, Ziv's remains the largest television collection in the archive. The Ziv-TV Productions portion of the United Artists collection includes 345 boxes of paper documentation (scripts and

Faye Emerson and her son Scoop, from Emerson's collection. Courtesy of WCFTR.

production files) and photographs along with 16mm prints of each episode of thirty-eight programs produced by Ziv. In addition to the prints, the collection also contains more than twelve thousand reels of picture and sound negatives from Ziv programs. The Ziv collection is exceptionally comprehensive for its era. The desire of its owners to exploit the works as widely as possible—through the distribution of copies and the production of derivatives—likely motivated the saving of so many programs, film and sound elements, and paper materials.

The Faye Emerson collection was donated to the WCFTR in 1998 by her son William "Scoop" Crawford III, who compiled the materials after Emerson's death in 1983. Skitch Henderson, Emerson's third husband, had previously donated his collection to UW-Madison; we think this is why Crawford approached the WCFTR. The archive cultivated fruitful relationships with many different media producers after the successful United Artists acquisition. These relationships included disparate industry personalities and creators, who had a vested interest in seeing their efforts preserved for future generations. Not only did the WCFTR provide an academic repository for their archival materials, institutional interest also had a legitimizing effect on the relatively new television me-

A photograph from the production of *Men of Annapolis* from the Ziv-TV collection. Courtesy of WCFTR.

dium. The archival efforts of institutions like the WCFTR signaled that broadcast media was not merely pop culture ephemera but a field worthy of academic study. Industry practitioners who were committed to elevating the cultural significance of their work could now collaborate with an archive that shared in their goal. This foresight into the future cultural value of television was evident in the Faye Emerson collection.[3] William Crawford exercised a great deal of thoughtfulness and care in saving and organizing his mother's materials, which included papers, clippings, photographs, and film prints. The care and foresight of someone else was evident too: Faye Emerson herself. It was Emerson who insisted on recording her live late-night television show to kinescope, enabling this early television series to enter the archive.[4]

Many researchers have used the Ziv-TV materials and the Faye Emerson collection, although the collections vary in the resources that make them discoverable. Fans of the series, genres, or actors represented in the Ziv-TV prints often request them for viewing, either in person on a Steenbeck or remotely through digitized copies provided by private links. Ziv programs, photographs, and related materials have also been sourced for documentaries and publications. For example, the U.S. Naval Institute's *Naval History* magazine featured a WCFTR photograph from the production of *Men of Annapolis* in an article about the Ziv series, an anthology program about trainees at the U.S. Naval Academy.[5] When the Ziv materials were processed, WCFTR staff produced a finding aid with a list of episode titles, making it possible to find both series and particular episodes. Researchers have mostly consulted *The Faye Emerson Show* for projects related to guests on the program, such as Edith Piaf or theatrical producer Daniel Blum. A detailed finding aid for the Emerson collection is in progress, and researchers have inquired about the materials after discovering the collection through the catalog record. WCFTR staff also added descriptions for audiovisual materials in the Emerson collection to the show's IMDb page, with notes explaining that episodes are available at the WCFTR.[6] Our ongoing efforts to digitize and contextualize *World of Giants* and *The Faye Emerson Show* will make these series and their collections more discoverable, hopefully leading to more research questions about their production and the industry and period they represent.

THE FAYE EMERSON SHOW

The Faye Emerson Show (CBS, 1949–51) was a trailblazing program—the first live, late-night television series in American broadcasting history. Broadcast regionally in real time, the show was pushed progressively later as broadcast schedules and stations expanded in the developing television landscape. It was not a conventional practice at the time to record programming to kinescope, but Faye ensured her brave contributions to the bursting TV landscape were maintained, not so much for posterity at that moment but for her own defense when critics or network executives criticized her on-air commentary or fashion choices. In a national magazine interview, when asked about baring too much cleavage on TV, Emerson retorted, "I have interviews of every show I ever made," and she challenged anyone with an issue to "watch them all and then say that my show hasn't always been the cleanest show on television."[7] Counterparts such as Ruth Lyons on daytime television refused to allow their programs to be taped as a defense mechanism against after-the-fact corporate or brand criticism, yet Emerson called her recordings to light as a way of defending herself and the production.[8] As *The Faye Emerson Show*'s popularity grew, CBS shipped the kinescopes to the West Coast for later air dates. CBS's records and archives, however, have been lost over time, while Faye Emerson's personal library of her series and appearances was preserved. She had once mentioned that she didn't see the need to write an autobiography: "My life is its own diary and my scrapbooks tell the story."[9] Emerson and her son seemed to recognize the significance of her story and the importance of maintaining it.

In the late 1940s Faye Emerson may have been new to New York and

A photograph of Faye Emerson from her collection. Courtesy of WCFTR.

the budding television scene, but she was familiar with the limelight. She had already gained notoriety as a Warner Bros. contracted film actress who then married Colonel Elliot Roosevelt during the time his father, FDR, was in the White House. Moving her life from Los Angeles to New York, the home of early TV, Emerson soon began making guest appearances on televised game shows such as CBS's *I've Got a Secret* and radio talk shows including *Hollywood's Open House*. She made her Broadway debut in *The Play's the Thing* in 1948. After she filled in as a guest host as well as successfully hosted *Paris Cavalcade of Fashions*, *Leave It to the Girls*, and *Author Meet the Critics*, Columbia Broadcast Network caught on to her on-air warmth, beauty, adaptability, and adroit conversational skills and created an evening show around her talent. *The Faye Emerson Show* began airing in October 1949 to East Coast markets. With the program fully sponsored by Pepsi-Cola, Emerson advertised the beverage's "more bounce to the ounce" fizz, serving drinks to her guests on air while her own effervescent personality and power captivated live TV viewers.

A dynamic range of guests and topics were featured on *The Faye Emerson Show*, including Duke Ellington, Tennessee Williams, Frank Sinatra, Salvador Dalí, and Edith Piaf. She even gave Steve Allen his first foray into late-night TV. Well liked and respected by her crew due to her egalitarian and progressive approach, Emerson was also known to be demanding and comprehensive in ensuring her show's details were spot on—from lighting to set design. The set featured a living room decked out for entertaining, including a piano, which she often encouraged musical guests, including Skitch Henderson, whom she'd later marry, to play. Her show generated a great deal of viewer mail, including feedback and considerations on Emerson's neckline, commendations and criticisms on her insistence that politics were for everyone—including women, and democratic messaging surrounding free speech and equal rights. While Emerson did not save the viewer mail in her collection, she occasionally read choice letters on her program. These viewer letters were sometimes included in show episodes titled "Viewer Mail" and in other instances utilized as a thematic launch into a particular episode on "Tomboys" or "North Korea" or other topics. While *The Faye Emerson Show* ended in 1951, her new show, *Wonderful Town* (CBS, 1951–52), launched the very next day, also on CBS. The program was sold as a travel show that never left its New York City TV studio and featured a new city or location each week. At the time, *Wonderful Town*, which was also preserved in the Faye Emerson collection, was considered to be the most expensive TV series on air.[10]

Largely forgotten in cultural history if not for the work of the archivists, researchers, and William Crawford III, *The Faye Emerson Show* kinescopes are significant for two major reasons. First, the show's preservation reframes Faye Emerson's pioneering voice and contributions to media history as a feminist who understood the power of her platform. Second, the safeguarding and eventual digitization of Emerson's show completely reframed TV history, establishing the demonstrable fact that *The Faye Emerson Show* was actually America's first late-night television talk show.

Hailed as "Television's First Lady" at the height of her stardom in the early 1950s, Faye Emerson eventually left the TV business altogether, retiring to Majorca, Spain.[11] Sexist news commentary on Emerson's age, physical appearance, refusal to dial down political conversations as the daughter-in-law to Eleanor Roosevelt, and sharing her democratic ideals and personal opinions eventually led to an almost virtual wipe of her name in popular history, save a few media history scholars who noted Emerson's significance.[12] Even one of her two stars on Hollywood's Walk of Fame contains a typo in her name. The opportunity to embrace her digitized archives allowed a rewriting of her story. It is a restoration of not only kinescopes but also justice to the creative and political work done by women in the late 1940s and early 1950s during the genesis of television broadcasting in the United States.

WORLD OF GIANTS

Independent companies began to create prerecorded programs produced exclusively for television during the 1950s, selling them to local stations for distribution.[13] The Frederick W. Ziv Company was a leader in this midcentury boom in first-run syndication, producing more than 2,300 episodes of primarily action/adventure or crime television, with many adaptations of popular radio series.[14] The WCFTR's Ziv collection houses 16mm prints of all episodes of the thirty-eight produced Ziv series, as well as more than twelve thousand reels of picture and sound negatives. Most series lasted 38 or 39 episodes, with a few running 77 or 78 episodes, like *Ripcord, Mr. District Attorney,* and *Favorite Story,* or even more than 100 episodes, such as *Bat Masterson, I Led 3 Lives,* or *Sports Album.* The longest-running Ziv production was *Sea Hunt* at 155 episodes. In addition to the audiovisual materials, the 345 boxes of Ziv-TV papers and photographs document many aspects of production for the completed series, as well as records related to some unproduced series. Papers include correspondence, script drafts, contracts, filming reports, and shooting schedules. While some of the shorter series in the collection offer less documentation than the more successful Ziv productions, they still present opportunities for formal and cultural analysis, as scholars have found in using this collection.

One largely unremarked diamond in this celluloid rough is 1958's *World of Giants,* or as the announcer's voice booms in the show's introduction, "WOG!" *WOG* stars Marshall Thompson as Mel Hunter, a "special, special agent" who was exposed to dangerous rocket fuel in a mission behind the Iron Curtain. On his return home, he began to shrink until he was a mere six inches tall, and no doctor knows how to return him to his original size. However, his diminutive stature provides new opportunities for his work as a secret agent, allowing him to sneak unseen into gambling dens, carrier pigeon coops, and the purses of nefarious lady agents. With the help of his "normal" sized partner, Bill Winters, and their kindhearted secretary, Miss Brown, Mel must combat foreign powers and ferocious possums alike in the *World of Giants.*

WOG aired haphazardly on CBS in the twilight of Ziv's earlier successes. Ziv favored cost-saving measures like recutting stock news footage or rebooting older, proven radio shows in new televisual format, and this

A telephone prop on the *World of Giants* set from the Ziv-TV collection. Courtesy of WCFTR.

was reflected in their productions' comparatively low budgets and inexpensive visual quality. *WOG*, however, eschewed the company's low-cost strategies in favor of spectacular and expensive visual effects. The show's most compelling feature are its massive props and sets designed to make the regular-human-sized actor Thompson appear tiny by comparison. For example, *WOG* featured a massive telephone prop the size of a car, which Mel dramatically struggles to dial for help in the pilot. Although diverging in terms of budget, *WOG* aligned with past and future Ziv winners such as *Science Fiction Theatre* (1955) and *Sea Hunt* (1958) in its nonrealist genre. Ultimately, however, *WOG*'s expensive sets and novel combination of science fiction and spy drama were not realized in profits or longevity. Only thirteen episodes of *WOG* were produced, as the show evidently did not fit Ziv's already-failing profit model, which relied on money from rerun sales to balance the high costs of initial production.

WOG was not a success story in its time, but it can be of great interest to scholars today, as it contains numerous avenues for productive historiographic, formal, and cultural study. For instance, in viewing the early episodes, one finds traces of radio-style storytelling lingering in the television form. Mel's impassioned voiceover (trying to make his way down a garden trellis, he's attacked by a lawn sprinkler that's "like a thunderstorm!") attempts to compensate for insufficiently dramatic imagery (we observe

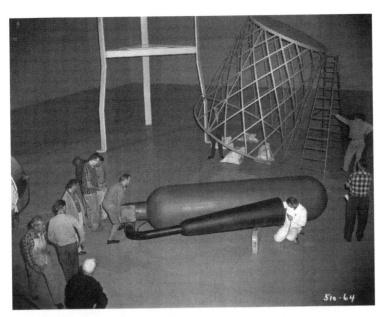

A fire extinguisher prop on the *World of Giants* set from the Ziv-TV collection. Courtesy of WCFTR.

Mel standing on a ladder in a stationary medium shot while someone off camera presumably sprays him with a hose—not exactly dynamic visuals). *World of Giants* also represents a relatively early televisual foray into spy thrillers and Cold War dramas, situated as Michael Kackman notes between earnest espionage dramas of the 1950s and spy parodies like *The Man from U.N.C.L.E* in the 1960s.[15] Further, the visual effects employed in *WOG* are worthy of study in and of themselves, as *WOG*'s set director, Robert Kinoshita, went on to construct one of TV's most famous robots in the show *Lost in Space* (1965), demonstrating the power of imaginative sets and props in creating engaging speculative television. Finally, *WOG* offers rich analytical fodder for representational and ideological analysis, a critical mode that may seem more naturally associated with the increase in racial and gender diversity seen in 1960s TV. Particularly, *WOG* acts as evidence of midcentury speculative televisual exploration of the perspectives and experiences of disability.

Mel Hunter experiences bodily impairment and limitations due to his small stature, and his embodiment is considered negatively nonnormative by those around him. Thus, following Sami Schalk's exploration of defamiliarization and nonrealist disability, we can clearly locate Hunter within an obscured history of disability in media.[16] Mel is disabled, and moreover, the show is deeply concerned with exploring problems of ableism and inaccessibility. *WOG*'s premise and hook is that it allows viewers compassionate access to its disabled protagonist's point of view as he survives in our "World of Giants." Mel is not steeped in tiresome disability tropes such as pity, ostracization, monstrosity, or overcoming. Instead, the show mounts a critical crip critique of the inaccessible structures of living that disabled people must navigate in order to survive—albeit couched in near-campy scenes of Mel climbing curtain drawstrings and dodging giant pencils. Thus, *WOG* can be understood as part of a longer lineage of genre fare that not only deals in fistfights and femmes fatale but engages meaningfully with issues of identity and acceptance that are still deeply relevant to modern audiences. Analyzing *World of Giants* presents an excellent opportunity to mobilize contemporary disability media studies theories and tools such as the "ideology of ability" and the "ableist habitus" to demonstrate the historical duration of disability and accessibility thought in popular culture.

Given that *WOG*'s broadcast run was abbreviated relative to other programs in the Ziv collection, it is significant that anything at all is known about the show. The absence of star power or an auteur narrative meant that there were few obvious points of entry for scholarship, and the paper materials for this program are relatively spare compared to other Ziv series. However, preservation and access to this midcentury curiosity enabled researchers to find these modern resonances in these historical texts. Had this program been lost to time, this important link to past iterations of disability representation would have been severed. Analyses from scholars such as Olivia Riley demonstrate why the continued care of these kinds of collections are so essential to the continued richness and diversity of the media studies discipline.[17]

FILM PRESERVATION, CATALOGING, AND SCANNING OF THE PROGRAMS

The contemporary significance of *The Faye Emerson Show*, *Faye Emerson's Wonderful Town*, and *World of Giants* became clear to us through the research of Maureen Mauk and Olivia Riley, both of whom developed graduate school class projects using the collections that later turned into publications and other outreach activities.[18] We at the WCFTR found their energy and passion to be infectious. When it came time to identify collections and programs to direct our digitization resources toward, we decided to prioritize the 150 *Faye Emerson* kinescopes and thirteen episodes of *World of Giants*.

The WCFTR's Lasergraphics ScanStation. Courtesy of WCFTR.

The subsequent film digitization process, led by Amanda Smith, took nearly a year to complete. All 150 episodes of *The Faye Emerson Show* and *Faye Emerson's Wonderful Town*, as well as the entire thirteen-episode run of *World of Giants*, were scanned at UW-Madison using the WCFTR's and Department of Communication Arts' Lasergraphics ScanStation scanner. Over the past decade, the WCFTR has developed and refined our digital preservation workflow, a process that is still being finessed as we learn more and tackle new projects.

Before a film is scanned, extensive prep work was required to ready the films. Each episode was inspected, loose splices were repaired, and six feet of leader was added to the head and tail of the film. To streamline the scanning process, we made the decision to splice several episodes together, which saved time loading and unloading the scanner. To keep track of these linked episodes, we created a spreadsheet with the episode titles, unique call numbers, condition notes, and a record of where in the process each film was: requested from cold storage, prepped, transferred, files received.

Many of the *Faye Emerson* kinescopes were exhibiting advanced stages of vinegar syndrome; deterioration of the acetate base was causing the film to curl and warp. Fortunately, the Faye Emerson collection includes multiple copies of most of the episodes, so we were able to choose the best version out of two to sometimes five different options. After making this choice, severely curled films were spliced together separately from the films in good condition. These curled films would require the use of a warp gate to hold the film flat during scanning. Without the gate to hold it flat, the resulting scanned image would be blurry and uneven. The gate helps generate a crisp image from even badly warped film, but it does result in a much longer scanning time.

Other than the condition issues described above, we found that the *Faye Emerson* and *World of Giants* films were intact and clean. Particulate rollers on the Lasergraphics ScanStation would remove surface dust and dirt during the scanning process. The films were in good enough condition that they did not require cleaning beyond this feature.

From the scan we generated three file types: DPX preservation files, ProRes 4444 mezzanine files, and H264 access files. Access files are stored on a secure local server for quick retrieval and researcher use. Preservation and mezzanine files are stored on redundant LTO tapes, kept in separate buildings. These files are bagged with their metadata and managed for fixity and file obsolescence by the WCFTR alongside our IT staff. We used MediaInfo to generate sidecar .xml metadata files and Library of Congress's Bagger application to store files with their metadata and create checksums.

As another step, we updated existing catalog records and the *World of Giants* online film list with the new digital file information. Like the other series in the Ziv collection, *World of Giants* already had an episode list created by archivists when the materials were processed, and the digitization details now make those episodes more immediately available to researchers. Faye Emerson's collection was previously processed and accessible to researchers who requested information from WCFTR's staff, and a finding aid is currently being developed for the papers. This online resource will list all episodes of *The Faye Emerson Show* and *Faye Emerson's Wonderful Town* along with paper materials and photographs in this collection.

Finding aids are helpful for scholars interested in visiting the archive and viewing the materials. However, we knew from Maureen Mauk's and Olivia Riley's research that there was public interest and relevance for these programs that extended beyond the academy. We wanted to publicly share the scanned episodes online as widely as we could. Inevitably, our attention turned to the question of intellectual property. Surely these programs were protected by copyright and our hands were tied—or were they?

INVESTIGATING COPYRIGHT STATUS

The WCFTR does not hold the copyright for the vast majority of materials that we preserve and care for. The same is true for almost all other noncorporate audiovisual archives and libraries. We possess the physical materials and provide research access to them. But the original donor—or sometimes another entity entirely—retains the underlying intellectual property rights. Additionally, some deeds of gifts contractually place limits on accessibility and usage. While the donation of the Faye Emerson collection used the WCFTR's standard deed of gift, the United Artists deed of gift included additional restrictions. For example, it specified that film prints could only be screened on the University of Wisconsin–Madison campus, instead of being available to circulate to other venues for screenings, like many WCFTR prints. Based on such deed of gifts restrictions, there may be legal limitations even for materials that are out of copyright. For these reasons, the WCFTR, along with most of our peer institutions, must approach digitization and online distribution with care, diligence, and caution.

Yet excessive caution carries its own risk. When saying no becomes the unchangeable default setting, libraries and archives lose out on opportunities to extend the reach of their collections, connect with new communities, and demonstrate their relevance.

Additionally, we learned firsthand through our work on the Media History Digital Library that most American books and periodicals published before 1964 belong in the public domain. The reason is tied up with the history of copyright policymaking: beginning in 1964, Congress began granting automatic one-year copyright extensions every year to new works as it worked on the legislation that would ultimately become the Copyright Act of 1976. The previous governing policy, the Copyright Act of 1909, had set the duration of copyright protection at twenty-eight years. Publishers had to opt in by registering, with the option for one twenty-eight-year renewal. Although the big movie studios and leading New York publishing houses generally applied for copyright renewals, the majority of media creators and publishers did not. Today, the best way to determine whether a particular work published between the mid-1920s and mid-1960s is protected by copyright is to run a search at the Library of Congress for copyright registrations and renewals. We decided it was time to take this step for our television collections.

In 2022 we hired one of the nation's leading copyright search consultants to investigate the copyright registration and renewal histories of both the Faye Emerson and Ziv programs in the WCFTR's collection. We knew in advance that both programs had been syndicated, which is important for establishing that they had indeed been "published" (thus avoiding the thornier copyright ground of kinescoped live television programs that were not distributed beyond their initial broadcast). When we received the report, we found the results to be encouraging for our goals to extend access to the collections, as well as revealing about the perceived value of the television programs that most intrigued us today.

The copyright search found no registrations and/or renewals for any episodes of *The Faye Emerson Show*, *Faye Emerson's Wonderful Town*, or *World of Giants*. By all indications, the creators never pursued copyright protection for these particular shows. This was unusual in the case of Ziv Television Productions; the company registered the copyrights for most of its other series produced during this same era, including *Dr. Christian* (1956–57), *Harbor Command* (1957–58), *Highway Patrol* (1955–59), *Man and the Challenge* (1959–60), and *This Man Dawson* (1959–60). All of those other series, however, lasted for a minimum of thirty-nine episodes. But having pulled the plug on *World of Giants* after a mere thirteen episodes, Ziv most likely did not see any long-term value in the program and did not bother to register the show for copyright protection.

Similarly, *The Faye Emerson Show*'s producing team probably assumed that the live TV show would not have long-term value. And they were largely correct—for seventy years. While there is no clear indication as to Faye Emerson and her son's decision to hang on to her show kinescopes and records, it is evident that she, and later her son Scoop, understood the significance of her contributions and her experiences in the television and cultural sphere from the 1940s to the 1960s. Before his donation and his death, Scoop sought to write a biography of his mother, interviewing some of her colleagues and star cohort of the time, such as TV personalities Garry Moore and Hugh Downes. With historical consciousness, it is easy to see how Faye Emerson's tremendous energy and pioneering work in the television arena happened so quickly and faded so fast. Reviewing her archive and the recollections captured through her son's work, we can speculate that those in the arena with Emerson understood her power and sought to find a way to document its significance.

SHARING THE DIGITAL FILES VIA
OPEN ACCESS WITHIN CURATED EXHIBITS

Because of our findings related to the copyright status for *The Faye Emerson Show* and *World of Giants*, we are able to share the digitized files with a broader audience. Thanks to an arrangement with the distributor ClassicFlix, the entire thirteen-episode series of *World of Giants* is now available through affordable DVD and Blu-ray editions. These discs contain scans we generated, of both episodes and publicity photographs.

Additionally, we are currently in the process of making a number of *Faye Emerson Show* and *World of Giants* episodes available via open access on a website with curated exhibits and pages showing the full digitized episodes. The exhibits will present items from the Faye Emerson and Ziv Television collections, including clips, sample episodes, and photographs, alongside introductions that offer users various entry points to appreciating the programs and understanding the historical conditions that produced them. We are using Omeka to produce these exhibits—a framework we've employed for other projects stemming from WCFTR collections because of its utility in presenting and describing digitized materials.

Across three exhibits, the website will address the overall project and both series. The exhibit focusing on the project as a whole will discuss how two television series from the 1950s, likely unfamiliar to users, are now available, explaining the trajectory from appearing on broadcast television decades ago to internet browsers today. This section will stress the amount of television that is lost after initial broadcast, especially from this period, and how these were preserved, summarizing some of the narrative that is detailed in this chapter. The exhibit on *The Faye Emerson Show* will contextualize the series through two of its key components: its historical importance as a late-night television show with a woman as the host, and its status as an example of live television from the period. The *World of Giants* exhibit will frame the series through the Ziv television company and the history of syndicated genre programs, as well as the show's connections with the history of visual effects in television.

These exhibits will highlight historical context and contemporary connections by referencing examples from the lineages of the genres and strategies represented by *The Faye Emerson Show* and *World of Giants*. We expect that scholars will discover these series, which are rich with possible directions for research and analysis, but we also hope that the Omeka website and the exhibits will provide a way to reach users beyond the typical researchers who know archives and the work we do. The exhibits could be resources for educators or anyone interested in broadcast history, women in media, genre television, or the variety of other topics related to the programs. While older films and television shows do not always seem accessible to general audiences, we plan for the exhibits to offer entry points to anyone who visits the website. Like so much of television history, *The Faye Emerson Show* and *World of Giants* contain abundant connections with the programs produced in the decades after them. We aim to foreground those contemporary connections and the specific contexts that produced the series, allowing users to learn what has changed and what has stayed the same through television history.

CONCLUSION

As archivists at the WCFTR, we never truly neglected *The Faye Emerson Show*, *Faye Emerson's Wonderful Town*, or *World of Giants*. We processed the collections, rehoused and cared for the materials, preserved the papers and film prints. We also included digitized clips within conference presentations and nudged researchers toward using them.

And yet it would be difficult to contend that neglect did not play a role—and a quite generative one—throughout the process of reviving these programs and collections. Even if the collections were not neglected by archivists, they had been underutilized by scholars. Fortunately, Maureen Mauk and Olivia Riley formulated original research questions exploring 1950s television programs that were not well remembered in broadcasting history. This resulted in their publishing articles and blog posts that shared new knowledge and put the past and present together in exciting ways. But it also resulted in our decision at the WCFTR to invest resources into scanning the collections and investigating their rights statuses.

As we learned in the process, the original creators of the programs did not pursue copyright registrations. This is most likely because the producers did not foresee long-term commercial value in programs that were live and topical (Faye Emerson) or so short-lived they could not be profitably licensed for syndication (Ziv's *World of Giants*). The research value and contemporary relevance of these programs is clear, however, and the lack of copyright protection has enabled us to extend their reach online. We are currently developing open-access websites and exhibits for the Faye Emerson collection and Ziv's *World of Giants* that contain digitized episodes and other production documents.

By sharing these project histories and our process, we hope that other archivists in the field will explore the full range of possibilities that may be available to revive neglected programs, extend the online reach of their collections, and highlight contemporary significance. Not everything can be digitized or freely distributed online, but our experience suggests that many early TV programs can be openly shared. Doing so requires the infrastructure and labor resources. Just as importantly, it requires curiosity and the willingness to ask questions, particularly "Why?" and "Why not?"

NOTES

1. Tino Balio details the acquisition process, including working with UA leadership and the challenges of housing and processing such a large collection, in the preface to his book, *United Artists*, vol. 1, *1919–1950: The Company Built by the Stars* (Madison: University of Wisconsin Press, 2009).
2. For more on the story of how these film libraries were bought and sold for television, see Eric Hoyt, *Hollywood Vault: Film Libraries before Home Video* (Berkeley: University of California Press, 2014), 142–94.
3. Lauren Bratslavsky provides a historical analysis of the role of the WCFTR and academic archives generally as a legitimizing force for television studies in the 1970s in her dissertation, "From Ephemeral to Legitimate: An Inquiry into Television's Material Traces in Archival Spaces, 1950s–1970s" (PhD diss., University of Oregon, 2013).
4. Margaret Compton has discussed the fragility of television and related challenges for archivists, and she notes kinescopes of early live broadcasts as the only way that such programs still physically exist. Margaret Compton, "The Archivist, the Scholar, and Access to Historic Television Materials," *Cinema Journal* 46, no. 3 (Spring 2007): 129–33.
5. Sherman G. Alexander, "Men of Annapolis: Good Show?" *Naval History* 16, no. 2 (April 2002), https://www.usni.org/magazines/naval-history-magazine/2002/april/men-annapolis-good-show.
6. The episode descriptions that the WCFTR contributed to the Internet Movie Database (IMDb) are available, as of August 13, 2024, at https://www.imdb.com/title/tt0053554/episodes?ref_=tt_eps_sm.
7. "Fifteen Minutes with Faye Emerson," *Pageant*, October 1951, 109, Faye Emerson Collection, WCFTR; Maureen Mauk, "Politics Is Everybody's Business: Resurrecting Faye Emerson, America's Forgotten First Lady of Television," *JCMS: Journal of Cinema and Media Studies* 59, no. 4 (2020): 129–52.

8. Marsha Francis Cassidy and Mimi White, "Innovating Women's Television in Local and National Networks: Ruth Lyons and Arlene Francis," *Camera Obscura* 17, no. 3 (January 9, 2002): 31–69.
9. Harold L. Cail, "Faye's Keeping Her Memories," *Evening Express* (Portland, Me.), July 16, 1959, Faye Emerson Collection, WCFTR.
10. For more on this, see Mauk, "Politics Is Everybody's Business."
11. Mauk, "Politics Is Everybody's Business," 135.
12. A few key media scholars, namely, Christine Becker, Cary O'Dell, and Maureen Mauk, have worked to bring Faye Emerson's name back into contemporary cultural history and reclaim Emerson's position as "Television's First Lady." See Christine Becker, *It's the Pictures That Got Small* (Middletown, Conn.: Wesleyan University Press, 2008); Cary O'Dell, *Women Pioneers in Television: Biographies of Fifteen Industry Leaders* (Jefferson, N.C.: McFarland, 1997); Mauk, "Politics Is Everybody's Business."
13. For a broader history of the rise of independent companies in syndicated production, see chapter 3 on film and early television in Derek Kompare, *Rerun Nation: How Repeats Invented American Television* (London: Taylor & Francis, 2004), 39–68.
14. Kompare, *Rerun Nation*, 50.
15. Michael Kackman, *Citizen Spy: Television, Espionage, and Cold War Culture* (Minneapolis: University of Minnesota Press, 2005).
16. Sami Dawn Schalk, *Bodyminds Reimagined: (Dis)Ability, Race, and Gender in Black Women's Speculative Fiction* (Durham, N.C.: Duke University Press, 2018).
17. Olivia Johnston Riley, "'A Special, Special Agent': Defamiliarized Disability in *World of Giants*," *JCMS: Journal of Cinema and Media Studies* 64, no. 3 (2025).
18. Maureen Mauk's research in the Faye Emerson collection proved especially generative when the Society of Cinema and Media Studies awarded her the Student Writing Award for her article on Emerson's contributions to political discourse ("Politics Is Everybody's Business"). Olivia Riley published a journal article with her *World of Giants* research, "'A Special, Special Agent.'"

CHAPTER 9

HUGO LJUNGBÄCK

PRESERVING CAMPUS TELEVISION

OR, HOW AN UNDERGRAD FOUND WILLEM DAFOE IN THE ARCHIVE

Like many campuses across the United States, the University of Wisconsin–Milwaukee was once home to a thriving instructional television studio. Between 1969 and 2016, the studio produced thousands of programs for screenings in classrooms, for use by campus offices and service providers, or for broadcast on the campus cable station or local PBS affiliate. Although only a handful of these tapes and productions survive, the extant collection offers a compelling portrait of the university's pedagogical, intellectual, and administrative history. But it also showcases how the priorities and identities of the studio slowly shifted from being an "instructional media laboratory" in the 1970s, to merging into the Division of Information and Media Technologies in the mid-1990s, and finally being subsumed by Integrated Marketing Communications in the early 2010s, leading up to its closure in 2016.

From 2017 to 2020, while I was an undergraduate student at UWM, I was charged with reviewing, digitizing, and preserving the small collection of surviving videotapes—one-inch Type C, three-quarter-inch U-matic, VHS, DVCAM, and MiniDV—a passion project that quickly grew in scale and scope and an undertaking I soon realized I was ill prepared for with no prior experience working in archives, few resources to guide me, and little support at my disposal. In this chapter, I provide a more-or-less chronological narrative of this project, initially dubbed ECTSA—the Educational Communications and Television Services Archive—and the issues I faced and the solutions I managed to implement. My hope is that this chapter can serve as not only a guide to others taking on similar projects—the kind of guide I wish I had had when I started—but also an illustration of the common obstacles encountered in the preservation of "obsolete" media in a no-budget, nonprofessional archival context.

As a case study, the television studio and its history and surviving output serve to illuminate many of the common challenges of television's archivability: the technological obsolescence of recording and playback equipment, the constant migration of older media to newer formats, and the subsequent disappearance of master elements; the poor documentation of the studio's operations and history and the loss of institutional memory and technical knowledge; the perceived usefulness of an analog television studio in, and its struggle to keep up with, a rapidly changing and proliferating digital media landscape; and the perception of educational media's short-term utility rather than long-term value. As this chapter demonstrates, even within the "safe" institutional context of higher education, precarity and questions of value and legitimacy permeate the entire life cycle of the materials.

The chapter begins by offering a brief overview of the television studio's almost fifty-year history, and the development, success, and eventual demise of educational media production on campus. I then narrate my own experience working with the extant collection, "learning on the job," and building support for a new student-run campus media archive. I conclude by offering another brief case study, of the discovery and afterlife of a 1975 Theatre X production featuring Willem Dafoe as a theater student, to tease out how the university's conflicting priorities make the collection's future uncertain.

FIFTY YEARS OF CAMPUS TELEVISION, ALMOST

In the summer of 1966, the UWM Instructional Media Committee (IMC), a group composed of faculty and staff across several campus departments and divisions, delivered a formal proposal to vice chancellor Charles Vevier:

> The UWM center for instructional services is to be a facility designed for the management and distribution of information derived from non-book sources and the use of electronic and m[e]chanical media to serve the faculty in both their [teaching] and research functions.... The facility is to be located in one central building containing a core of equipment and service units surrounded by teaching laboratories.... The use of machines and

equipment will be programmed by the staff of the Center for the UWM community in the most effective and economical way possible.

The ambitious proposal included a request for the space to develop radio, television, and media production facilities along with language and teaching laboratories, a satellite computer center, information retrieval services, audiovisual service facilities, and an "instructional media demonstration laboratory." The estimated necessary budget totaled $8,680,000, and the requested space amounted to 130,300 square feet.[1]

The Instructional Media Committee had been meeting weekly since December 1964, with the aim of developing "language laboratories, computer functions, programmed learning, library services, radio, television, and audiovisual services" to harness the power of emerging media technologies in service of instruction on campus.[2] Led by Chairman Ruane B. Hill, a communications professor who also managed the campus radio station, WUWM, and coedited a 1967 volume on educational television,[3] the committee had been developing support across campus for the formation of an instructional media facility, and from the get-go, instructional television had been high on the list of priorities for the proposed center.

Although with a significantly smaller budget than was sought in their initial request, the Instructional Media Laboratory (IML) was officially founded that fall, and Robert E. Hoye was appointed its first director effective December 1, 1966. Hoye had the requisite background in both education and technology through his work in K–12 education, at IBM and Xerox subsidiaries, and as dean of Champlain College, and he became an important champion of the IML and its television studio during his seven-year tenure.

The first two years of the IML were shaky, as the center was first granted space in the old Kenwood Library building in spring 1967 but had to vacate a year later as the building underwent renovations. They found a new home in Mitchel Hall, but concerns about a permanent space remained unresolved, and as Hoye and his collaborators continued to make plans for the new television studio, one question lingered: where on campus would the television production facility be located?[4]

The television studio was eventually assigned space in the Fine Arts Building, where it was to take over the facilities of the WUWM FM station, which was relocating. In a September 19, 1968, letter to campus deans and directors, Hoye was finally able to announce that "the dream of a television production facility for UWM is now becoming a reality." Gary Olson, a recent communications and radio-television graduate from the University of Illinois at Urbana-Champaign, had been hired on July 1 as coordinator of instructional television, and Earl Lindgren would join the IML on October 1 as chief engineer. The School of Business Administration and the School of Nursing had already submitted proposals for televised course programs and been approved funding, and several other televised instruction initiatives were underway. As Hoye reported: "A complete package of RCA professional broadcast equipment is being installed in the UWM television studios. It is expected to be fully operational by January 1st. At that time UWM's first ITV course—Basic Accounting—will be videotaped for presentation in future semesters. . . . You will have our complete assistance and guidance in the preparation of any projects involving television at UWM."[5]

As Olson would go on to note in one of the studio's first reports, IML's television capabilities received significant interest from faculty across campus before they were even fully operational—it would take until the following summer, 1969, before production finally could commence as the result of a delay in moving WUWM out of the assigned space and in processing capital requisitions.[6] One of those expressions of interest was from a communications professor who wanted to use the studio to help him teach his television production and direction course. This query raised questions about the ultimate purposes of the studio and alternative ways it might be made useful to the campus. As vice chancellor William L. Walters put it to the IML Advisory Committee: "What we need is a policy which balances (1) the need to stimulate and facilitate additional uses of instructional media by our faculty and (2) the realities of the tight budget situation. The first of these dictates against an expensive system of charge-backs; the second against uncontrolled use without concomitant responsibilities for payment of services."[7] These tensions would continue to strain the studio's budget and functionality throughout the next five decades.

At the same time, the School of Nursing was making its own "plans for a major commitment to the use of television," which included designing its new building with media production in mind. "The television-oriented aspect of the building will work in conjunction with the UWM television studios in the Fine Arts Building and will be under the jurisdiction of the Instructional Media Laboratory," Olson reported.[8] Four years later, as anticipated, the School of Nursing's new Frances Cunningham Building included a fully functional, high-band color television production studio in the basement. Concurrent with the final installation of the Cunningham studio in fall 1973, the studio in the Fine Arts Building was also upgraded from a black-and-white production facility to color, and the IML now had two studios at its disposal.

In 1971 IML handed over control of its curriculum library to the UWM Libraries, and its remaining services and departments now included information and course development, computer-assisted instruction, media distribution, instructional graphics production, and instructional television (which in 1975 was split into television services and television engineering). Over the course of the 1970s IML eventually discontinued information and course development as well as media distribution, while rebranding instructional graphics production as visual design services. IML also added both photographic services and a cable department, and in 1978 IML was renamed the Educational Communications Division "to better reflect the wide range of work we perform."[9] Following these organizational changes, the scope of ECD's services and departments would remain more or less the same throughout the next decade.

University records and extant productions leave very little to be known about the studio's output throughout the first decade. Produced primarily on quadruplex, the tapes were large and bulky, and the first to be tossed when space became an issue.[10] The biggest clue is *IML Composite—Sampler of TV Productions*, a twenty-minute U-matic tape from 1976, which highlights some of the studio's greatest accomplishments from the past few years: a forum-style urban planning program with a host, invited guests, and live audience; an educational nursing program about helping patients make informed decisions about their health care; a legal program about handicapped students' rights to education; a puppet play about high-achieving students' mental health and sense of self-worth; a dramatic staging of domestic disputes for police training; an instructional video encouraging Black students to pursue careers in architecture, providing an introduction to early African building techniques and design; and an informational video about services available to foreign students through the Department of International Scholars.

The wide range of productions—all in full color, meaning they were produced between 1973 and 1976—evidence a busy studio schedule and a widespread interest in instructional television from across campus departments and units. They also showcase a sophisticated mix of on-location and in-house shooting, of staged acting, direct camera address, and B-roll, of constructed sets and green screen effects, and of voice-over, on-screen text, and other narrative, pedagogical, and technological devices. Television had finally come of age at UWM.

The early 1980s saw another boom in the television studio's produc-

Still images from four of the productions featured on the *IML Composite* sample reel, including urban planning, nursing, mental health, and architecture programs. Courtesy of the Educational Communications and Television Services Archive.

tion schedule and output—they were busier than they had ever been, partly thanks to a transition from quadruplex and U-matic production to new one-inch Type C machines, which allowed for faster editing. The studio created instructional videos for classroom use and informational videos about campus services, recorded and documented lectures, visiting speakers and artists, and other significant campus events and ceremonies, and produced documentaries both locally and internationally. In partnership with the Center for Latin American and Caribbean Studies, ECD produced several documentaries on location in Nicaragua, including *And Also Teach Them to Read . . .* , *Five Months That Changed a Nation*, and *Nicaragua 1982*, which won a distinguished broadcasting award.

At the same time, both studios were plagued by problems. The Cunningham studio had seen an air-conditioning failure that left heat and humidity issues unchecked for several years, making production conditions

Still image from *Nicaragua 1982*. Courtesy of the Educational Communications and Television Services Archive.

unbearable and equipment unusable during the summer months, until repairs were finally resolved in 1984. The Fine Arts studio also became largely unusable after the Music Department moved in upstairs, making it impossible to record any sound while students practiced their instruments, forcing the studio to frequently cancel or reschedule productions until, it appears, it was finally abandoned in the mid-1980s, fully consolidating all television production in Cunningham for the next thirty years.

In 1994 the Educational Communications Division merged with Information Systems (IS) and the Computer Services Division (CSD) to form Information and Media Technologies (I&MT), "a new division responsible for UWM's effective and efficient use of information and media technologies for teaching and learning," with the goal of "support[ing] communications, computing, and media services for the university."[11] I&MT became the "locus of centralized functions for information technology, networking, media production, telephony[,] and printing,"[12] and instructional television, which had been the pride of the IML and ECD, was more frequently seen as only one small part of a larger media and technology ecosystem, an analog relic in a new digital era.[13]

I&MT eventually became UITS, University Information Technology Services, in 2007, and Television Engineering and Multimedia Technologies (as they were then called) remained under its auspices until 2012. By 2014, Television Services had become part of Integrated Marketing Communications, a subunit of the Division of University Relations and Communications. The television team was responsible for "Video," as opposed to "Field Video," which was the designation for marketing, web, and news production. The move represented another shift in the conception of the utility of television and video on campus, as the studio was now a direct part of the same team responsible for the upkeep of UWM's image. In the fall of 2016 the television studio ceased regular production of academic, instructional, and educational media, and transitioned to only producing marketing and other videos. This is where I entered the picture.

That same fall, as a sophomore at UWM, I was hired as a production assistant for University Communications and Media Relations. UCMR Media Services maintained and operated the TV studio, where it still produced a weekly international affairs program for the local Milwaukee PBS affiliate. *International Focus*, which had been on the air since the early 1980s, was approaching its seven hundredth episode, and I had the chance to work as a production assistant on about ten episodes before my then-supervisor confirmed that the studio would cease production because academic video did not generate any substantial income for the division. My fellow production assistants and I got to take part in the final taping—of an episode titled "China's Water Crisis"—before production of the long-running program moved to Milwaukee Public Television's facilities.[14]

The chief engineer, who had worked at the studio for close to three decades, was laid off a few months before his retirement, and the senior producer promptly gave a four-week notice by the end of the year, never to be heard from again. The remaining engineer on the team became responsible for dismantling and surplussing as much of the equipment as he could before his contract expired in summer 2019, taking the last bit of institutional and technological know-how with him. And in the spring of 2017, whatever was left of our unit was merged into the Integrated Marketing Communications team, and the studio sat mostly dormant, except for the occasional commencement video and virtual campus tour audition.[15] The acronyms become a poignant reflection of the fate of campus television over fifty years: in December 1966 the IMC had succeeded in founding a campus center that would inspire instructional and educational uses of television and emerging media; in December 2016 another IMC had ensured its obsolescence.

MAKING A CASE FOR CAMPUS TELEVISION PRESERVATION

Rather than producing academic video, which is what I had been hired to do, I was now being asked to make and assist with marketing and social media videos. I tried to oblige, but my heart was elsewhere. During my brief tenure in the studio, I had become fascinated precisely by the massive and obsolete video decks and technologies, and with the significant and overlooked histories of media production they represented. Foreseeing the imminent closure of the studio—and the oncoming surplussing of the equipment—I raised some initial questions about what was going to happen to the studio's collection of videotapes. Faced with the dreary prospect of producing marketing videos for the next three years, I instead expressed my interest in being part of any potential effort to digitize the collections, not only because I was fascinated by the materials themselves but because it would give me an opportunity to play with the exciting machines. To my surprise, IMC's video manager was receptive to the idea and put me in charge of the entire project—and I quickly realized I had bitten off more than I could chew.

From May 2017 to May 2020, when I graduated, I was responsible for the preservation, digitization, and safekeeping of the whole videotape collection, which amounted to thousands of items and spanned several different analog and digital formats. I had no prior experience with collection management or digitization processes, nor any training in library and information sciences or archival studies. I did not even really understand how video functioned on a technical level, how the many different videotape and cassette formats had developed over the course of the past sixty years, or how the corresponding recorders, playback machines, time base correctors, and other equipment functioned. I had a lot to learn, and I needed to do so quickly.[16]

Before I could do anything, I needed to take stock of the collection and its contents and, more importantly, develop a goal for the project—what exactly did I hope to accomplish? Following our discussions, IMC's video manager and I arrived at a shared dream: to create a completely digital archive of all productions and programs deemed worth saving—documentaries, educational and informational videos, important visitors and historical campus events, as well as stock footage of campus throughout the decades.[17] The purposes were twofold: not only to keep a record of campus history (especially visual records that could be reused and repurposed in social media videos—more on this later) but also to make collection management and access requests easier to fulfill. Frequently, any given department of the university would ask: "Hey, remember that video we recorded nine years ago? Do you still have a copy?" Rather than sifting through thousands of disorganized videotapes in the media storage room in hopes of finding it, it would be possible to quickly cross-reference the digital archive for a quick yes or no.

A few of the one-inch Type C tapes in the extant collection.
Photo by author.

With this ambitious goal in mind, I tried to assess the collection's holdings, and gauge how much of it we might realistically try to digitize. According to my initial estimates, the collection comprised roughly 50 quadruplex tapes, 700 one-inch tapes, 25 U-matic tapes, 10 Betacam tapes, 250 VHS tapes, 150 MiniDV tapes, and 1,500 DVCAM tapes, for a total of somewhere between 2,500 and 3,000 items. The collection consisted of a mix of master tapes, dubs, work tapes, and raw material, so it was often difficult to determine whether something was a finished program, a first cut, or a second- or third-generation transfer from an older format, since many of the materials originally produced on one- or two-inch tape had already been migrated to U-matic, VHS, or DVCAM. Having concluded my quick assessment, I needed to develop a collection policy to help determine which tapes would ultimately be worth keeping and digitizing, and which should be deaccessioned: with a few exceptions, the general guideline was that finished programs would be kept while raw footage and work tapes would not. There were also very few paper records of the holdings, and the tapes themselves had varying degrees of identifying markers. Some followed a protocol listing titles, dates, clients, producers, and more, while others just had a title, or ambiguous identifying tags like "Racism Tape 1," or, worse, poorly handwritten, undecipherable sticky notes that frequently fell off or were misplaced. There were also those tapes that were mislabeled, or that once were correctly la-

A mystery tape labeled only "Racism Tape I" with no other identifying information. Photo by author.

beled but since had been recycled and rerecorded so that the information was no longer correct.

My original estimate was that roughly 25 percent of the collection would be saved and digitized. By the time I graduated in 2020, I had managed to digitize about 250 tapes and deaccessioned close to 1,500, and my estimate had shifted closer to 15 percent. Partly this was because new boxes of tapes seemed to emerge every other month, as they had been stored in different rooms that were cleaned out one by one, and partly because I did not have as much time at the beginning of the project as I would have liked to thoroughly review, inventory, and familiarize myself with the collection—I had originally been allotted just a year to work on the project and had approached it accordingly, largely skipping over a detailed assessment in favor of getting right to digitizing.

Armed with a rough sense of the collection's holdings, I next had to figure out the technical questions of what types of equipment I would need. Luckily, since the studio had remained more or less fully functional until it closed, I was able to repurpose a lot of its equipment for my digitization purposes: tape decks, time base correctors, monitors, video switchers, cables, and more. Transferring the many VHS, DVCAM, and MiniDV tapes in the collection to digital file formats would be relatively simple—in fact, it was a service the studio had offered up until its closure. I tested a few proprietary video capture cards and compared the results before deciding to stick with the studio's original method, which was also most readily compatible with the extant equipment: I would send the native, highest quality video signal (composite, S-video, or component) from the respective analog tape deck to a DVCAM/MiniDV deck and capture the digital video in Adobe Premiere Pro through FireWire. The resulting DV25 NTSC .mov files would serve as new master files and be quality-checked before being copied onto three separate hard drives in different locations. This process was the most reliable and most easily accommodated based on my skill level and the resources at my disposal, and I could quickly begin digitizing and capturing the U-matic, VHS, and digital tapes in the collection.

The biggest—but most exciting—challenge would be digitizing the significant collection of one-inch Type C tapes in the collection. We had three Ampex one-inch VTRs, but none of them was fully functional, so there was no way to digitize, or even review, the approximately seven hundred one-inch tapes in our collection. The remaining engineer, who had limited experience working the machines, concluded that there was nothing we could do without bringing in an expert repairman to fix the machines—which we did not have any funding for—so I spent a few weeks browsing eBay, trying to find a working machine that could do the job, and ended up investing about $1,900 out of my own pocket to purchase my own Ampex VPR-80 tape deck and TBC-80 time base corrector and installing them in my apartment. After tinkering with the machines over the course of a couple of weeks, mostly not having any real idea what I was doing, trying to search through and make sense of the instruction manuals without much luck, I finally managed to get a stable picture and was able to start reviewing the tapes that summer. The machine had limited operability—the shuttle function that lets you fast-forward and reverse failed twice, and I did not want to risk snapping any other tapes, so I had to review every tape in real time—but I eventually managed to get through about seventy tapes on my machine over the next few months, while still doing regular transfers of other tape formats on campus.

A couple of months later, the engineer emailed me to let me know that he had met for lunch with a retired engineer from the studio's heyday. He had asked him to stop by the studio to take a look at the one-inch VTRs, and in less than two hours he had been able to get one of them almost fully functional. After some initial frustration, my irritation quickly gave way to excitement that we finally had a machine on campus that was able to do the job not only properly but more efficiently, so I could stop

The new digitization setup in the old Cunningham studio control room. Photo by author.

bringing tapes home to my apartment. I was now able to work on all tape formats in the studio and made slow but consistent progress throughout the next year and a half until the machine gave up in early 2020. During this time I was able to review the vast majority of the one-inch collection and complete digitization of about 120 of them, including documentaries about Mayan languages, Native American arts and culture, and spiritist healing in Brazil, concert recordings of famed percussionists Andrew Cyrille and Daniel Ponce, documentation of a stage production of *La Bohème* by UWM students, public service announcements on safe dating, and much more. Roughly one hundred tapes remain to be reviewed and, possibly, digitized, if the machine ever becomes operable again, and if future students are interested in picking up where I left off.

The beginning of 2020 also marked a premature end to the project, as campus closed down and things ground to a halt because of the COVID-19 pandemic. Since I was working alone in the subbasement of the School of Nursing, I was eventually let back onto campus for my last month as a student, but though I continued to volunteer, unpaid, throughout the summer, there was only so much I could do to try to wrap up the project and prepare it for someone else to take over. I had devoted three years to this project—two-thirds of my college career—spending as much time as I was able, which was typically between ten and fifteen hours per week, to ensure that the studio's output would not be forgotten or discarded, as the university's priorities continued to shift. The scope of the project as initially conceived had also changed over the course of the three years, and there was still work left to be done. What would happen now?

Thankfully, concurrently with this project, I had gotten to know students and faculty in the film studies program who shared my interests in media preservation, and together we had revived another forgotten media collection on campus—a 16mm film teaching collection. We had been given an office with the Center for 21st Century Studies, which we quickly outgrew, and we founded a student organization that was put in charge of the film collection's safekeeping. We had spent a year and a half trying to find other campus partners, collaborators, and, most pressingly, additional space to be able to have students work on the collection. In June 2019, while on my way to an art exhibit, a possible solution suddenly struck me—I realized that we could combine the two collections and efforts and turn the studio's defunct control room into an archive, and I was so excited by this idea that I skipped the exhibit, took the bus right back home, and spent the whole night drafting an eight-page proposal. The next week, after a few more edits, I shared it with the IMC video manager and the film studies faculty coordinator, who were both receptive.

The proposal went through many drafts and entailed several meetings, including with the vice chancellor, but in February 2020 the film studies program and University Relations (under which IMC operates) were finally able to sign an agreement for space-sharing, though the pandemic would intervene with our collection-moving plans. In the summer of 2021, once we were finally able to return to campus, the control room was refashioned into an archive and collaborative workspace—an "instructional media (preservation) laboratory," if you will—and the first part of the film collection was transported across campus. Much work is left to be done—to make the new space fully functional, as well as to complete reviewing and digitizing the campus television collection—but I am reassured by the fact that a new group of students have expressed interest in taking these challenges on and ensuring the continued safekeeping of these collections. I hope they will learn, as I did, just how exciting campus television can be, so they can keep advocating for these materials.

WILLEM DAFOE AND THE AFTERLIFE OF CAMPUS TELEVISION

In the fall of 2017, as I was refining the priorities and scope of the collection, I sent the University Archives a sample list of about 130 titles from our collection, along with whatever limited descriptive information and metadata about each tape I had been able to gather. Out of those tapes,

Still image from *Civil Commitment Hearings*. Courtesy of the Educational Communications and Television Services Archive.

they estimated only ten or so had any long-term value, the majority of those being UWM chancellor events, a commencement ceremony, and a George W. Bush campus visit. The rest, they told me, I could "safely discard." Among the tapes on that list were the previously mentioned award-winning documentaries from the 1980s, a wide range of educational programming, and, as I would discover on closer examination, a Theatre X production, *Civil Commitment Hearings*, featuring Willem Dafoe, as a young UWM theater student, in his first screen performance.

Theatre X formed in the late 1960s as an informal workshop for UWM faculty and students, before developing into a professional touring company that performed well-known plays as well as original and improvised work. This 1975 production reenacted Milwaukee County court transcripts from cases in which people who had been deemed potential dangers to themselves were involuntarily committed to psychiatric institutions, and it is perhaps exemplary of the radical, experimental, and political plays Theatre X staged throughout the company's thirty-five years. Shot with a multicamera setup and featuring set design replete with judge's bench, witness stand, jury box, and defendant's and plaintiff's tables, the six actors continually swap their roles as judge, prosecutor, patient, and expert witness as the courtroom drama unfolds. The tape is a rare and exciting document of Theatre X's early work, and one of the only examples surviving in full that showcases the high production standards and level of sophistication the Instructional Media Laboratory was able to reach only two years after transitioning to color production.

When I discovered Willem Dafoe's involvement—on the heels of his third Oscar nomination for *The Florida Project*—IMC suddenly got very interested in the tape, exposing the department's commercial, rather than cultural, historical, or even educational interests in the preservation of these tapes. Dafoe had been a theater student at UWM for about two years, 1973–75, before leaving for New York and embarking on a long and celebrated film career, and the department leaped at the opportunity to capitalize on his Oscar buzz and claim him as an alum—although he never finished his degree—to generate excitement and pride on campus.[18] I was asked to make a short social media video for IMC featuring footage from *Civil Commitment Hearings* as well as a retired theater professor's personal documentation of a play in which Dafoe had performed. The video was published on YouTube at the beginning of 2018, along with the full forty-three-minute *Civil Commitment Hearings*, as well as a two-minute highlight reel.[19] As of September 2024, the full production has received almost 85,000 views, while the highlight reel has accumulated over one million views. A clip from the beginning of the tape, where the actors introduce themselves, was shown during an interview with Dafoe on Conan O'Brien's talk show in November 2019. "Willem Dafoe Pronounced His Name Wrong," as the YouTube video was titled, has been watched over five million times.[20]

As of this writing, this is largely the extent to which the digitized archive has been utilized and made public, and the legacy of my three-year project. Throughout, it has remained trying to prove the archive's value and find institutional support to maintain it. Early conversations with the University Archives made it clear that they did not have the resources to support the project in a substantial way, and they were more interested in leveraging the limited resources they did have to preserve any old marketing videos I might find rather than the educational programming that made up the core of the collection. Similarly, it became evident that IMC approached the project more like the cleanup of a messy media storage room that had been overstuffed for decades than as an attempt to reckon with a five-decade media production legacy, and they were not really interested in turning the archive into a public resource but were rather looking for material they could reuse in new marketing videos: stock footage of campus, campy videos of people with 1980s hairstyles, or a quick insert of a chancellor, president, or Oscar nominee.[21]

I return to my tale of two IMCs and the way they represent the ideals of video communication and emerging media technologies in the university fifty years apart. The Instructional Media Laboratory and its successors were never as well funded as they needed to be, but it is clear from a cursory glance over the list of videos that were produced—with clients and collaborators in every UWM department, shot on location across Wisconsin and sometimes around the world, and reaching hundreds of thousands of students on campus and far beyond—and the quality of the productions that survive that the studio's value was measured in more ways than just financially, and that, when they *were* able to, departments were eager to cough up the necessary funds to use video technology as part of their pedagogical efforts, integrating instructional media in all of its forms into the classroom. It was a media laboratory in the truest sense of the word, and I hope that the archive that remains, featuring full-length documentaries, lectures by prominent speakers, performances by renowned musicians, and documentation of significant campus events, not only represents the wide range of educational and intellectual pursuits of the studio and its collaborators but will someday be reactivated by contemporary scholars' and other viewers' curiosity for these fascinating media productions.

While the tapes themselves should be of interest to wide constituencies within the humanities and beyond, television scholars and those working in the subfield of nontheatrical film and media studies might be particularly interested in the kinds of programming produced by campus television, an area that has received little attention in these fields but is ripe for further exploration. They could also be the loudest champions of these collections and could help raise the profile of instructional television within the media-archival field to ensure that these collections are taken seriously—culturally, historically, and aesthetically—as significant media artifacts worth studying and keeping around. That way, maybe next time, an instructional television archive's survival might not hinge on the blood, sweat, and tears of a passionate but unprepared undergrad. It's time to give these videotapes the attention they deserve.

NOTES   Early versions of this chapter were presented at University Film and Video Association and Association of Moving Image Archivists conferences. I thank the respective audiences for their thoughtful engagement with this material, and for welcoming me to the archival community with warmth and generosity. I also thank the editors for their persistent patience and enthusiasm for this chapter.

1. Letter from UWM Instructional Media Committee to Vice Chancellor Charles Vevier, June 24, 1966, UWM AC 101, box 1, folder 29, University of Wisconsin–Milwaukee Libraries, Archives Department.
2. Faculty Development Plan, attached to memo from O'Myers, November 25, 1968, UWM AC 101, box 1, folder 29.

3. See Allen E. Koenig and Ruane B. Hill, eds., *The Farther Vision: Educational Television Today* (Madison: University of Wisconsin Press, 1967).
4. Letter from Robert E. Hoye to James Robertson (director, Radio-Television at UW Extension), October 31, 1967, UWM AC 101, box 1, folder 29.
5. Memo from Robert E. Hoye to deans and directors, September 19, 1968, UWM AC 101, box 1, folder 29.
6. Report from Gary Olson to Robert E. Hoye, June 9, 1969, UWM AC 101, box 1, folder 30.
7. Memo from William L. Walters to Kenneth Frandsen (chairman, IML Advisory Committee), November 1, 1968, UWM AC 101, box 1, folder 29.
8. Olson to Hoye, June 9, 1969.
9. "ECD MEDIAlogue" newsletter, February 1979, UWM AC 101, box 3, folder 1.
10. Throughout this project, I was frequently told stories of tapes from the studio being thrown in the dumpsters outside of Cunningham Hall when space became scarce in the early 2000s.
11. "The University of Wisconsin–Milwaukee Information and Media Technologies (I&MT) Budget Planning Document, 1995–96," December 16, 1994, UWM AC 192, box 1, folder 2.
12. "Overview of the Office of Information Technology & Division of Information & Media Technologies," July 2004, UWM AC 46, box 200, folder 45.
13. Until its closure, much of the studio remained analog. While the early 2000s saw some movement toward digital production, with the introduction of DVCAM and MiniDV tape decks as well as nonlinear editing on Media-100, the studio continued to use analog cameras, switchers, and character generators as a digital upgrade of the studio was deemed too expensive. One-inch tape was still in use in 2002, and likely later.
14. "China's Water Crisis," International Focus, 2017, https://www.youtube.com/watch?v=XUPfbwG-N-0. *International Focus* continued to be produced at Milwaukee Public Television until spring 2020, when the COVID-19 pandemic "paused" the program indefinitely. The final episode, taped January 28, 2020, focused on the initial responses to the outbreak in Wuhan. "Outbreak in Wuhan," *International Focus*, 2020, https://www.youtube.com/watch?v=tYju6CoZmFQ.
15. The *Wisconsin HIV/AIDS Oral History Project* was the final academic production to be recorded in the Cunningham studio, taped between April 2017 and June 2018, but using IMC's own "field" equipment rather than the studio's cameras. As of 2024, the studio is the new home of IMC's photo team.
16. The project's relative success was in large part thanks to Igor Solunskiy's bemusement with what he perceived as my weird interest in obsolete television equipment. I thank him for offering advice and guidance, and for humoring me about television technology and institutional history.
17. While I conceived of the archive as a publicly available resource, IMC saw its value as primarily for internal use. Our ideas about what was worth saving, as I would soon discover, were also quite different.
18. Willem Dafoe was awarded an honorary doctor of arts degree from UWM in

May 2022. I'd like to think my finding and digitizing that tape had something to do with it.

19. "Willem Dafoe: From UWM Stage to Oscar Nominee," UW-Milwaukee, 2018, https://www.youtube.com/watch?v=cpwCDR1a6M0; "Willem Dafoe in a 1975 Theatre X Production," UW-Milwaukee, 2018, https://www.youtube.com/watch?v=lJRF6YyMD8o; "Willem Dafoe Highlights from a 1975 Theatre X Production at UW-Milwaukee," UW-Milwaukee, 2018, https://www.youtube.com/watch?v=RZqh5lFgSHg.

20. "Willem Dafoe Pronounced His Name Wrong," Team Coco (Conan O'Brien), 2020, https://www.youtube.com/watch?v=vt7hu9RB51Q.

21. The lack of paper records has also made the copyright status of many of the productions uncertain. Without records confirming copyright, publicity, and other rights clearances, any plans to make the videos publicly available will remain on hold.

CHAPTER 10

QUINLAN MILLER

ARCHIVE CAMARADERIE

THE MEDIA ECOLOGY PROJECT'S DIGITAL QUEER FEMINIST CAMP AND ANTI-RACIST TRANS TV POST-POST-PRODUCTION

PRELUDE (TO CAMARADERIE)

Asked to contribute a chapter about personal archives, I pivot to my involvement in the Media Ecology Project, relaying my experience cultivating a linked archive of digital annotations, as well as other responses on the part of some of my students at the University of Oregon, to the online repository currently streaming *In the Life* (PBS, 1992–2012), an idiosyncratic outlier of a television program that is a kind of LGBTQ NPR (National Public Radio). Like other Media Ecology Projects, the one on *In the Life* uses Mediathread, a password-protected database platform for annotation for "tagging" clips. This practice is typically accessed/mobilized in an academic context for ostensibly objective recording of content in the style of an index presumed impartial—as opposed to, for example, in the mode of queer feminist Tumblr, where a plethora of creative and ironic (self-) tagging practices abound.

The Media Ecology Project (MEP), sponsored by Dartmouth College, seeks to jumpstart the preservation efforts at various international archives with outreach, using MediaThread for broader scholarly engagement, connecting preserved video records and access to this annotation software through which those records are routed, which allows scholars and their students to tag the digitized material for better and more transparent retrievability. In this context, the Media Ecology Project on *In the Life* illuminates questions of intersectional feminism and academic activist archive labor, as well as the role of each in long-term projects that assemble through counterpublic (amorphous, ambiguously anonymous, queer) collaboration rather than a more normative consistent, clarified, identity-streamlined form of institutionally sanctioned collective work.

Straight annotation is not enough for queer studies, or for this TV unicorn that debuted at the height of ACT UP outings, quickly jumped the shark, and then persisted as an emblem of nonprofit press relations and one-per-center pink-dollar industrial lobbies, doing good and important work, no doubt, yet leaving much to be desired and demanded, within and without. As this discussion of my teaching details, I allowed but did not encourage the elementary tagging of seemingly self-evident topics. I seeded and awaited and replanted and continued to instigate other lines of inquiry. This came to look like "slow" TV and intermedial studies, with *In the Life* as a heuristic learning tool within the frame of feminist criticism.

Working with a place-based decolonizing framework buttressed by the general University of Oregon acknowledgment of operating on occupied Indigenous land, we imagined, sometimes implemented, and by way of both processes accumulated minoritized historical interventions into liberatory claims about *In the Life*'s role in social progress and change. To do so, we used more "amateur" tagging methods, which we understood not as unprofessional but rather as part of a strategy to construe such tagging alternatives as authoritative first-person self-production at the point of archival contact. Doing the unschooling work of abolition in the years leading up to the momentary mainstreaming of Black Lives Matter, I encouraged the people enrolled in my classes to question institutional authority and standardized instructions with respect to this database and beyond. This framing produced papers with titles including "Paradoxical Feminism" and "Is *In the Life* Racist?" As a result of that process and our findings, which accentuate the need for aversion to the letter and law and procedure and policy of the Media Ecology Project, this essay is an experiment in "bad affect," on display in difficult prose that "channel[s] . . . negativity" in order to "push . . . in another direction."[1]

The chapter airdrops you within the depths of the Media Ecology Project on *In the Life* from my perspective as someone ambivalent, enmeshed, and resistant. Rather than delivering *In the Life* and the Media Ecology Project to you for ease of consumption, I exteriorize and grapple with my disgruntlement. I enlist readers in the project as I have students, principally by relaying a relatively recent Gayatri Spivak concept, affirmative sabotage, a mode of appropriating resources from within dominant institutions in ways "contextually . . . dependent on the agency of subjects."[2] According to the manifesto of the Institute for Affirmative Sabotage, the mode "disturbs and destroys," with "a gentle threat": "We want the (dis)disruption of the status quo. We want lasting change. We work with and against Theater. We work with and against Academia. We work with and against Diversity Politics." My work with students on the Media Ecology Project used affirmative sabotage, along with a series of other concepts, to (re)produce *In the Life* as a trans archive.

FINDING CAMARADERIE IN THE ARCHIVE

I could not deny the archive camaraderie called for and called forth by the Media Ecology Project on *In the Life*, especially because of its emphasis on intergenerational exchange. I am, after all, *in the life*, or at least always aspiring to be; "in the life" is how I live and what I live for, ever since I learned.

The expression "in the life" is about immersive subaltern subcultural experience, criminalized affiliation, primary firsthand encounters with the unique immediacy of a particular lifeworld and its ways of life, usually consistent (even if intermittent) and more generally constant, continual, lived ongoingly, even down low.

In the case of *In the Life*, this framework of being in the life recognizes the significance of how archival, televisual knowledge, like various things in the context of cultural production, "take[s] shape in material and in the process of working it, and no imagination is great enough to know before they are done what they will be like."[3] Alfoldy, writing in the context of art historical and studio art approaches to the discourses and practice of "crafting," elaborates: "Push[ing] against . . . desire for control . . . produc[es] ostensibly uncontrolled, sloppy, raw objects. However, a very careful control underscores this aesthetic. In the hands of the sloppy crafter even, or especially, manipulated mass-produced objects give rise to a form of aesthetic conceptualism that can infiltrate . . . elitist spaces."[4] Alfoldy is concerned here with the elitist spaces of high art, but the arguments resonate with the power dynamics of queer television studies and experiments in legitimacy with the elitism of education even at our nominally public university. As students worked in computer labs and other classrooms, I prized the "sloppy" tagging of "minor" elements and keywords related to fleeting ideas and ephemeral emotional response, for example, or whatever else they could think of beyond subject categories typically cataloged. To follow Alfoldy's argument with respect to this work, sloppy tagging was an option the group as a whole used to "appropriate . . .

cultural consumption," in this case of television, television archiving, and PBS activism, where we could "remake the meanings" of television, archives, and the *In the Life* Media Ecology Project, "while defying cultural expectations and creating conceptually challenging material statements," in our case statements preserved in digital space and collective (interpersonal labor-love-hate) institutional memory.[5]

While it may be the case that thinking of an archive as something personal is perhaps counterintuitive for some, it is crucial to attempt to account for personal archives and their intimate, interpersonal potential.[6] One dimension of this is that I approached the Media Ecology Project's *In the Life* project in the context of and as a continuation of my work in *Camp TV: Trans Gender Queer Sitcom History*—in other words, as part of my experience researching television archives from within my own unique and internally complex queer and trans and LGBTQ+ studies perspective. I question more than celebrate the *In the Life* Project, and this is evident in student work and the database of tags we developed in the digital archive.

In the context of teaching, I presented *In the Life* as a personal archive open to all. It is a personal archive in that it overlaps with my own collections (of VHS tapes, for example) and in that it is an archive I have a personal and interpersonal relationship with (through encounter, memory, self-identification, fandom, anti-fandom, and the time of research). I instructed students to assess whether they too would consider *In the Life* a personal archive of theirs and what that would mean and entail.

I compelled this decentralized network of contributors, disproportionately students working with me, to approach *In the Life* principally by being or becoming more (or realizing they were not, or not yet) "in the life." I emphasized a manner of understanding and of potentially transforming our relationships to the program by which we would work with the sense memory and sensory sentiments within the phrase, where the phrase refers to much more than the show and may oppose the show.

To do so I brought together several collaborating concepts (an excess, from which to pick and choose, to mix and match) perhaps all mediated by a particular blend of off-the-books neuroqueer camp production: "radical schlock," "affirmative sabotage," "pleasure activism," "emergent strategy," "access aesthetics," "sleazy realism," "fearless vulgarity," and "sloppy craft."

Additionally, in terms of re-archiving this series and comprehending and representing the significance of the preservation of it in all its details and excesses, I have been motivated by the tortured disorder of my attempts to narrate my work and the work of my students. As a result, I present this chapter as a "feminist killjoy" involved in the Media Ecology Project, a relentless downer (an admitted if devoted "hater") in a perpetual face-off with the amnesiac buzz of would-be trans-positivity. In other words, it is all about this dis-play and unease, longing for another way and another world with respect to the MEP, *In the Life*, and the institutions involved.

ABOUT *IN THE LIFE*

For the better part of the 1990s, and throughout the 2000s and into the 2010s, people including John Scagliotti, Katherine Linton, Charles Ignacio, Jac Gares, Andre Poulin, Uri Gal-Ed, Carlos Anaya, and Carlos Mayorga produced *In the Life*, an LGBTQ+ comedy–variety–news show, out of a studio on Fifth Avenue in Manhattan. Each season has several episodes, whether four or seven or nine, with six episodes each season from 1996 to 2000 and twelve annually from 2000 to 2012. There are segments on education, discrimination, housing, health care, employment, violence, activism, youth, sports, independent filmmaking, and the arts generally, with a national, regional, state-based, and international scope. The seasons began every October, following a pilot episode that debuted in June 1992. The show was not produced or officially distributed by PBS; it was "produced on a shoestring budget by In the Life Media Inc" and WNYC aired it, with the producers needing to convince individual PBS stations to carry it locally.[7]

Throughout its run, the series never really regularly included trans news coverage. When the program does cover trans topics, especially earlier on, it routinely defers to non-trans doctors or filmmakers for information on trans experience. Yet, approached from the perspective of camp TV, *In the Life* is a trans archive. The show's tagline is "documentary stories from the gay experience," and documentary segments are a hallmark of *In the Life*, as detailed by David R. Coon in *Turning the Page: Storytelling as Activism in Queer Film and Media*.[8] However, this is one of many modes, merely the more easily legitimized and also the most dated. In scholarship, press coverage, and the awards context, hierarchies of legitimacy have trumpeted *In the Life*'s news reporting as if this series were entirely journalistic and positive, when it is more literary, conceptual, and eclectic than its canonizing descriptions suggest—and more heartbreaking for it, sometimes hilariously so. Genre hybridity permeates as a queer factor in the "magazine" format of discontinuous montage; this is camp

TV production akin to that found in the integrated ad breaks of in-show sponsorship during the 1950s network TV era, an early industry period indicative of, decades later, the innovation as well as the market and level of commercialism *In the Life* was denied yet nevertheless typified.

The dominant public news–public service mission framework minoritizes "entertainment." This discourse compounds across, first, the initial (partial) "PBS" (outlet) era of "live" broadcast, as part of the calendar-based television schedule, and, second, the MEP context of database development and outreach decades later, during which the program tethers to the time of academic schedules and contemporary news and TV cycles.

Abiding the industry (television, TV studies) terms, *In the Life* is technically a PBS program. In a similar register, the archiving of the program is technically a part of the Media Ecology Project; predictable double standards render belonging more ambivalent in practice, as for gender and sexual minorities generally. This follows from the cultural politics of *In the Life* doubling as, among other things, YouTube TV, by virtue of being routed through a commercial player in order that we may annotate in Columbia University's Mediathread, another of, again, several compromising partners and parameters in the class projects and classification system history. The space of interaction supported by these data management institutions, as well as infrastructure provided by Dartmouth College, all normalize classification systems of many kinds beyond and above tagging. Camp TV renders and requires the scrambling of these taken-for-granted commonsense categories.

GETTING IN (THE LIFE)

In the Life skews white-centric; it does so in an instructive manner. Its white-normativity is egregious and obvious, requiring at times extra effort to comprehend its crystallization of structural racism while gleaning also that the show is exceptional in being relatively inclusive for white lesbian and gay activist cultural production in its period. The white-centrism is a problem manifest in the very title of the program, which signals cultural appropriation, because the phrase "in the life" was innovated and given life by and mostly in circulation among people of color, queer and trans people especially, including prior to and independent of these terms as hegemonic identity configurations. I feel it is important to say (here, as I did repeatedly in class discussions from multiple meta perspectives), that *In the Life* is not only or even primarily this TV show text.

In the Life is also the 1986 Joseph Beam–edited book *In the Life: A Black Gay Anthology*,[9] an unconnected publication released half a decade prior to the launch of this PBS program.

Keeping that separate publication and other projects like Yvonne Welbon's Sisters in the Life in play as intertexts supports an intersectional approach to the politics of canon formation, the ethics of canon expansion, and the work of revamping TV history.[10] Apart from the TV show, "in the life" is a mixed queer-and-trans-of-color colloquialism ambiguously related to criminalized activity. It has meant "in the family," or "one of us," in a street and same-gender-loving sense within Black vernacular specifically. To be in the life is to participate in marginalized spaces—to be self-identified, or (allow yourself to) be identified by others, as participating in worlds of which still others, outside those worlds, are oblivious. The phrase indicated a person was privy to a particular social scene, generally one in which white norms are not the presumed default. The television show, meanwhile, links the phrase to an investment in people being "out" about their sexual identities. This transformation of the "in the life" idiom is, I argue, the *In the Life* transformation that is most urgent to address. Focusing on this "appropriating Blackness" rather than a shift in the series' first season from comedy to documentary, which currently overshadows most popular discussion of the show, speaks to the need to address *In the Life* as feminist and trans in order to reckon with the structuring white supremacy manifest in the series, the In the Life Media nonprofit, and the institutions currently involved.

While *In the Life* is a public service–oriented series, it is like commercial television of the period, prior, and since in falling so remarkably short of ideals of representational justice. Reeling in politically disparate viewer groups who had varying degrees of experience and tolerance for social diversity cultivated a production context for *In the Life* that resembles the environment within which the makers of situation comedy in the United States worked in the 1950s (and which I elaborate in my book *Camp TV* and stretch here). When people working in television at that time reinvented situation comedy for the system, they distinguished the format from comedy variety, which had a salacious reputation. Both television comedy producers in the 1950s and *In the Life*'s producers in the 1990s oriented the success of their formats around the jettisoning of drag routines and displacement of both overtly and coyly humorous delivery, especially delivered in direct address.

The production teams that created the various segments that constitute the episodes of *In the Life* were working, alongside those who edited and distributed the program, in a camp TV context. Like the camp TV in the 1950s that constitutes network programming, *In the Life* appears to have been sanitized, but queer trans content not only remains but flourishes with standardizing changes. The producers of *In the Life* strategically left out more radical, sexual, and camp content, but content of that kind is still there, surrounding and fully infused within *In the Life*'s widely acclaimed news coverage and its extensive hosted interviews and investigative, sometimes undercover, reports. Camp TV is a critique culled from and within the display of oppression. In the context of *In the Life*, later on appear what had come out of the 1950s network era: forms of assimilation and censorship that create "trans gender queer" representation (a term from *Camp TV* that means both "transgender queer" and "trans gender-queer" and more).

Toying with tagging protocols in the database and exploring student research, I attune my antireverential account to the feminism of *In the Life*. The show's most obvious feminism is a white lesbian feminism indicative of a U.S. mode and historical moment of tokenizing multiculturalism. This feminism and other feminisms, along with their coinciding white supremacy, have so far been sidelined in the written record, if not across popular memory, by *In the Life*'s reputation as a historic lesbian and gay series.

WHICH *IN THE LIFE*?

According to histories as they are currently written, *In the Life* is an anomaly within U.S. LGBT TV in being long-running and thoroughly archived. All episodes are accounted for, apart perhaps from some lost audio on a YouTube transfer or two; the paper collection of the *In the Life* Records at the Arts Library Special Collections appears to be extensive; and there are other collections at UCLA of related people, as Bratslavsky put it while piecing through my process, thereby discerning my commitment and attention to the unarchivable (the lived unlivable) and that it has, in this case, kept me out of the archive.[11] I have not visited (or forgot or didn't have time or skipped it when I went to that campus for *Camp TV* in 2016). There are about two hundred episodes total, each an hour long, and they are complete except for sequences flagged for copyright violation. The missing pieces of trademarked texts and their promotional materials intrude glaringly at times, as one student who took this as their research topic found. I think we brainstormed a supercut of audience reaction shots, because the crowd scenes of in-studio audiences are also prominent and noteworthy. Those were of interest to several students focused on interrelated topics of their own design. *In the Life* is a bit bizarre, highly televisual, and simultaneously an outlier with respect to these elements, missing or not. The show is also representatively anomalous in the context of the common practices of its "network," PBS, the free education station in the United States, which distributed *In the Life* to a subset of its stations but without backing the series financially. Private donors and contributing members funded these episodes, as title cards during the opening credits of each indicate. As documented by the archival items that are part of a portal provided within the UCLA Film and Television Archive Library's online exhibit, initially some stations would schedule the program but not air it, or run it having never announced it, prompting viewers to insist their local stations air episodes that they, in donating to *In the Life*, had paid to produce.[12]

According to the director of the Media Ecology Project, television historian Mark Williams, *In the Life* is a vital piece of queer history, and queer history, as implied by the inclusion of this pilot in the project, is important.[13] Jan-Christopher Horak, a former director of the UCLA archive, attributes to *In the Life* a "unique importance": the series holds a "singular place in LGBTQ history," making "the opportunity to catalog and preserve this material, contextualize it and make it accessible online . . . a privilege."[14] Yet the Media Ecology Project has so far focused more on its many other projects, none of which are treated as LGBTQIA+-specific or flagged from the start as relevant to queer history.

What, then, of the importance of archiving the archivable, and what about our archiving of the-unarchivable-of-the-archiving-moment, the process of encounter, in this classroom and scholarly context?

In the repository of *In the Life*, there are mid-1990s segments with Leslie Feinberg, Kate Bornstein, Shannon Minter, and Riki Anne Wilchins. *In the Life* also features Laverne Cox, Imani Henry, Miss Elizabeth Latex, Venus DeMars, Paisley Currah, Mara Keisling, Janet Mock, and Isis King. Nothing stops there; the program also showcases myriad other trans artists, activists, and icons. Why would any other TV ever be necessary? *In the Life* is, based on these segments, a trans archive. At the same time, this gay and lesbian series overwhelmingly skews cissexist. On top of that, it insults us. For me as a trans professor and for trans students and other students, the transphobia in the text, transmitted to us as usual through school, media, seriousness, moralizing lecturing, and so on, was rough.

Thankfully, as some reprieve, the tension of *In the Life*'s combined white-centrism and its stellar cast list of both luminaries and underappreciated cultural producers of color is an incongruity that can be understood as camp—camp, as in, "fuck you, fuck this system" (a voice from within, a surface expression, a glitching). For example, queer gender, or genderqueer, or nonbinary, or "trans gender queer" dynamics at the level of industry and audience that I detail in *Camp TV* allowed *In the Life* to energize queer-and-trans-of-color cultural production while supporting an ideology of cis white male authority slightly transmogrified. This *In the Life* is an example of white-normative TV canonized through the white-normative narrative of the "pioneeringness" of the series as a serious news program. Apprehending the camp necessitates sidestepping the show's status as a purported landmark "first" for TV conferring dignity—a reputation that emerges through the normative origin story about *In the Life*'s aborted debut as a variety show.

I generated and absorbed this continuity as a counterdiscourse as I obsessed over the question. I recognized the hagiography only in order to reject it, taking on in order to undo, ignoring, not interacting, and orienting otherwise, instead toward fractured, composite perspectives of "archive camaraderie" in accordance with Bratslavsky and Peterson's emphasis here on preservation of process. That taking interwoven strata of camp TV as the backdrop of *In the Life* while producing *In the Life* as a trans archive supports insight-salvaging methods of study, affect as mourning through a queer approach to television history as trans history, supplying a medium for interconnected ways of negotiating the cyclical racisms of dominant media lesbian and gay politics.

Trans people appear in the later years of the series as experts on their own lives, as Coon's study *Turning the Page* compellingly details.[15] The key is to not focus exclusively on those participants or the documentary mode. Those tendencies, which cut across cis and trans and LGBTQ and straight distinctions, reproduce biases toward status quo realism, racialized hypersexuality norms, and a clarity of simplicity in identity construction.

THE MEDIATIONS OF THE MEDIA ECOLOGY PROJECT

The standardized process of logging proper names and obvious topics from *In the Life* episodes for the Media Ecology Project facilitates a reproduction of the status quo, using a largely conservative interface to index a progressive text.

For example, the collection of episodes preserves significant in-studio and on-location work by many artists, activists, and producers of color, such as Ivy Young, Kye Allums, Kevin Cata, Pamela Sneed, Karen Williams, Tanya Barfield, Bobby Rivers, Darius de Haas, Keith Boykin, Paris Barclay, Staceyann Chin, Wendi Moore-O'Neal, and Adrianne Prioleau—to name just a few. But as evident when using the now publicly accessible archive of *In the Life*, not all of these people, as proper names, are locatable for their on-screen appearances. Moreover, people such as these sometimes appear in secondary footage supplied by independent filmmakers, indicating a web of producers of color beyond those given credit, and not always tagged accordingly. What you can still find in the searchable database: a segment on Simon Nkoli is excerpted from Beverley Ditsie's *Simon and I* (episode 1209). And what you can't find: Nickie Charles's "Reliving My Alabama," likewise, is seamlessly integrated into *In the Life* within an intact segment of *Homoteens* (episode 1308). *In the Life*'s incorporation of this material constitutes QTBIPOC-centered critique and could be a vital source of anti-racist intergenerational exchange.

The process of logging names and generating the interface provides an anarchic playground capable perhaps of instigating what la paperson calls the third university, a school of poetics beyond colonization as colonization, that can occur within the dominance of exploitative first and second university systems.[16] In the realm of the third university, annotating *In the Life* might produce, instead of straightforward subject categories, "radical schlock," that is, technology-attuned thought experiments and performance art, such as that rendered in practice and in prose, by collectives such as the Electronic Disturbance Theater and namely by the poet, publisher, and performer Raquel Gutiérrez. Gutiérrez's "Radical Schlock," a "queer media manifesto" that appears among others in a special section of the journal *GLQ*, calls for a sensibility of indulgent disruption since elaborated in *Brown Neon*.[17] It demonstrates tactics for reorganizing the basic terms of perception and value in systems designed to profit off of difference as hierarchy, in the type of adjacent monetization evidenced by *In the Life*'s preservation and professionalizing possibilities, and in microcosm in the question of professionalizing best practices for assigning digital humanities labor to students enrolled in contemporary college courses. The database, a seemingly neutral application, mobilizes standard processes for codifying content. Gutiérrez's Yiddish term "schlock" signals a conflicting value system. Gutiérrez's "radical schlock" suggests ways of reworking seriousness and prestige, such as of the kind characterizing *In the Life*'s success, and thus influencing its perceived suitability for the Media Ecology Project, into camp. Merging Gutiérrez's "radical schlock" with Feil's "fearless vulgarity" and the "sleazy realism" they discuss, and in the context of these other models including "sloppy craft" and "affirmative sabotage," I advocate approaching *In the Life* and its archive (both as manifest principally in the interface of the Media Ecology *In the Life* Project and broadly, on YouTube, at UCLA, and beyond) as an icon with experimental legitimacy; in other words, given the prominence of celebrity, microcelebrities, eponymity, anonymity, euphemism, genre, "queer irony" intricacies, and "trans gender queer" dynamics, I approach *In the Life* and its artists as interrelated texts and a vast composite along the lines of Feil's consideration of Jacqueline Susann.

There is nothing that is actually necessary to do to convert *In the Life* to models of camp excess and counterpublic production. The show innovated in these modes. However, the conventional tagging process would evaporate all evidence. For example, episodes 1208 ("The Fundamental Fight," May 2003) and 1308 ("The Art World," May 2004) showcase a Pamela Sneed performance, a brief monologue about a specific LGBTQIA+ television event. In Sneed's segment, Black and trans and feminist and queer representation coincide, in a queer trans temporality and "trans gender queer" media characterization and performance system. In this segment, part feature, part interlude, Sneed tells audiences about the 1977 debut and development of Billy Crystal's Jodie Dallas character in the ABC series *Soap*—a fascinating figure, including by virtue of being so thoroughly misclassified as cis by television historians. Sneed and the others who produced the piece articulate the satire through several performance elements. Sneed, delivering scripted lines in direct address, treats the copy like an interim snippet or a capsule report, while at the same time the aesthetics are not that of a conventional newsroom. Sneed's vocals and gestures convey both a style of public service announcement and an affect beyond other cited genre forms, that of the comic monologue, the critical review, and the network press release. These aspects of Sneed's performance ground the brilliant askewness of addressing a storyline from the distant TV past as if it were breaking news in the early 2000s.

How should we tag this segment? How should we not tag this segment? Those underserved, undermined, and opposed by dominant systems will sense the importance of not taking tagging or the terms of annotation and classification for granted, will appreciate the centering of self-understanding and self-representation, the call for access, the impossibility of playing by the rules. Among the tags added to the system in the spring of 2017 is a banal but provocative typo, made in an attempt to log a term that I, personally, never would have "allowed," had I had true control. The tag is "gay transvestitie," which we must imagine resulted from my student accidentally putting an extra "i" into the second word, which creates a pseudo-suffix, "-titie," a homophone of "titty." This phrase "gay transvestitie" is an instructive slipup in relation to *In the Life*'s overall white-centrism. It shows the insufficiencies of the default academic apparatus according to which *In the Life* is supposed to be revived for future scholars.

The phrase appears in place of a term, "transvestite," that has come to be disavowed in many trans-centric circles and generally understood as transphobic in the years since Sneed's monologue, although there is pushback and reclamation and continued identification, as extensively explored in the journal *TSQ*. The inadvertent reference to trans-reinvented body taxonomies through the "transvestitie" tag in the context of annotating Sneed's work is significant because of the injustice in there being so disproportionately less documented queer-of-color commentary than there is canonized and archived white queer cultural production. Instead of a faithful transcription of the language in the program (i.e., the cis-centric and trans activist–canceled term), there is absurdly explicit slang, suggestive of "breast" or "chest," in a "bad" trans context. The language dissonance and the whole concept of error in this context points up disparities resulting from racialization, specifically the racism of education systems, the racism of the epistemology of the closet, the racism of transphobia and gender normativity, and the racist appropriation of nonwhite anti-racist knowledge and culture production.[18] No matter how nonsensical this error tag is, it is better, from an ethical standpoint, than "transvestite," the annotation phrase that the participant presumably intended to add. While there are movements to work within existing systems to "correct" terminology in classification systems, such as the Library of Congress, at this point I'm barely interested in that sphere of engagement.[19] By that I mean that in sharing this work from my classes I'm describing an endeavor largely without library resources. I was granted library rooms at times and, at times, University Library–supplied desktop computers with login access for students. It is a long time ago now, though, since I've looked or encouraged students to look for holdings that might return off-putting (triggering, dehumanizing) classifications like transvestism, transgenderism, and homosexuality.

To cut to the chase, transvestitie is a schlock tag linked to Sneed's enunciation of network TV relations for the initial PBS-identified or -affiliated audience. This, my own firsthand experience, rather than gatekept scholarship or "good gay" community virtue signaling, confirms for me the need to reorient the Media Ecology Project from a standard generic non-LGBTQIA+ approach to annotation. The better mis-tag is an inadvertent redaction, an inspired human/machine-generated improvement. This instance of partial "censorship" intrudes on a category that is commonly relied on in dominant discourse in ways that undermine trans-affirming understandings of bodies, identities, presentations, and their various combinations. Of the two terms, "transvestitie" and "transvestite," "transvestitie" would be considered wrong, from a point of view deemed objective. Even though "transvestite" is outgroup-sourced and insulting, it would be considered more correct, meaning more accurate and appropriate, according to the standard Media Ecology Project rhetoric.

My analysis may seem to make too much out of an inconsequential accident. The transvestitie example may seem to chastise the carelessness of a student (a self-identified straight white cis woman, doing work in the database as part of my class, for a grade, who did not expect to care about *In the Life* but became fiercely committed). Trans-centered queer media analysis for intersectional feminism in big data can benefit in seemingly outsized ways from blips and sparks and dug-in heels. What's the connection between the student's experience, their work, their labor, and my use of "transvestitie" here? Their contribution displaces my "Vincent Manicotti," a tag produced by following the rules through literal transcription of comedy lines, and one I took for the title of a paper I gave on this project, as a kind of failed pilot. It also stands in, for me, for another flirtation, a nonce taxonomy too taboo, the deadpan "purse nelly" for "personally" in dialogue attributed by Lily Tomlin to Chita Rivera. How to tag that in a way that displaces the white-centrism of the mediated setting and text? There is an enunciative factor, a performance element, a sphere of affectation, self-creation, and queer authorship, that creates trans culture in linking these *In the Life* moments. Some of the unarchivable of the archive experience can be accessed in this way, through annotation.

THE LIFE OF THIS *IN THE LIFE*

The annotation work on *In the Life* is still relatively uncharted. High-profile people (of color) featured prominently are easy to find and tag straightforwardly for the first time in the database because they appear often, and some episodes have not been annotated at all. Participants can also add the names of those who appear in supporting and other seemingly minor roles within investigative reports and other footage, which entails reading an underside to the uplifting narrative of this *In the Life*.

Tagging can focus on the unnamed, especially in segments perceived as filler as opposed to featured content. We can devote resources to documenting the trans-and-queer-of-color cast, crew, and executive labor. Researchers can link moments from across episodes in order to transmit multiracial histories of nonwhite-centrism within white cis supremacy.

The program's use of hosts and their omniscient voiceover narration telegraphs a belabored inclusivity. The awkwardness of *In the Life*'s flagging of a cutting-edge, progressive veneer and its earnest, activist, documentary agenda combine in a cringeworthiness especially striking in the presentational mode of episode hosts. Given this, centering hosts of color and correspondents of color interrupts the replication of an implicit white norm. Researchers Beau Gaines, Trevor Nau, and Kiana Pontrelli have shown that the patterns of casting, scripting, and performance in the production of the program invested in the white star power of presenters Harvey Fierstein and Katherine Linton, as well as that of Charles Busch, in Busch's many roles, such as the lesbian feminist filmmaker from Santa Cruz.[20] Linton was an executive producer who hosted the most episodes of anyone. So far only the Ford Foundation, a recurring sponsor, surpasses Linton in number of tags.

Comparing Linton's delivery and longevity as a host to Black femme Karen Williams's comic energy and early appearances is instructive with respect to the series' racism-amid-multiculturalism and with regard to the persistence of the camp sensibility and comedy variety mode the show ostensibly abandoned in order to continue production. Its critical acclaim (Emmy nominations and awards from GLAAD and Lambda Legal) and success within big-money respectability politics has hinged on this narrative of a reinvented image. In my reading of the materials online, supplied by the program press relations and the archivists at UCLA, the dominant narrative about the series, beyond its "pioneering" firstness, is that it changed abruptly from cheeky entertainment to sober journalism, following producer Linton's and others' personal appeals for airtime, amid backlash, to individual PBS employees. The use of white authority figures as experts in many profile pieces indicates the context of *In the Life*'s producers' calculated appeal to gatekeepers and imagined viewers with a fragile conformist mindset, who are assumed alienated by gender variance and the decentering of whiteness. In light of this, the final product of completed episodes constitutes a camp space of compromise. Williams's comic persona, also evident in her essay "Cash Flow Makes Me Come" (1995), shines camp survival tactics through *In the Life*, including when she may seem to be doing straightforward newscasting.[21]

Drawing attention to these and other tactics, we attempted to circumvent the whiteness of *In the Life* in order to produce the text differently. Whiteness self-embeds through standardized academic spaces and tools. In this context, tagging can collapse support for entrenched hierarchies at the foundation of the project's infrastructure and archive of programming. Idiosyncratic tagging and "misuse" of the tag field/function can embed intersectional standpoints, with annotations that scramble anti-trans sentiments that attach to and traffic in other normative subject categories. In response to my request for tags so specific to their own perception, personal history, and reception experience that no one else would be able to provide them, students have logged self-representation, word and memory associations, satirical impulses, and feelings ("lost hope," "failed hope," "sadness," "pain," "pain of being trans"). M. Ahler "realized that as a potential feminist heuristic tool, *In the Life* cannot exclude the documentation of emotions without rendering the series as apathetic to its viewerbase and perpetuating heteronormative ideas of queer identity."[22]

In a related case, researcher Andrew Robbins, dissatisfied with the "expert" voices on trans people that the program's producers included, set out "to decenter what can now be interpreted as transphobic."[23] Robbins added previously unused tags including "misgendering" and "transphobia" to the database several times, describing these contributions as acts of aggression against the credibility granted to cis ideas about trans people and against the ways in which that authority is aesthetically conferred. The annotation "misgendering" refers to the effects of the language of *In the Life* interviewees who use "assigned birth names instead of chosen names" when referring to trans icons such as Billy Tipton. In the case of the compendium episode 1610, titled "Gender Revolution," that tag and another Robbins added, "gid not disorder," respond simultaneously to the video content and the existing "GID" tags in the database. Robbins's work represents an attempt to "capture the pathologization embedded in the historical use of the term GID," and "tag this as a violent history" at work in *In the Life* and in the Media Ecology Project, one that made the program's 1998 segment on the 1997 film *Ma Vie en Rose* (in episode 703) and others "painful to watch with trans eyes." The annotation is an implicit statement. It is also a near transcription of the sentence "Gender Identity Is Not a Disorder," which appears on a protest sign in a series of trans activist placards pictured in quick montage. Others read: "Gender Expression Is Not a Disease"; "Stop GID Misuse"; and "STOP GID Misuse ON Children." Such tags elevate trans people within *In the Life*, and they also represent our collaborative work done to expose the extent to which the series, through its narrative frame, grounds rhetoric of human rights as well as the patina of objectivity in white privilege.

In the Life's use of hosts, expert interviews, and voiceover, over the years, conveys investments in a serious tone, the tone Williams transcends by way of demeanor, affect, and inflection. Against this background, Linton's attire, vocal modulations, and comportment in gesture and movement convey a deadpan camp quality. The queer temporality of sober satire, which is presented as the winning approach of the program, indexes compromises and constraints perceived by its producers and their funders in their historical moment. Linton is a chosen token whose gravity of demeanor suggests a functional prop, a crowdsourced puppet doing "white female" martyr shtick dialed back from unacceptable dykeyness. Linton's benevolent affect and "articulate host" persona spotlights the high-concept, "passing" camp aesthetic tied to the series' coerced serious-news mode. How archivable is this satire (loose, broad, underlying, intertextual, minority)? Could we institute a requisite annotation for this type of parody?

Specifying further, Coon explains, "as the form and content of *In the Life* evolved, the program moved away from using performers and artists to tell stories, highlighting instead the actual experiences of real people and using the words of those individuals to tell their own stories."[24] Trans people appear in the latter representative role, but there is also trans content elsewhere, in the seemingly non-trans-related tone dissonance of the blatant white-centrism, which transmits cis limitations, and in those "performers and artists" who are "real [trans] people." Coon refers to mainstream celebrities with the phrase "performers and artists," somewhat as a stand-in, still, for the show's comedy-variety era. Those elements continue throughout the "news" years, as Coon's account documents in explaining that, during its heavily journalistic seasons, the program's producers at times organized episodes by theme but also produced programs that mixed subject matter. As a rule, *In the Life* juxtaposed documentary segments and disparate interstitial content: spoofs, skits, drag, monologues, and cabaret-style spoken word and stand-up (and sit-down barstool) comedy performance. Television historians present *In the Life* straightforwardly as a news show, but the somber white newscaster mode is a joke, a camp scene of dated, inspired hypocrisy doubled back on itself. The feminism, trans and anti-racist, racist and cissexist, is within this camp turn and everywhere, along with the unarchivable, and everything else that haunts our archives.

NOTES

1. Sara Ahmed, *The Feminist Killjoy Handbook: The Radical Potential of Getting in the Way* (New York: Seal Press, 2023), 15. The channeled negativity referenced here includes (1) negativity directed toward trans "killjoys" such as myself in my various institutional contexts as well as (2) our negativity in response to the constrained administration and policing of access to trans representation within institutions.
2. Institut für Affirmative Sabotage, "Manifesto," Institut für Affirmative Sabotage, https://affirmativesabotage.org/en/manifesto/, accessed August 15, 2024.
3. Albers quoted in Sandra Alfoldy, "Doomed to Failure," in *Sloppy Craft: Postdisciplinarity and the Crafts*, ed. Elaine Cheasley Paterson and Susan Surette (London: Bloomsbury Academic, 2015), 81.
4. Alfoldy, 89.
5. Alfoldy, 89. The group to which I refer consisted of me and various students, working on projects independently, occasionally in pairs, in small- and large-group discussions, in class sessions with multiple different classes, sometimes dispersed discontinuously over years.
6. See Jalen Thompson and Quinn Miller, "Inter-Inner-Personal Archives: Pandemic-Induced Introspection and Television Studies (a Dialogue)," *Television and New Media* 25, no. 6 (2024): 609–25.
7. Stephen Tropiano, n.d., "The Time of Our Lives: In the Life—America's LGBT News Magazine," UCLA Film and Television Archive, https://www.cinema.ucla.edu/collections/inthelife/history/time-of-our-lives, accessed January 29, 2021.
8. David R. Coon, *Turning the Page: Storytelling as Activism in Queer Film and Media* (New Brunswick, N.J.: Rutgers University Press, 2018).
9. Joseph Beam, ed., *In the Life: A Black Gay Anthology* (Boston: Alyson, 1986).
10. Yvonne Welbon, "Sisters in the Life," 2023, http://sistersinthelife.com.
11. All programs are now digitized and viewable at https://www.cinema.ucla.edu/collections/inthelife/episodes. For the manuscript collection, see In the Life Records (Collection 2178), UCLA Library Special Collections, Charles E. Young Research Library, UCLA, https://oac.cdlib.org/findaid/ark:/13030/c8x350tk/.
12. Tropiano, "Time of Our Lives."
13. Mark Williams, "Networking Moving Image History: Archives, Scholars, and the Media Ecology Project," in *The Arclight Guidebook to Media History and the Digital Humanities*, ed. Charles R. Acland and Eric Hoyt (Sussex, U.K.: Reframe, 2016), 335–45.
14. Jan-Christopher Horak, "In the Life: Introduction," UCLA Film and Television Archive, https://www.cinema.ucla.edu/collections/inthelife/introduction, accessed January 29, 2021.
15. Coon, *Turning the Page*.
16. la paperson, *A Third University Is Possible* (Minneapolis: University of Minnesota Press, 2017).
17. Raquel Gutiérrez, "Radical Schlock," *GLQ* 19, no. 4 (2013): 572–73.
18. For example, see Adrienne Shaw and Katherine Sender, "Queer Technologies: Affordances, Affect, Ambivalence," *Critical Studies in Media Communication*

33, no. 1 (2016): 1–5; Legacy Russell, *Glitch Feminism: A Manifesto* (New York: Verso, 2020); Marquis Bey, *Cistem Failure: Essays on Blackness and Cisgender* (Durham, N.C.: Duke University Press, 2022).

19. Emily Drabinski, "Queering the Catalog: Queer Theory and the Politics of Correction," *Library Quarterly: Information, Community, Policy* 83, no. 2 (2013): 94–111.
20. Student papers for Feminist Film Criticism, University of Oregon, Eugene: Beau Gaines, "Is *In the Life* Racist?," March 13, 2018; Trevor Nau, "Paradoxical Feminism When Hosting *In the Life*," March 22, 2018; Kiana Pontrelli, "Comedy and Characters in Queer Television and Cinema," March 22, 2018.
21. Karen Williams, "Cash Flow Makes Me Come," in *Out, Loud, and Laughing: A Collection of Gay and Lesbian Humor*, ed. Charles Flowers (New York: Anchor Books, 1995) 191–201.
22. M. Ahler, "Documenting Sentimental Citizenship of *In the Life*," March 19, 2018, Feminist Film Criticism paper.
23. Andrew Robbins, "Archiving Hermeneutic Violence: *In the Life* as a (Trans)Feminist Heuristic," March 19, 2018, Feminist Film Criticism paper.
24. Coon, *Turning the Page*, 56.

CHAPTER 11

ELIZABETH PETERSON

VISIBILITY AND VALUE

A CITATION ANALYSIS OF
TELEVISION ARCHIVE MATERIALS

As we consider the archivability of television and discuss notions of value, one of the underlying assumptions of this book is that television archives are essential to the work of media historians. Yet how much do scholars actually use television archives in their work? What repositories are represented, and how visible are the collections used? The proliferation of online finding aids and aggregators such as ArchiveGrid and World-Cat within the last twenty years has made it easier than ever for scholars to discover primary source collections in libraries, archives, and other cultural heritage organizations. More and more of these institutions provide online collections of digitized primary sources, and free platforms such as YouTube have revolutionized access to historical moving images. Likewise, digitized newspapers and digital collections of historical periodicals have transformed the ability of researchers to access information about media history. One might safely assume that archival materials are well represented in recent television scholarship. But are they? And why does it matter?

To answer these questions, this chapter examines the use of archival materials related to television in media scholarship in ten television, media, and communications studies journals from 2016 to 2021. The data collected in this citation analysis documents the extent to which media scholars use television archives relative to other types of sources, as well as the types of libraries and archival repositories from which scholars accessed materials.[1] While much attention is often devoted to the programs on air as an object of study, this analysis will also note the record types and formats of materials used in television scholarship, a distinction that Lauren Bratslavsky terms the processes and products of television.[2] Based on the study data, the chapter explores characteristics of frequently cited libraries and archival repositories, the capacity in which archival television materials function in media scholarship, and implications for libraries based on the findings.

WHY DO A CITATION ANALYSIS?

The importance of archives to historians and television historians in particular may seem self-evident, but the value of a citation analysis is to test those assumptions. At its most basic, a citation analysis identifies the sources used in research publications, providing "an auditable trail of scholarship" that provides "more reliable evidence beyond anecdotes and gut feelings about what is taking place in scholarship."[3] For example, one recent citation study revealed that in the field of communication studies the use of monographs in journal literature declined over a five-year period compared to references to journal articles.[4] The authors suggest that their findings are concrete evidence of the impact of the "crisis in scholarly publishing," in which academic and commercial publishers have struggled with the expense of producing scholarly monographs in a shrinking marketplace, in turn making it more difficult for authors to find publishers for their work. Another study found that research on representations of women in advertising cited print materials far more than audiovisual materials such as television advertisements, concluding that ease of access to different formats likely determines the objects of study.[5] This information can be especially useful for librarians to inform collection development decisions, and for shaping library services and instruction.

According to Richard Heinzkill, most citation studies analyze scientific literature to answer questions about research impact of particular journals and types of journals such as open access or e-journals, the identification of emerging disciplines and subfields, and the influence and interactions among scientists.[6] Citation studies on the humanities and social sciences can be useful for answering these questions as well, although these disciplines present different challenges. Journals are the main outlet for sharing research in the sciences, so the unit of comparison in these citation studies is largely the same. The humanities and social sciences are much "messier" with their mix of primary and secondary sources, archival records, monographs, and references to nonscholarly materials.[7]

WHAT IS AN ARCHIVE? WHAT IS AN ARCHIVAL RECORD?

Media historiography makes plentiful use of primary sources for original evidence, contemporaneous accounts, and context, as a cursory scan of any journal or monograph dedicated to the discipline will show. In addition to the audiovisual programs themselves, these sources include the trade press, industry reports and data, photographs, television programs, popular print media, interviews, advertising, and government documents, as well as archival records, diaries, correspondence, and so on. Louise M. Benjamin provides a good argument for focusing on the use of archival materials in a citation study centered on television history. Primary sources are the foundation of historical research, she writes, but "original, unpublished materials" such as diaries, letters, unedited audiovisual materials, and photographs are the most important primary sources for their authenticity and evidentiary value within and among sources.[8] Archival materials are in a special class because of their uniqueness and closeness to the individual or organization that created the records, and the evidentiary value that results from that closeness. Archival materials bring us close to the genesis of the many decisions—creative, financial, legal, personal—that reveal the processes of how and why television is produced, promoted, and distributed.

Nonetheless, as I set about designing my citation study, I had to grapple with the question of what we mean by "archival materials." Definitions from professional literature are helpful, but the terms are slippery in their use. Are they only unpublished, original manuscript materials? Must they be located within official archival repositories? For example, Benjamin's framework notably positions corporate and government records—sources often located within archives—below "original manuscript materials" in her hierarchy of primary sources.[9] The Society of American Archivists' "Dictionary of Archives Terminology" places the record creator at the center of its definition of an "archival record" and emphasizes the "enduring value" of the materials because of the information they contain: "Materials created or received by a person, family, or organization, public or private, in the conduct of their affairs that are preserved because of the enduring value contained in the information they contain or as evidence of the functions and responsibilities of their creator."[10]

The entry goes on to note that archival records can be in any format, including paper, audiovisual, or electronic, and collections may include artifacts and books as well. By this definition, an archival record can still be an archival record even if it hasn't been collected by an official repository. While it's become common for scholars to talk about "the archive" as an abstract concept (Jacques Derrida's *Archive Fever* is one well-known example), these discussions often elide the physical and intellectual labor of the human beings charged with building and caring for archives, not to mention the myriad challenges of maintaining the brick-and-mortar buildings where archives reside. Archives don't just happen; they are the outcome of a host of human decisions and actions that eventually result in a piece of historical information being accessible for research (or not). Guy Pessach reinforces this point with his definition of "memory institutions"—a term that includes archival organizations—as "social entities that select, document, contextualize, preserve, index, and thus canonize elements of humanity's culture, historical narratives, individual and collective memories."[11] Archival organizations marshal the human and financial resources to accomplish this work to make scholarly research—the citations—possible.

Therefore, for the purposes of this study, I chose to document sources that reside within archival institutions for several reasons related to the hands-on contributions of archivists, which I explain below. Materials within archival institutions share the following characteristics:

Provenance

Provenance is "a fundamental principle of archives, referring to the individual, family, or organization that created or received the items in a collection. The *principle of provenance* or the *respect des fonds* dictates that records of different origins (provenance) be kept separate to preserve their context."[12] Provenance helps answer questions of why, where, and how records were created, which is critical for situating them within a historical context and relying on them as evidence. Professional archival practice ensures that provenance will be documented and preserved along with the records themselves. Archival records or their digital surrogates located outside of archival institutions are often fragmented from their provenance and the contextual connections to the creator that give them meaning and value as historical evidence.

Access

Access refers to both intellectual and physical access to archival records. Intellectual access indicates that the records exist, explains what they are, and describes how one goes about finding and using them. Intellectual access results from the archival practice of processing—describing, arranging, performing conservation work, and making records discoverable and available for research. Physical access refers to the ways researchers can see and use archival materials, whether in person with the original materials or virtually with digitized surrogates of the originals. Are the materials open to researchers? What are the hours of the repository? What policies and restrictions guide use of the materials? Not all archives are open to the public, but for those that are, researchers can expect both intellectual and physical access to the collections housed there.

Persistence

Archival institutions have caveats—cultural gatekeeping, hegemonic power, legacies of colonialism, heterosexism, and racism—but they are also designed to persist. Yes, archives burn down, or get flooded, but the common mission is to preserve materials in perpetuity. That persistence distinguishes sources in archival repositories from other types of sources. Consider TV clips on YouTube: the platform provides free physical access and some intellectual access through keyword searching and the descriptions provided by the channel owner. However, description varies widely, there are no requirements or standards, and the original item—wherever it resides—may not actually be preserved, because the channel owner can delete the videos at any time without notice. Even a robust database like the historical *New York Times* is licensed through the for-profit vendor ProQuest and requires a library subscription for full access. It's a very shaky foundation for sources used as evidence in historical research.

Along with books, journals, reference tools, and other scholarly materials found in research libraries, archival materials in repositories help support the notion of the "library as laboratory," a popular notion for humanities scholars and librarians alike.[13] If a fundamental principle of academic research is to engage in the scholarly conversation within a discipline and to grow knowledge within that discipline, the products of research must be available to scholars, as well as those sources used to create scholarship, for the purposes of reproducibility to assess the validity of arguments and reported results. These principles hold true in the sciences, social sciences, and humanities alike. This is why we cite our sources, so others can follow our trail of evidence and see if they come to the same or different conclusions. With these criteria of provenance, access, and persistence in mind, I narrowed my study to document citations to archival records held within a named institution or organization. A further explanation of methods follows.

METHODOLOGY

Journal Selection

In a citation study, selection criteria may vary according to the desired scope of the project, which may be shaped by time and resources available. For this project I focus on scholarly journals, since incorporating books and dissertations would be much more ambitious and unwieldy for a single person to do, and impossible to automate the labor of harvesting citations. I selected the journals based on a combination of three criteria. The first criterion is the journal's primary coverage: does it focus on television or is television a dominant topic? With this criterion in mind, I excluded the well-known communications studies journals such as *Journal of Communication* and *Media, Culture and Society* because their scope extends far beyond television, even though I knew I might miss some relevant citations by excluding those titles. A recent article by Francisco Segado-Boj et al. reinforced this decision and recommended several of the journal titles that did find a place on my list for the study. "Even though Communication is the central field for television series studies and is one of the most productive disciplines in this regard, it only comprises less than 20% of the global cites for television . . . while the remaining come from a wide variety of disciplines, some of them very far from traditional audiovisual studies."[14]

Some tools I used to generate the list of titles include the MLA International Bibliography's Directory of Periodicals (which also provides circulation data), research guides created by media studies librarians, advice from media studies colleagues, and the Journal Citation Reports database.[15] The latter tool points to the second selection criterion, which is the importance of the journal within the scholarly community, or its impact factor. I wanted to analyze journals that are well regarded within the scholarly community and that are routinely part of the scholarly conversation. In other words, these are journals that television scholars frequently cite in their own research. The Journal Citation Reports database pulls data from other bibliographic databases to analyze cited references at the journal title level and even at the level of specific articles. Journal titles receive a number rating, or journal citation indicator (JCI), that indicates how often they are cited in research publications over a three-year period. The average JCI is 1, so journals with a JCI of 1.5 have 50 percent more "citation impact" than the average of other journals in their category.

I wanted to create a list of journals that would generate a sufficient

TABLE 11.1

Journal Titles Included in This Study

Title	ISSN	Journal citation indicator
Television and New Media	1552–8316	3.252
Journal of Cinema and Media Studies (formerly Journal of Cinema Studies)	2578–4919	1.10
Critical Studies in Television	1749–6039	1.10
Feminist Media History	2373–7492	0.97
Continuum: Journal of Media and Cultural Studies	1469–3666	0.902
New Review of Film and Television Studies	1740–7923	0.64
Historical Journal of Film, Radio, and Television	1465–3451	0.55
Journal of Popular Television	2046–987X	0.52
Journal of Popular Film and Television	1930–6458	0.33
The Moving Image	1542–4235	0.02

sample size of articles to analyze in order to make something meaningful out of the data. My initial plan to analyze five journals quickly swelled to ten to account for television journals that print historical articles less frequently than others. So even though the *Historical Journal of Film, Radio, and Television* has a relatively low impact factor compared to *Television and New Media*, its primary mission is to publish articles that take a historical approach to the study of the three media in its title, so I couldn't possibly leave it out of the study.

Lastly, I selected the journals based on language—English—which skews the results toward articles about the United States and United Kingdom, although there are many articles in the data set that are from a global perspective.

Table 11.1 is a list of the journals included in this study, along with their journal citation indicator number.

Article Selection

The next level of selection involved the articles themselves. There were just over 2,260 articles in the data set (excluding book reviews and editors' introductions), but I wanted to narrow the list of articles to those most likely to cite archival materials, that is, articles that take a historical approach. I thought this would be much more straightforward than it actually was. What is "historical," after all? A topic about television from fifty years ago? Twenty years ago? Last year? I decided that for the purposes of this study, a "historical approach" would be any article that "looked back" at something within television studies, no matter how near or far that past actually was. Working off that definition, I would select articles that reflected on something from the past, whether a TV show, technology, or government regulation, or topics within media industries broadly defined, such as audience analysis or the globalization of streaming media. Within this framework, an article about how Netflix contributed to the phenomenon of binge-watching television shows would be considered a historical approach even though this is recent history and Netflix and other streaming platforms are still very much part of the current scholarly conversation about new media. Indeed, according to Helen Wheatley, "It is not always clear where historical television research and other television scholarship begins and ends, as most, if not all, studies of television usually contain some historical contextualization on a textual, industrial or sociocultural level."[16]

Even within the broad framework of "historical approach," it is important to acknowledge that there are still multiple ways of "doing history" within film and television studies, as described by Robert C. Allen and Douglas Gomery, David Bordwell, John Corner, and others,[17] and depending on one's research question, original manuscript materials may not be necessary to achieve one's goals. For example, an aesthetic approach that analyzes the look and sound of a television program, or a sociocultural approach that critiques and contextualizes a TV show's representations of race, gender, and sexuality—even if these studies are about programs from the past—most often rely on the program itself as the primary text, and archival sources aren't necessary for the argument. Additionally, amid the apparent abundance of digitized video and documents, one must acknowledge the scarcity of sources in some areas of television studies, and creative historians may still write these histories without access to the original archival sources. A number of articles in the data set analyze television from the last thirty years—*Friends*, *Gilmore Girls*—for which no archives are available as yet, so the authors rely on more accessible trade industry sources or create their own primary documents by conducting oral history interviews with screenwriters, producers, and other key media personnel.[18]

Citation Selection

The full data set of articles amounted to 2,262, and by reading titles and abstracts—and scanning full articles when necessary—I determined that

202 of those took a "historical approach" to a topic. The next step was to scan through the cited references in each of those 202 articles and copy the citations to archival materials and repository information into a spreadsheet. Even with my definitions firmly in mind, within the 9,434 citations I still encountered ambiguities that required further distinctions, and thus I developed a more restrictive criteria for exclusion:

- A citation that seems to indicate an archival record but does not include repository information.[19]
- Government documents that do not indicate an archival repository location, such as records of the U.S. Congress, the census, or annual reports of the BBC. Although these are primary sources that are important to historical media research, unlike other archival materials they are not unique and are often published and widely available in federal depository libraries in the United States, and in academic libraries.
- Industry reports that do not indicate an archival repository location.[20]
- Online media players associated with an archival institution, such as the BBC's iPlayer or UC Berkeley's Media Vault. The issue is instability: some of the URLs provided in citations worked, while others did not.
- Citations to media in the Internet Archive. The Internet Archive does have a mission to provide a digital archive and has proved to be quite stable, but given the crowdsourced nature of the content—including the metadata, which can be scant—and the decontextualized nature of the items (removal from the *fonds* or provenance), I have excluded these citations.

FINDINGS AND DISCUSSION

These data represent a snapshot of one slice of scholarly publishing, so they can provide some illumination about the field but the picture is incomplete. Nevertheless, the data suggest several conclusions about trends in recent scholarship in television and media studies. First, there are not many articles that take a historical approach, even with my generous definition, and there are even fewer that cite archival materials.

Nearly a hundred archival repositories are cited, with 91 percent of them in the United States and England. The BBC's Written Archives Centre in Reading, England, alone accounts for 28 percent of the total citations. This finding confirms Helen Wheatley's assertion about the im-

TABLE 11.2

Number of Journals and Articles Reviewed

Data element	Data value	Percentage of total (%)
Journals reviewed	10	
Journal dates reviewed	2016–21	
Journal issues reviewed	254	
Journal articles reviewed	2,262	
Selected journal articles with a "historical approach"	202	9
Citations reviewed from selected journal articles	9,434	
Number of articles with citations to archival materials	80	3
Number of citations to archival materials	1,044	11
Number of archival repositories cited (a complete list of cited repositories is in the data set)	95	

This table lists the number of journals and articles reviewed; of these, the number of articles that take a "historical approach" to television; of these, the number of articles with citations to archival materials; and of these, the number of citations to archival materials.

pact of this repository on the kinds of television history research that can be done: "the relatively rich archive of institutional documents held at the BBC's Written Archives Center (WAC) has arguably led to an uneven emphasis on this particular national institution and its policies and management structures, within broader histories of the medium."[21] Likewise, Alexander Dhoest recognizes that the preponderance of scholarship on British television is the result of the existence of national and regional archives, the extent of the records they hold, and the relatively easy intellectual and physical access to these materials, a "luxury" that British researchers should see as a privilege compared to "the sorry state (or even absence) of broadcasting archives in other nations." In Spain, for example, "due to strong state control over broadcasting, the lack of (accessible) broadcasting archives in Spain makes historical research all but impossible. While British archives may have their limitations, comparatively they offer a wealth of material."[22]

Table 11.3 cites the geographic representation of archival repositories. Within the United States, the cited repositories represent nineteen

TABLE 11.3
Geographic Representation of Archival Repositories Cited in This Study

United States	489 citations	47 percent
England	456 citations	44 percent
Other countries*	99 citations	9 percent

*These countries include Australia, Croatia, Finland, Germany, Ireland, Northern Ireland, Sweden, and "unknown."

states and twenty-seven different institutions, with a fairly even distribution among those organizations. At the top is the Wisconsin Center for Film and Theater Research (WCFTR), which was cited in six articles. The New York Public Library (NYPL) comes in second with citations in five articles. The U.S. National Archives and Records Administration (across all regions) was cited in four articles. The Library of Congress, the UCLA Film and Television Archive, and the Margaret Herrick Library at the Academy of Motion Picture Arts and Sciences all were cited in three articles apiece. All of the other repositories were each cited in only one or two articles. It's not surprising that WCFTR and NYPL are the most cited, since their respective collections are long-standing, extensive, and very accessible to researchers. It is surprising that the data don't skew more dramatically toward these institutions but instead are spread broadly and in diverse locations.

The number of articles with citations to archival materials sorted out as follows within the different journals. Predictably, the *Historical Journal of Film, Radio, and Television* provided the highest number of articles with citations to archival materials, but it is notable that the other journals included far fewer, particularly since many of the journals in the study publish far more issues per year. *Historical Journal of Film, Radio, and Television* publishes quarterly, while *Television and New Media* publishes eight issues each year and *Continuum: Journal of Media and Cultural Studies* six issues per year. *The Moving Image*, in contrast, publishes only two issues per year.

One might assume that the number of articles that cite archival materials would increase over the time period of the study because of increased discoverability of and access to archival collections. However, the number remained fairly steady, with a peak in 2018, and a decline in 2020–21,

TABLE 11.4

Journals in This Study Containing Articles with Citations to Archival Material

Journal title	Number of articles with citations to archival materials
Historical Journal of Film, Radio, and Television	38
Television and New Media	10
Journal of Cinema and Media Studies [formerly *Cinema Studies*]	6
Journal of Popular Television	6
Feminist Media Histories	5
Critical Studies in Television	5
Journal of Popular Film and Television	4
Continuum: Journal of Media and Cultural Studies	3
The Moving Image	2
New Review of Film and Television Studies	2

perhaps due to the effects of the coronavirus pandemic shutdowns, which made access to physical archives nearly impossible.

AUDIOVISUAL MATERIALS

There are only forty-four citations to audiovisual materials held in repositories, or less than 1 percent of the total number of citations. Most citations of AV items had no source or format information at all, such as "DVD," but just listed details such as the item's program title and airdate. The implication seems to be that scholars and readers may take for granted that the programs are simply accessible somewhere and there is no need to specify where or how one may access them. There were some citations with links to YouTube and the Internet Archive, but I did not document them in the data set per the guidelines I established about materials in archival institutions. The vast majority of the articles in this study did not cite AV media that are accessible only within archives, which suggests that scholars do not have to visit institutions to gain access to the products of TV, a longtime dream of television historians that seems to be coming true, albeit with many gaps and caveats.[23]

TABLE 11.5
Number of Articles Published That Cite Archival Material by Year

Year of publication	Number of articles published that cite archival materials
2016	30
2017	35
2018	43
2019	37
2020	28
2021	29

TYPES OF COLLECTIONS REPRESENTED

Many of the citations are to collections that are clearly *about* television, such as records of screenwriters, producers, and studios. Other citations reference archival materials that are not obviously about television but contain information about television and/or provide context for television histories.

The following are some examples from the data set:

- Records of the United States District Court, Record Group 21, held in the (U.S.) National Archives at Riverside, Perris, California. Jennifer Porst's article about Gene Autry's legal disputes relied heavily on these records.[24]
- Records of the National Organization for Women, held in the Schlesinger Library at Harvard University. M. Alison Kibler used these records extensively in her article about the impact of women's activism on the programming content on television station WGAL in Pennsylvania.[25]
- The Truth About Cuba Committee, Inc., Records, which are part of the Cuban Heritage Collection at the University of Miami Libraries in Coral Gables, Florida. Richard M. Mwakasege-Minaya incorporated these records in his article about the media activism of Cuban exiles in the 1960s and 1970s.[26]
- Ronald Reagan Presidential Library and Museum in Simi Valley, California. Adrian Hänni used a variety of collections and sources from this archive in her article about how the Reagan Administra-

tion leveraged the TV movie *The Day After* (1983) to create a propaganda campaign to promote its own nuclear weapons policies.[27]

- University of Brighton Design Archives, Brighton, England. Deborah Chambers referenced sources in the Council of Industrial Design collection in her article about the role of architects and industrial designers in the design of early television receivers and in popularizing television in Britain from the 1930s to the 1950s.[28]

The range of collections cited in the data set show the potential for new insights about television in sources beyond those tagged as "Television" in a finding aid. "Particularly in television," writes Craig Allen, "new ideas demand the uncovering of historical data that no one else has seen. The objective is to peel back TV's visible effects and processes of production in order to discover less visible historical truths."[29] Television histories may be found not just in the papers of NBC and Rod Serling but in archival sources that document the social, cultural, and political context around television: in government documents that define regulations; in FBI surveillance files; in the records of advertisers; in the meeting minutes of community organizations; and in the photographs of an early telecommunications company.

CONNECTING SCHOLARS TO COLLECTIONS

"Here are the materials, where are the scholars?" asked Milo Ryan in an essay musing on the lack of researcher interest in his institution's remarkable collection of unique CBS radio broadcasts. Ryan wrote in 1970, long before EAD finding aids, digital collections, and streaming video, but he and his colleagues had done all of the standard outreach and publicity available at the time to promote the materials to faculty and students to make them aware of the materials and their research potential. "We're surprised," he wrote, "because we had assumed the scholars would be beating a path to our door. As it is, the trail is scarcely blazed."[30]

The results of this citation study suggest that Ryan's question is still relevant. "Imagine how many more unseen programs exist in archives holding television programs, and how many of them remain unstudied," wrote archivist Margie Compton nearly forty years later. "In order for archives to succeed in their missions, they need the patronage and support of scholars."[31] This citation study does not tell us what topics remain unstudied, but it does suggest how creative scholars can be in finding relevant archival sources in sometimes surprising places. Additionally, we can know how much potential there is within existing archival collections held in publicly accessible institutions. ArchiveGrid and Archives Portal Europe are two of the major databases that aggregate online finding aids and enable research across multiple institutions.[32] ArchiveGrid returns 752 collections worldwide labeled with the topic "Television," and Archives Portal Europe returns 611 collections. The materials in these collections are in a mix of formats that document the products and processes of television—the paper records and the audiovisual records.

Archives are messy. They require more effort to access and use than other research materials. They are not like published books that librarians can purchase with a click from vendors who will ship them "shelf-ready" with spine labels attached and readymade electronic catalog records. Researchers can find them on their own in the catalog and on the shelf, and take them home for months at a time. Books are abundant, with multiple copies in circulation. Archives are unique, often fragile; they require special storage, careful handling, and security measures to keep them safe and intact. They can seem fragmentary and arcane, and they require more research to make sense of them. We can assign Library of Congress subject headings to indicate what they are about, but the items within collections defy tidy classification. It is extremely labor-intensive to describe archival records at the item level, so many of them remain hidden to researchers. And there are gaps, great gaping holes in the historical record from all eras of television. The urgency to collect and preserve television's history remains very urgent, particularly for more recent history and even more particularly for born-digital materials.[33]

Digitization and online access are part of the solution, but they are not the only answer to ensuring greater use of archival materials, even for established institutions. In fact, an overreliance on digital materials—especially free ones outside of established institutions—runs the risk of skewing our sense of television history toward a particular, narrow version. Nelson and Cooke emphasize this point: "Much remains to be done by archivists and other researchers to ensure that the cultural memories mobilized by television are not unduly selective. Amidst understandable excitement about the possibilities of digital technologies, care is needed to avoid distortions simply because significant materials remain undiscovered or because access to such materials as may be readily available online eclipses fuller, more scholarly accounts based on cross-referencing a range of sources."[34]

The precarity of the digital is a fact that scholars must confront as they conduct their research, document their sources, and contribute to the scholarly conversation and the building of new knowledge. Persistent access to sources should be a goal, not something we just hope for or shrug off as inevitable as the internet shifts and changes. "The very fragility of digital data and Internet sites, the fact that digital content is so prone to disappearance and loss, means that no Internet archive should be regarded as a structure that will last into perpetuity. Most, if not all, digital archives that currently exist will not survive into the next century," argues Abigail De Kosnik.[35] This is not the time for complacency born of technological utopianism or the illusion of abundance. Scholars should not assume that television history—in all its forms—will be preserved and accessible when they need it. Scholars and archivists should partner to share their expertise in identifying donors with materials and collections in need of preservation. Television as an ephemeral medium is a long-accepted idea, but television's archival traces do not have to be.

NOTES

1. The data set for this citation study is available in the University of Oregon's institutional repository, Scholars' Bank: https://scholarsbank.uoregon.edu/xmlui/handle/1794/27964.
2. Lauren Michelle Bratslavsky, "From Ephemeral to Legitimate: An Inquiry into Television's Material Traces in Archival Spaces, 1950s–1970s" (PhD diss., University of Oregon, 2013).
3. John Laurence Kelland and Arthur P. Young, "Citation Patterns and Library Use," in *Encyclopedia of Library and Information Science*, vol. 61, ed. Allen Kent (New York: Marcel Dekker, 1998), 62; Richard Heinzkill, "References in Scholarly English and American Literary Journals Thirty Years Later: A Citation Study," *College and Research Libraries* 68, no. 2 (2007): 141–53.
4. Karen Chapman and Steven D. Yates, "The Impact of the Monographs Crisis on the Field of Communication," *Journal of Academic Librarianship* 43, no. 3 (2017): 163–69.
5. Marian Navarro-Beltrá and Marta Martín-Llaguno, "Bibliometric Analysis of Research on Women and Advertising: Differences in Print and Audiovisual Media," *Comunicar* 41 (2013): 105–14.
6. Heinzkill, "References in Scholarly English."
7. Diana M. Hicks, "The Four Literatures of Social Science," in *Handbook of Quantitative Science and Technology Research*, ed. Henk Moed, Wolfgang Glänzel, and Ulrich Schmoch (Dordrecht: Kluwer Academic, 2004), 473–96.
8. Louise M. Benjamin, "Historical Evidence: Facts, Proof and Probability," in *Methods of Historical Analysis in Electronic Media*, ed. Donald G. Godfrey (Mahwah, N.J.: Lawrence Erlbaum, 2006), 25–46.
9. Benjamin, "Historical Evidence."

10. Society of American Archivists, *Dictionary of Archives Terminology* (2005–23), https://dictionary.archivists.org/, accessed December 12, 2022.
11. Guy Pessach, "[Networked] Memory Institutions: Social Remembering, Privatization, and Its Discontents," *Cardozo Arts and Entertainment Law Journal* 26, no. 1 (2008): 71–149.
12. Society of American Archivists, *Dictionary of Archives Terminology*.
13. Carolyn E. Lipscomb, "The Library as Laboratory," *Bulletin of the Medical Library Association* 89, no. 1 (2001): 79–80.
14. Francisco Segado-Boj, Juan Martín Quevedo, and Erika Fernández-Gómez, "Research on Television Series: A Bibliometric Analysis," *Serials Librarian* 81, nos. 3–4 (2022): 265–81.
15. Clarivate, *Journal Citation Reports* (2023), http://jcr.clarivate.com, accessed December 15, 2022.
16. Helen Wheatley, *Re-viewing Television History: Critical Issues in Television Historiography* (London: I. B. Tauris, 2007), 2.
17. Robert C. Allen and Douglas Gomery, *Film History: Theory and Practice* (New York: Knopf, 1985); David Bordwell, "Doing Film History," *David Bordwell's Website on Cinema* (2008), http://www.davidbordwell.net/essays/doing.php, accessed December 22, 2022; John Corner, "Finding Data, Reading Patterns, Telling Stories: Issues in the Historiography of Television," *Media, Culture and Society* 25, no. 2 (2003): 273–80.
18. Some examples of "history without archives" include Jean K. Chalaby, "Drama without Drama: The Late Rise of Scripted TV Formats," *Television and New Media* 17, no. 1 (2016): 3–20; Ben Dibley and Gay Hawkins, "Making Animals Public: Early Wildlife Television and the Emergence of Environmental Nationalism on the ABC," *Continuum: Journal of Media and Cultural Studies* 33, no. 6 (2019): 744–58; Hannah Hamad, "The One with the Feminist Critique: Revisiting Millennial Postfeminism with *Friends*," *Television and New Media* 19, no. 8 (2018): 692–707; Ryan Lizardi, "Mourning and Melancholia: Conflicting Approaches to Reviving *Gilmore Girls* One Season at a Time," *Television and New Media* 19, no. 4 (2018): 379–95; Travis Vogan, "*Monday Night Football* and the Racial *Roots* of the Network TV Event," *Television and New Media* 18, no. 3 (2017): 235–51.
19. The following are some examples of ambiguous citations that seem to indicate an archival record but do not include repository information. The citations are formatted as they appeared in the original publications followed by a citation to the article in which they appeared: Sense of Place (1978) BBC2. BBC NorthWest (cited in Billy Smart, "Television History: Archives, Excavation and the Future," *Critical Studies in Television* 11, no. 1 [2016]: 96–109); Bielby, William, and Denise Bielby. 1998. *The 1998 Hollywood Writers' Report: Telling ALL Our Stories*. Los Angeles: Writers Guild of America (cited in Josh Heuman, "What Happens in the Writers' Room Stays in the Writers' Room? Professional Authority in *Lyle v. Warner Bros*," *Television and New Media* 17, no. 3 [2016]: 195–211); America for Me (1953) Production Co: Jerry Fairbanks Productions. Sponsor:

Greyhound Lines (cited in Kit Hughes, "Disposable: Useful Cinema on Early Television," *Critical Studies in Television* 12, no. 2 [2017]: 102–20); Mackenzie, P. (2011) (unpublished), "Proposal to MG ALBA," Glasgow: STV Productions (cited in Paul Tucker et al., "Scheduling for Christmas: How an 'Ordinary' Piece of Television Became Extraordinary," *Journal of Popular Television* 5, no. 1 [2017]: 31–48); Commission nationale de la communication et des libertés (1987) Note terminologique. 31 December (cited in Ana Vinuela, "Television Documentary Production in France: Policy Interventions and the Assessment of Quality," *Critical Studies in Television* 13, no. 2 [2018]: 227–43).

20. The following are examples of citations to media industry reports that do not indicate an archival repository location. The citations are formatted as they appeared in the original publications followed by a citation to the article in which they appeared: FRAPA. 2009. *The FRAPA Report 2009: TV Formats to the World*. Cologne: FRAPA (Format Recognition and Protection Association) (cited in Jean K. Chalaby, "Drama without Drama: The Late Rise of Scripted TV Formats," *Television and New Media* 17, no. 1 (2016): 3–20); BBC Trust, MTM London. 2011. "The BBC's Processes for the Management of Sports Rights." Review by MTM London Ltd. Presented to the BBC Trust's Finance and Compliance Committee, 13th January 2011. London: BBC Trust (cited in Phil Ramsey, "Commercial Public Service Broadcasting in the United Kingdom: Public Service Television, Regulation, and the Market," *Television and New Media* 18, no. 7 (2017): 639–54); ITV. 2012. "Delivering Growth through Transformation." ITV plc Annual Report and Accounts for the Year Ended 31 December 2012. London: ITV (cited in Ramsey, "Commercial Public Service Broadcasting in the United Kingdom"); Conseil supérieur de l'audiovisuel (2016) Étude sur le tissu économique du secteur de la production audiovisuelle. Paris: Direction des études, des affaires économiques et de la perspective, January (cited in Vinuela, "Television Documentary Production in France").

21. Wheatley, *Re-viewing Television History*, 9.

22. Alexander Dhoest, "Breaking Boundaries in Television Historiography: Historical Research and the Television Archive, University of Reading, 9 January 2004," *Screen* 45, no. 3 (2004): 245–49.

23. Sonja de Leeuw, "European Television History Online: History and Challenges," *VIEW Journal of European Television History and Culture* 1, no. 1 (2012): 3–11; Julia Noordegraaf, "Who Knows Television? Online Access and the Gatekeepers of Knowledge," *Critical Studies in Television* 5, no. 2 (2010): 1–19; Helle Strandgaard Jensen, "Doing Media History in a Digital Age: Change and Continuity in Historiographical Practices," *Media, Culture and Society* 38, no. 1 (2016): 119–28; Kathleen Collins, "The Trouble with Archie: Locating and Accessing Primary Sources for the Study of the 1970s U.S. Sitcom, All in the Family," *Critical Studies in Television* 5, no. 2 (2010): 118–32.

24. Jennifer Porst, "Roy Rogers and Gene Autry Do Not Endorse This Project: Actors, Advertising, and Feature Films on Early Television," *Television and New Media* 22, no. 4 (2021): 420–39.

25. M. Alison Kibler, "'Feminists for Media Rights': A Case Study in Television Activism," *Historical Journal of Film, Radio and Television* 40, no. 1 (2020): 210–31.
26. Richard M. Mwakasege-Minaya, "Cold War Bedfellows: Cuban Exiles, U.S. Conservatives, and Media Activism in the 1960s and 1970s," *Historical Journal of Film, Radio and Television* 41, no. 1 (2021): 114–35.
27. Adrian Hänni, "A Chance for a Propaganda Coup? The Reagan Administration and *The Day After* (1983)," *Historical Journal of Film, Radio and Television* 36, no. 3 (2016): 415–35.
28. Deborah Chambers, "Designing Early Television for the Ideal Home: The Roles of Industrial Designers and Exhibitions, 1930s–50s," *Journal of Popular Television* 7, no. 2 (2019): 145–59.
29. Craig Allen, "Television Broadcast Records," in Godfrey, *Methods of Historical Analysis*, 207–31.
30. Milo Ryan, "Here Are the Materials, Where Are the Scholars?" *Journal—Association for Recorded Sound Collections* 2, nos. 2–3 (1970).
31. Margie Compton, "The Archivist, the Scholar, and Access to Historic Television Materials," *Cinema Journal* 46, no. 3 (2007): 129–33.
32. ArchiveGrid, https://researchworks.oclc.org/archivegrid/; Archives Portal Europe, https://www.archivesportaleurope.net/.
33. See Nan Rubin, "Preserving Digital Public Television: Not Just an Archive, but a New Attitude to Preserve Public Broadcasting," *Library Trends* 57, no. 3 (2009): 393–412; J. P. Kelly, "'This Title Is No Longer Available': Preserving Television in the Streaming Age," *Television and New Media* 23, no. 1 (2022): 3–21.
34. Robin Nelson and Lez Cooke, "Editorial: Television Archives: Accessing History," *Critical Studies in Television* 5, no. 2 (2010): xvii–xix.
35. Abigail De Kosnik, *Rogue Archives: Digital Cultural Memory and Media Fandom* (Cambridge, Mass.: MIT Press, 2016), 7.

CONTRIBUTORS

RUTA ABOLINS is director of the Walter J. Brown Media Archives and Peabody Awards Collection at the University of Georgia Libraries. She has worked in moving image archives for more than thirty years. She currently manages a collection of more than 350,000 analog audiovisual items and more than 200,000 digital files with collections ranging from home movies and local news to the Peabody Awards Collection. She has written and presented on the importance of local news content and the licensing of archival content for documentary use to help support archives.

LAUREN BRATSLAVSKY is an associate professor at Illinois State University, where she teaches media criticism, broadcast history, and visual communication. The work in this volume originates from her dissertation, which won the Broadcast Education Association's Harwood Outstanding Dissertation Award in 2014. Her archives-related research has been published in *American Journalism*, the *Moving Image*, *Film and History*, and the inaugural issue of the *Journal of 20th Century Media History*. Her other research falls broadly under cultural studies and media ecology, with interest in critical analyses about contemporary television as well as online infrastructures and political communication.

LYNNE CARMICHAEL has a doctorate from Monash University (Australia)'s School of Media, Film, and Journalism, focusing on a cultural history of the Australian Broadcasting Commission/Corporation (ABC) in the twentieth century, specifically the national public service broadcaster's contribution to the Australian classical music "art world." This work arises from her forty years' experience as a librarian—including more than twenty-five years in ABC libraries and archives. Over a decade as the music collections coordinator for the ABC, the author created a data set of some forty thousand recordings from a wide range of archival sources.

KATE CRONIN has a master's degree in film and media preservation from the University of Rochester and a PhD in media studies from the University of Texas at Austin. Her research focuses on the labor and practices of information professionals within the U.S. film and television industries.

CAROLINE FRICK is an associate professor in the Department of Radio-TV-Film at the University of Texas at Austin and founded the award-winning organization the Texas Archive of the Moving Image. Dr. Frick has worked in film preservation at Warner Bros., the Library of Congress, and the National Archives in Washington, D.C., and programmed cable for AMC networks. Her book, *Saving Cinema: The Politics of Preservation* (2010), was published by Oxford University Press. Dr. Frick currently serves as the cochair for the Association of Moving Image Archivists' national task force for the preservation of U.S. local television materials.

OWEN GOTTLIEB is Associate Professor of Interactive Games and Media at the Rochester Institute of Technology and the founder and director of the Interaction, Media, and Learning Lab at RIT. His research traverses the learning sciences, media studies, and interactive design. His latest project on instructional design history focuses on American and Canadian instructional television during the late Cold War, its aesthetic and historical importance, and its implications for contemporary instructional design.

ERIC HOYT is the Kahl Family Professor of Media Production in the Department of Communication Arts at the University of Wisconsin–Madison. He is the director of the Wisconsin Center for Film and Theater Research and Media History Digital Library. His books include *Hollywood Vault: Film Libraries before Home Video* (2014) and *Ink-Stained Hollywood: The Triumph of American Cinema's Trade Press* (2022), as well as the coedited anthologies *The Arclight Guidebook to Media History and the Digital Humanities* (2016), *Saving New Sounds: Podcast Preservation and Historiography* (2021), and *Global Movie Magazine Networks* (2025).

MARY HUELSBECK has been the assistant director of the Wisconsin Center for Film and Theater Research at the University of Wisconsin–Madison since March 2012. She has more than twenty-five years of experience managing film, videotape, audio, photograph, manuscript, and three-dimensional object collections in museums, libraries, and archives. She is a longtime member of the Association of Moving Image Archivists.

PAULINE LAMPERT is completing her dissertation in film studies at the University of Wisconsin–Madison. Her research focuses on political activism, independent filmmaking, and labor practices among actors in the postwar era. In addition to her scholarship, she has served as a production assistant for the Wisconsin Center for Film and Theater Research, processing new material for the archive.

HUGO LJUNGBÄCK is a filmmaker, archivist, and scholar whose work examines the intersections of experimental film and video, media archaeology, and archival studies. His research has appeared in *Found Footage Magazine*, *Cinema & Cie*, and *Media, War & Conflict*, and his films have screened at festivals, art galleries, and museums internationally. He is a PhD candidate in cinema and media studies at the University of Chicago.

MAUREEN MAUK is a visiting research fellow at York University's Institute for Research on Digital Literacies and serves as the senior standards and practices analyst at Sony Crunchyroll. Her research focuses on the intertwined relationship between parents, policy, and industry as it relates to television history and the current platformized media landscape. She carries a decade of experience serving in Los Angeles as a television standards and practices executive both with FOX Broadcasting and Mattel. Her research has been published with MIT Press and several journals, including the *Journal of Cinema and Media Studies*, *Learning, Media and Technology*, and the *Spectator*.

QUINLAN MILLER is an associate professor in English at the University of Oregon. He is the author of *Camp TV: Trans Gender Queer Sitcom History* (2019) and the coauthor, with Marty Fink, of "Trans Media Moments: Tumblr, 2011–2013" (*Television and New Media*, 2014), as well as the coauthor, with Jalen Thompson, of "Inter-Inner-Personal Archives: Pandemic-Induced Introspection and Television Studies (A Dialogue)" (*Television and New Media*, 2024).

ELIZABETH PETERSON is a digital collections librarian at the University of Oregon, with prior roles as the curator of moving images and as subject specialist librarian for cinema studies. She received her MLIS from San Jose State University, and her master's in English/film studies from the University of Oregon. She has published articles on Oregon film history and archival film in the *Moving Image*, *Film History*, *Oregon Historical Quarterly*, and *Iluminace*. She is cofounder and editor of the Oregon Theater Project, a digital project documenting the early history of Oregon movie theaters. She is the author of *Tribal Libraries in the United States: A Directory of American Indian and Alaska Native Facilities* (2007).

WALTER PODRAZIK is a television historian, analyst, and media planner. He is an adjunct lecturer at the University of Illinois at Chicago, where he teaches about television history and the intersection of mass media and politics. Prominent roles include serving as a member on the Library of American

Broadcasting Foundation's board of directors, a TV curator at the Museum of Broadcast Communications in Chicago, and an on-camera expert in the CNN *Decades* miniseries. He is the coauthor of ten books, including *Watching TV: American Television Season by Season.*

OLIVIA JOHNSTON RILEY is completing their dissertation in media and cultural studies at the University of Wisconsin–Madison. They study disability and queerness in speculative media, as well as how fans of these media take up, interpret, and transform these texts. They have been published in *Participations* and *Transformative Works and Cultures* and have an article on Ziv TV's *World of Giants* forthcoming from the *Journal of Cinema and Media Studies.*

AMANDA SMITH is the head film archivist at the Wisconsin Center for Film and Theater Research. She is an instructor for graduate students in the archives track at the UW-Madison Information School. Previously, Smith was the cinematic arts cataloger at the HMH Foundation Moving Image Archive, part of the USC School of Cinematic Arts. She holds a master's degree in moving image archive studies from UCLA and a bachelor's in geology from Colby College.

HANNAH SPAULDING is a lecturer in digital screen studies at the University of Liverpool. Her work examines the relationship between technology, domesticity, and surveillance with a focus on television. She has a PhD in screen cultures from Northwestern University and has been published in *Screen, JCMS, Television and New Media,* and the *Journal of Sonic Studies.* Her current project traces a history of "useful television" in the American home.

MATT ST. JOHN is a manuscript archivist at the Wisconsin Center for Film and Theater Research and earned his PhD in film at the University of Wisconsin–Madison. His research focuses on film and media circulation, with specific interests in film festivals, documentary media, and educational and public media.

LESLEY STEVENSON is a PhD candidate in media and cultural studies at the University of Wisconsin–Madison. She received her master's from UW and her bachelor's in film, television, and theater and American studies from Notre Dame. She has served as a communications project assistant for the Media History Digital Library and Wisconsin Center for Film and Theater Research since 2019. Her research explores the intersections of identity, power, and labor in the media and entertainment industries, particularly at the early career level.

INDEX

Page numbers in italics refer to tables and images.

ABC (American Broadcasting Company), 52, 105, 109n43, 150, 233
ABC (Australian Broadcasting Commission/Corporation), 19, 167–68; archives, 171–73; musical recordings, 177, 179n15; NAA collaboration, 173–74; organizational structure, 169–71, 178n2; televised ballet, 174–76, 177–78
Abolins, Ruta, 19
Academy of Television Arts and Sciences. *See* National Academy of Television Arts and Sciences
access to archives, 150–52; to audiovisual materials, 252; BFI search function for, 146n35; copyright and, 197, 199; COVID-19 restrictions and, 154–55, 156–57; intellectual and physical, 244–45; to MACE's collection, 130–31, 139–43, 146n30; MBC exhibits and, 158; open access, 174, 199–201, 242; paywalls versus free, 148–49; to Peabody Awards Collection, 119, 121, 123–25; public restrictions, 72, 74–75, 76, 79; to regional media archives, 134, 250; for researchers, 166–67, 174, 178, 196, 244, 250; in Spain, 250; television scholarship and, 241–42, 254–55; to WCFTR's collections, 199–201. *See also* online databases
Adams, Edie, 17

administrative research, 92–94, 96, 101, 105
advertising, 42, 242; for access to news stock footage, 36, 37–38; Pepsi-Cola, 189
affirmative sabotage, 223–24, 225, 233
Agee, Warren, 116
Agency for Instructional Technology (AIT), 59–60, 84n33; Cohen's proposal to NPBA, 63–68; collection at Moving Image Archive, 72–76, 78, 79, 84n41; institutional evolution and programs, 60–63, 84n33; public broadcasting and, 68–69, 77
Alfoldy, Sandra, 224
Allen, Craig, 254
Alley, Paul, 33
Allman, John, 78
American Archives of Public Broadcasting (AAPB), 75, 85nn42–43, 125
American Heritage Center, University of Wyoming, 14, 23n25
American Television and Radio Archive, 90
Ampex Corporation, 3, 214
annotation. *See* tagging
archivability: common challenges of, 204; four dimensions to, 166, 174; selection process, 168–69, 171–73, 177; term usage, 3–4
archival materials: characteristics of, 241, 243–45; citation analysis on, 247–49, 249–52, *251*, *252*, *253*; journals as, 246–47, *247*, *250*

archival record, definition, 243–45, 249, 255
archival space, 2–3, 4, 5, 6, 17; climate control and, 116, 117, 124, 171; for film, 12–13; formation of new, 97–98; operational demands and costs of, 99; repositories by geographic representation, 250–51, *251*; resource limitations and, 70, 72, 76, 80, 96, 169; storage space and, 122, 126, 218, 255
archival theory, 6, 10–11; Jenkinson and Schellenberg's, 7–9
archival turn, 7, 11, 87, 88, 106n9
archive, the: term usage, x–xi, xiii, 7–8, 10, 121, 244; traces on, 88
Archive 81 (2021), xi–xii
ArchiveGrid, 241, 255
Archives of Ontario, 80, 81n2
Archives Portal Europe, 255
archivists: fans and collectors as, 20–21; film and video, xi, 12–13; international community of, 90; for Peabody Awards Collection, 116, 119, 122–24; of popular culture materials, 12, 13–14; professionalization of, 7–8, 12, 67, 88; regional media, 135; role and attitudes, 10, 11, 23n25, 74, 79, 255–56
Associated-Rediffusion Television, 144n11
Association of Moving Image Archivists (AMIA), 79, 119
ATV (Associated Television), 136–37, 139, 142, 145n20, 146n27
audiences, 5, 20, 194; Australian, 175, 176; British, 131, 134, 135, 138, 139, 142; home recording and, 151; in-studio, 229; news, 38, 40, 41, 43, 54–55; online viewing, 140, 148–49, 158, 159–60, 161
audiovisual content, 56n3, 91, 93, 166, 242; citations to, 252; collection and curation in broadcasting, 168–69, 178; Peabody Awards Collection of, 117–18, 119–20, 121–27. *See also* playback
Australia: composers and performers, 176–77, 180n24, 180n26; geography, 170–71, 179nn5–6; national archives, 173–74, 178, 180n26. *See also* ABC (Australian Broadcasting Commission/Corporation)

Balio, Tino, 185, 201n1
Ball, Lucille, 15
ballets, 168, 174–76, 177–78, 180n24
BBC (British Broadcasting Corporation), 47, 130, 134, 145n15, 157, 170; archives, 19, 132–33, 135, 144n10, 249–50; *Doctor Who*, 4; internal recordkeeping process, 9, 102; *The Wednesday Play*, 131
Beam, Joseph, 228
Becker, Howard, 167
Benjamin, Louise M., 243
Betamax court case, 151
Bishop, Aileen, 157, 159
Black Country, UK, 138
Blake, Barbara, 146n27
Bloch, Marc, 166
Bluem, William B., 91, 92–94
Bluem Report, 88, 104–5, 108n32, 110n72; administrative research and methodology, 92, 93–94, 108n35, 110n68; classification system, 99–101; inventories of institutional and corporate holdings, 94–97; opening of the MoB and, 101–4; recommendation for a centralized institution, 97–99
Booms, Hans, 13
Bratslavsky, Lauren, ix, 201n3, 229, 231, 242
British Film Institute (BFI), 130, 131, 142, 144n10, 145n13, 146n35; relationship with ITV, 133, 144n11; television archival policy, 132–34, 144n5
Broadcasting Act (UK), 133
broadcasting system. *See* commercial broadcasting system
Brown, Lauren R., 65, 66–67, 70, 76, 83n17
Brown, Walter J., 123
Brown Media Archives. *See* Peabody Awards Collection
Burton, LeVar, 155

camaraderie, 224, 231
Camel News Caravan, The (NBC), 42, 53

camp aesthetic, 227, 229, 231, 233, 236, 238
campus television. *See* University of Wisconsin–Milwaukee
"captive" media, 72, 74
Carlisle, Robert D. B., 66
Carmichael, Lynne, 19
Carnegie Commission, 68, 70
Case, Fox, 113
Caswell, Michelle, x
catalogs/cataloging, 4, 76, 98; ABC (Australia) materials, 168, 172, 175; books, 255; CBS and NBC holdings, 95–97; computerized methods, 104, 105; *The Faye Emerson* and *World of Giants* collections, 188, 195, 196; institutional holdings, 94–95; newsfilm, 35–38, 50–51; Peabody Awards Collection, 116, 119–20, 121–24; regional television archives, 133, 135, 137, 140, 144n11; tiered system of, 99–101
CBC (Canadian Broadcasting Corporation), 102
CBS (Columbia Broadcasting System), 16, 52, 97, 110n72, 150, 152; documentary production and editorial collaboration, 38–39, 41–46; *The Faye Emerson Show*, 183, 184, 188–91; *Faye Emerson's Wonderful Town*, 190, 194–95, 196, 198, 200; film library and value of newsfilm, 18, 30, 31, 32, 36–38, 53–55; holdings, 95–96; inventories, 93; MoB's content, 105; newsmen and programming decisions, 38–39, 41–46, 55; radio broadcasts, 254; *World of Giants*, 183, 184, 191–94
celluloid film, 15, 30, 32, 34, 43–44; cameras and projectors, 61; splicing and scanning, 195–96
Central Television, 136–37, 139, 145n20
Century of Radio exhibit (2021), 156–57
Chambers, Deborah, 254
Chicago broadcasters. *See* Museum of Broadcast Communications
Chicago History Museum (CHM), 149, 151, 158–59, 160
children's television, 59, 158–60
Children's Television Workshop, 62
Churchill, Winston, 42, 47

citation analysis, 20, 241–42; article and citation selection criteria, 247–49, 257n19, 258n20; of audiovisual materials, 252; characteristics of archival materials and, 243–45; findings and discussion, 249–52, *250, 251, 252*; journal selection criteria, 246–47, *247*; scholarly access to collections, 254–56; types of collections, 253–54
Civil Commitment Hearings (1975), *217*, 217–18
civil rights releases, 34
classical music, 167, 169–71, 172
classification/classifying, 92, 93, 98, 169, 227; broadcast content, 99–101, 106; LGBTQ terminology and, 234–35; Library of Congress, 169, 234, 255; logics, 102
Cohen, Edwin G.: institutional lineage, 61, 73, 81n4; oral history, 62, 70–72, 81n2, 83n20, 84n28; paper collection at NPBA, 70–71, 75, 76, 77–78, 83n17; proposal to NPBA, 63–66, 67–70, 76–77
colonization, 232
commercial broadcasting system, 88, 89, 96, 99, 148; in Australia, 173, 174; public broadcasting system and, 90, 102, 170, 177
commerciality, 21; value of newsfilm, 31, 32–38, 42–43, 49, 52–53
communication studies, 92, 241, 242, 246
Compton, Margaret, 124, 201n4, 254
Connors, Thomas, 66–68, 70–72, 76, 83n21, 84n28
Continuum, *247*, 251, *252*
Cook, Terry, 10
Cooke, Lez, 255
Coon, David R., 226, 231, 238
cooperative consortia, 61–62, 65, 67
copyright, 19, 95, 150, 221n21; British law, 132, 144n10; for *In the Life* series, 229; Library of Congress and, 90; litigation between CBS and Vanderbilt TV News Archive, 16, 110n72; MACE collection and, 137; registration, 148, 197; restrictions to archives and, 72, 74, 75; status of WCFTR

copyright (*continued*)
    materials, 184, 197–98, 200; streaming services and, 151–52
Copyright Acts, 197
Cornelius, Don, 152
corporate archives, 9, 93, 185; CBS and NBC holdings, 95–96; classification system for, 99–101; institutional setting for, 97–99
Corporation for Public Broadcasting (CPB), 64, 67–70, 71, 77, 83n17, 83n21, 105
COVID-19, xi, 215, 220n14, 252; exhibitory projects and, 153–55, 156–57, 161
Crawford, William "Scoop," III, *186*, 186–87, 190, 198
Critical Studies in Television, 130, *247*, 252
Cronin, Katie, 18
cultural production, 224, 227, 231, 234
cultural systems, 3–4
Curtin, Michael, 50, 54
Cutlip, Scott, 118

Dafoe, Willem, 204, *217*, 217–18, 220n18
Day, John F., 39
deeds of gifts, 197
De Kosnik, Abigail, 256
Derrida, Jacques, 10, 244
destroyed or lost materials, 17, 79, 80, 81n2; of AIT programs, 59–60, 84n33; lack of storage space and, 220n10; of NBC stock footage, 9, 21, 37, 51–52; Peabody Awards Collection and, 115, 117
Dhoest, Alexander, 250
digitization, 79, 85n42, 144n10, 166; of Australian archival collections, 171, 173, 175; of *The Faye Emerson Show* and *World of Giants* episodes, 183–84, 190, 194–96, 199, 200, 201; initiative at IU Bloomington, 74, 75, 76; of *Kukla, Fran and Ollie* episodes, 159; of MACE's collection, 137, 140, 141; of Peabody Awards Collection, 123–26; precarity of, 255–56; tagging and, 222; of UW-Milwaukee's television collection, 210–16, *215*, 218
disability, 193–94, 207
documentary: ATV and Central Television programs, 136–37, 138, 142; ballet, 175, 177, 180n24; *In the Life* show and, 236, 238; news network productions, 30, 31, 37, 49–51, 55, 58n62; use of Ziv programs for, 187; UW-Milwaukee's collection, 208, 211, 215, 217, 219
domestic spaces, 86
donations, 118, 159, 230; Cohen's collection, 70–71, 75, 76, 77–78, 83n17; types of, 185. *See also Faye Emerson Show, The*
Drennen, Marcia, 40
Drewry, John E., 113, 114, 116
DuMont, Bruce, 148
Durica, Paul, 158, 159, 160
DVCAM, 203, 212, 213–14, 220n13
DVDs, 134; MACE's collection, 131, 141–42, 143

educational television, 18, 59, 60–63, 68, 80, 81n1, 96; racial inequality and, 137. *See also* instructional television
Edwards, Douglas, 41, 45
Edwards, John, 119
Emerson, Faye, *186*, *189*, 202n12. *See also Faye Emerson Show, The*
entertainment programming, 32, 42, 99–100, 238
Ernie Kovacs Show, 17
exhibits, 19, 161, 167, 177; of *The Faye Emerson Show* and *World of Giants*, 199–201; LABF's, 153–56; MBC and CHM's, 152–53, 156–58; spaces at UGA Libraries, 120, 124–25

Faye Emerson Show, The (1949–51), 183–84; about, 188–91; collection at WCFTR, 184–88; copyright and, 198; digitization and exhibits, 183–84, 190, 194–96, 199–201
Faye Emerson's Wonderful Town (1951–52), 190, 194–95, 196, 198, 200
FCC (Federal Communications Commission), 36, 100
feminism, 190, 222–23, 235, 238; lesbian, 229, 236
film archives, 12–13, 24n30, 89, 185; IU's Moving Image Archive, 69, 72–76, 77, 78, 79, 84n35; NFL Films Archives, 56n3; scanning technology,

268   INDEX

195, 195–96; television network film libraries, 29–33, 46–55. *See also* British Film Institute; Media Archive for Central England
Fletcher, James, 119
Ford Foundation, 68, 73, 77, 236
Foucault, Michel, 10
Fox, Bob, 61, 67, 71
franchises, 131, 134, 136–39, 144n11, 145n20
Franklin, Ieuan, 144n3
Frick, Caroline, 13, 79

Gable, Clark, 39, 41, 57n30
Garroway, Dave, 42, 160
GBH, 75, 85n42; *Zoom* program, 85n43
gender, 23, 40–41, 190, 234; misgendering, 237. *See also* trans people
George VI, King, 46–47
Georgia Museum of Art (GMOA), 122–23
Giants of Broadcasting and Electronic Arts event (2020), 153
Gilbert, Vera, 137
Gleason, David, 155
Google, 148–49, 151
Gottlieb, Owen, 18
governmental archives, 8, 9, 243, 249
GPTV (Georgia Public Broadcasting), 122
Gray, Frank, 43
Great Plains National ITV Library, 66, 81n2
Greene, Mark A., 23n25
Grinberg, Sherman, 49
Gudaitis, David, 59–60, 63, 71, 72, 74, 75, 79
Gutiérrez, Raquel, 232

Hacks (2022), xii
Hänni, Adrian, 253
Head, R. C., 11
Heinzkill, Richard, 242
Henneberger, Bob, 128n17
Henry, Michael, 161
Here and Now (1980–90), 137, 139
heritage, 13, 14, 97; American cultural, 90, 103, 104; American television, 80, 89, 91, 104; British television, 130, 131, 133, 134, 141, 143; film as, 89
Hill, Ruane B., 205

Historical Journal of Film, Radio, and Television, 247, *247*, 251, *252*
Hixon, Chip, 71
Horak, Jan-Christopher, 230
Hoye, Robert E., 205–6
Hoyt, Eric, 19, 56n3, 184
Huelsbeck, Mary, 19, 184

identity, 194; institutional, 60, 146n30; locality and, 135, 138; national, 13, 19; of newsmen, 38–41, 46–47; sexual, 227–29, 231
IMDB, 188
immigrant communities, 139
Indiana University (IU) Bloomington: Audio-Visual Center (AVC), 73, 77; ERIC (Educational Resources Information Center), 75, 82n9; Media Digitization Preservation Initiative (MDPI), 74; Moving Image Archive, 69, 72–76, 77, 78, 79, 84n35
Inside/Out (1973), 59, 63, 65, 71, 78
institutional space, 4, 7–8, 19, 20, 150, 223, 244; centralization of, 97–98, 103; for events and exhibits, 152–53, 161–62, 165n65; formation of, 18–19, 91–92, 93, 101–6; holdings retained by, 94–95, 108n35; resource limitations of, 70, 72, 77, 80, 96. *See also* archival space
Instructional Media Laboratory (IML), UW-Milwaukee, 205–9, *208*, 217, 218
instructional television (ITV): Cohen's role in, 71–72; history and programming, 59, 60–63, 81n1; lost or destroyed materials, 80, 81n2; net and, 73; preserving, 63–66, 70, 76, 78–80; public broadcasting and narrowcasting, 68–70, 77; understudied nature of, 63, 82n9; UW-Milwaukee's studio productions, 203, 204–10, *208*, *209*, 216, 219
Integrated Marketing Communications (IMC), UW-Milwaukee, 210, 211, 216, 218, 220n17; Instructional Media Committee (IMC) and, 204–5, 210, 218
intellectual property. *See* copyright
International Focus (TV series), 210, 220n14
International Instructional Television Cooperative, 81n2

INDEX   269

Internet Archive, 249, 252
In the Life (Media Ecology Project): LGBTQ television history and, 229–31; overview and project approach, 222–26, 239n5; about show and critique, 226–29, 235–36; tagging process and archivability, 231–34
inventories/inventorying, 65; CBS and NBC holdings, 93, 95–96, 108n41; institutional holdings, 94–95, 108n35
ITV (Independent Television), 131, 134–35, 138, 145n15; ATV and Central Television franchises, 136, 137, 145n20; relationship with BFI, 133, 144n11

James, William, 176, 177
Jenkinson, Hilary, 7–10, 12
Johnston, Andy, 117
Johnston, Russ, 29
journalists, 154; Black and Brown, 139, 146n27; CBS and NBC, 31, 43, 46, 50, 54
journals, 20, 93, 241, 242, 243; citations to archival materials, *250*, *251*, *252*; titles of scholarly television, 246–47, *247*

Kackman, Michael, 193
Kay, Lambdin, 114
Kelly, Ray, 34
Kersta, Noran, 33
Kibler, M. Alison, 253
kinescope recordings, 15, 17, 71, 94, 168, 171, 201n4; of *The Faye Emerson Show*, 184, 188–90, 194; NBC, 52–53, 96; in Peabody Awards Collection, 115, 117
Kinoshita, Robert, 193
Knapskog, Karl, 144n10
knowledge production, 4, 6, 11, 13, 17, 105, 106; social, 88, 107n9
Kogan, Rick, 160
Kompare, Derek, 91, 121
Korean War, 48–49
Kothor, Marius, xiii
Kukla, Fran and Ollie (TV series), 153, 156, 158–60
Kula, Sam, 24n30

Lampert, Pauline, 19, 184
Langlois, Henri, 74
Lepore, Frank, 36
Levine, Elana, 14, 20–21
LGBTQ, 222, 225, 226, 229–31, 233. See also *In the Life*; trans people
Library of American Broadcasting Foundation (LABF), University of Maryland, 149, 151, 153–56, 164n23, 165n39
Library of Congress, 16–17, 93, 108n28, 128n17, 196, 251; AAPB collaboration, 75, 85n42, 125; American Television and Radio Archive, 90; classification system, 169, 234, 255; copyright registrations, 148, 197; Motion Picture Division, 95; Radio Preservation Task Force, 79; Television and Preservation Study, 91
Life Magazine, 42
Lindgren, Earl, 206
Lindgren, Ernest, 74
Linton, Katherine, 226, 236, 238
Ljungbäck, Hugo, 19
Lost in Space (1965), 193
Lyons, Ruth, 188

magnetic tape, 3, 15–16. See also videotape
Margaret Herrick Library, 251
Mary of Teck, Queen, 46–47
Mashon, Mike, 66, 68–70, 83n21
mass media, 11, 14, 88, 90, 99, 105
Matter of Fiction, A (1970), 76, 84n33
Mauk, Maureen, 19, 184, 194, 196, 202n12, 202n18
Mbembe, Achille, 3
McCall, Frank, 48–49
McDougald, Worth, 114, 116, 117
McNeil, Donald R., 63, 67, 70, 76, 77, 83n17
McRobbie, Michael, 74, 79
Media Archive for Central England (MACE), 130–31, 146n32; collection and access to, 136–43, 145n21, 146n30
Media Ecology Project. See *In the Life*
media studies, x, 2, 5, 80; disability and, 193–94; mass communication programs, 92; spatial turn in, 144n3

270 INDEX

Mediathread, 222, 227
memory, 5, 10–11, 88, 89, 97, 166; institutional, 204, 225, 244; local, 131, 135, 143; nostalgia and, 152; popular, 87, 103; sense, 225
Men of Annapolis (TV series), 187–88
metadata, 167, 169, 196, 216, 249
Mickelson, Sig, 38–39, 44, 46
Midlands, UK, 130, 133, 136–40, 142, 145n20
Miller, Quinlan, 20
MiniDV, 203, 212, 213–14, 220n13
Morris, Ginny, 154
Moving Image, The (journal), 247, 251, 252
Moving Image Archive, IU Bloomington, 69, 72–76, 78, 79
Museum of Broadcast Communications (MBC), 148, 149, 151, 152–53; "Back with You Again" project, 156–58; *A Century of Radio* exhibit, 156–58
Museum of Broadcasting (MoB), 18, 86–88, 93, 106n3, 150–51; legitimation of, 104–6; museum label and opening of, 101–4; origin of, 89–92. *See also* Bluem Report
Museum of Modern Art (MoMA) Film Library, 12, 107n17
music production, 167, 168, 169–71, 179n15; televised, 176, 177, 178
Mwakasege-Minaya, Richard M., 253

National Academy of Television Arts and Sciences (NATAS), 71, 93, 95, 110n72, 150
National Archives and Records Administration, xi, 121, 251
National Archives of Australia (NAA), 173–74
National Association of Broadcasters (NAB), 114, 153, 154–56
National Capital Radio and Television Museum, 151
National Educational Television (NET), 61, 71, 73, 74, 77, 81n4
National Endowment for the Humanities (NEH), 118–19, 122
National Film and Sound Archive (NFSA), 173–74

National Historical Publications and Records Commission (NHPRC), 123, 125
National Instructional Television Library (NITL), 61, 62, 73. *See also* Agency for Instructional Technology
National Library of Australia (NLA), 173–74
National Public Broadcasting Archives (NPBA), University of Maryland: Cohen Papers, 70–71, 75, 76, 77–78, 83n17; proposal for ITV and radio collection, 63–70, 76–77
NBC (National Broadcasting Corporation), 9–10, 21, 105, 150, 152; documentary production and editorial collaboration, 46–51; film library and value of newsfilm, 18, 29, 30, 31, 32–38, 52–55; holdings, 93, 95–96, 108n41; news personalities and programming, 40–46, 55
Nelson, Robin, 255
Netflix, 149, 248; *Archive 81* (2021), xi–xii
Newberry Library, 149, 158, 159
newsfilm: ABC (Australia) footage, 172; commercial and historical value of, 18, 29, 32–38, 41–46, 51–55; for documentary production, 46–51; local television, 135, 136–37, 142, 145n20; network film libraries, 29–32; WSB collection, 123
newsmen, 154, 238; film librarians and, 46, 48, 51; integrity and programming decisions, 41–46, 54; public persona, 32–34, 38–41, 55
newspapers, 11–12, 42, 82n9; *New York Times*, 86, 245; *The Red and Black* (UGA), 117, 118
newsreels, 30, 32, 33, 40, 43–44; edited, 48, 49, 50; obituary, 46–47; syndicated, 37
New York Public Library (NYPL), 251
Nigocia, Harry, 156

objectivity: archivists and, 7, 10, 12, 14; newsmen and, 31, 38–39, 54
Olson, Gary, 205–6
100 Years of Broadcast News (2020), 154–55

INDEX   271

online databases: for AIT collection, 75, 85n42; for Australian archival collections, 174, 178; bibliographic, 246; digitization details for, 196; finding aids and aggregators, 241, 255; for MACE collection, 140, 142, 145n21; overreliance and precarity of, 255–56; for Peabody Awards Collection, 123, 124, 126; tagging *In the Life*, 232–35, 237. *See also* streaming services
online media players, 249
On the Level (1980), 68
open access, 174, 199–201, 242
Orphan Film Symposium, 85n47
Oswald, Lee Harvey, 151

Packer, Jeremy, 6
Page, Wilson, 119–20
Paley, William, 86, 87–88, 89–91, 106n3, 107n17, 150
Paley Center for Media. *See* Museum of Broadcasting
Paley Foundation, 91, 92, 95, 97, 102, 110n68
paper medium, 4–5, 11–12, 103–4, 166; books, 255; magazines, 39, 42, 175, 187; monographs, 242, 243; Peabody Award Collection and, 115–16, 119–20, 125, 127; Ziv-TV collection and, 185–86, 191
PBS (Public Broadcasting Service), 73, 80, 81n3; AIT programs, 59, 68, 77; *In the Life* series, 222, 226–27; Milwaukee affiliate, 203, 210, 220n14; scheduling and viewers, 69, 227
Peabody, George Foster, 114, 123
Peabody Awards Collection, 19, 95, 108n38, 113–14; creation and entry criteria, 114–17; preservation plan and renaming to Brown Media, 121–27; transfer to UGA libraries, 117–19
Peace Program (1940), 115
persistence principle, 245, 256
personal archives, 222, 225
Pessach, Guy, 244
Peterson, Elizabeth, ix, 20, 231
photographs, 125, 175, 186, 187, 243, 254
playback, 4, 89, 104, 119; equipment, 115, 120, 149–50, 166, 204, 213–14, 215

Plier, David, 158
podcasting, 155–56, 161
Podrazik, Walter, 19
Poker Face (2023), xii
popular culture, 6, 98, 158, 187, 194; informational value of, 4, 11–14
Porst, Jennifer, 253
post-broadcast records, 87, 94, 96, 97, 98, 105; value of, 91–92, 101, 104, 106
Potter, William Gray, 121–22, 124
primary sources, 17, 18, 21, 30, 241, 243, 249; creating, 248
provenance principle, 244, 245, 249
public affairs programming, 73, 87, 100; CBS and NBC, 31, 36–37, 41–45, 96
Public Broadcasting Service (PBS). *See* PBS
public relations strategies, 36, 50; MoB and, 87, 91, 105
public service, 87, 90, 92, 96, 102, 228; award, 114, 115; broadcasters, 168, 170, 176, 177
Public Service Broadcast (PSB) archives, 144n10
puppetry, 160, 207

queer television studies, 223, 224–25, 226, 229; annotation and classification and, 231–35, 237–38; history, 230, 231

race and racism, 137, 139, 146n27, 232; Blackness, 228; transphobia and, 234; white-centrism, 227, 231, 234–35, 236–37, 238
"radical schlock," 225, 232–33
radio, 91, 92, 99, 148, 151, 155; ABC (Australia), 167, 170–71, 174; BBC, 144n10; CBS, 254; instructional, 60, 63–66, 76–78; KDKA News, 154, 156, 157; MBC's exhibit, 156–58; preservation, 79, 94, 103, 150; programs, 157, 160, 167, 168; public service award for, 114; receivers, 162n3; recordings, 96, 115; WJBW, 156; WUWM campus, 205, 206; WVON, 152
Radio Hall of Fame (RHOF), 156, 157–58
Raphael, Heidi, 154, 165n39

Reagan, Ronald, 253
recordkeeping, 9–10, 90, 102
regional media archives, 19, 144n3, 250; in Australia, 173; locations and objectives of, 133–34, 145nn13–14; MACE collection, 130–32, 136–43; television in, 134–36, 145n17
Richert, Larry, 154
Riley, Olivia, 19, 184, 194, 196, 200, 202n18
Ripples (1970), 62
Rita, Fran and Dragon (2022), 159–60, 164n35
R. J. Reynolds, 42, 52–53
Robbins, Andrew, 237
Robinson, Julie E., 138
Rockman, Saul, 66, 68, 71, 83n16, 84n25
Ryan, Milo, 254

Saudek, Robert, 103
scanning/scanners, *195*, 195–96, 200, 248
Scargill, Alexis, 81n2
Schaden, Chuck, 156
Schalk, Samantha, 193
Schellenberg, T. R., 7–10
Schwartz, Ruth, 16, 108n36
science fiction, 192, 193
scrapbooks, 114–15, 120, 188
scripts, 4, 21, 50, 103, 115, 167
Segado-Boj, Francisco, 246
Sesame Street, 59, 62, 63, 68, 69
situation comedy, 228
Slow Horses (2022), xii
Smith, Amanda, 19, 184
Smith, Gordon, 154
Sneed, Pamela, 232, 233–34
soap operas, 14, 20
social media, 21, 156, 210, 211, 218; Tumblr, 222. *See also* YouTube
Society for Cinema and Media Studies (SCMS), 79
Socolow, Michael, 36
Spaulding, Hannah, 19
Spigel, Lynn, 91, 93, 108n28
spy dramas, 192, 193
State Historical Society of Wisconsin, 9, 14
St. John, Matt, 19, 184

stock footage, 191, 211, 218; NBC and CBS news, 32, 34, 36–38, 49–50, 52
Stoeltje, Rachael, 72–76, 77, 78
streaming services, 4, 21, 151–52, 170, 254; for events or exhibits, 154, 160, 161, 163; Netflix, xi–xii, 149, 248. *See also* YouTube
Sullivan, Mike, 71
Swayze, John Cameron, 41
syndication: of *I Love Lucy*, 15; of news content, 37–38, 49; of Ziv-TV productions, 184, 185, 191, 198, 199, 200

Tadic, Linda, 122
tagging, 222–23, 224, 229, 232–38, 254
telerecordings. *See* kinescope recordings
Television and New Media (journal), 247, *247*, 251, 252
television awards, 115–16; for documentaries, 50, 208, 217; Emmy, 59, 60, 71, 76, 78, 84n33; Insight Award, 155. *See also* Peabody Awards Collection
television broadcasting schedules, 4, 97, 98, 188, 227, 230; for ITV programs, 68, 69, 82n29
television products and processes, 4–5, 14, 21, 242; physicality or materiality of, 15–17, 93–94
television programming, 4, 14, 17, 253; aesthetic and sociocultural approaches to, 248; copyright and, 197–98; early recording technology, 15–16; game shows, 189; hosts, 236; instructional, 59, 62–63, 77, 84n33; live performances, 168, 171, 174–78, 180n24, 187, 188–91; prerecorded, 15, 55, 191; regional, 131, 134–35; revival of, 183; system for classifying, 99–101. *See also* syndication
television scholarship, 20, 79, 142, 241–42; access to archives, 254–55; analysis of articles and citations, 247–49, *249*–52, *251*, *252*, *253*; frequently cited journals, 246–47, *247*; scarcity of sources, 248; types of collections, 254–55
television technology, 3, 168, 171; newsfilm gathering, 43–44; obsolescence of equipment, 126, 166, 175, 204;

television technology (*continued*)
props, *192*, 192–93, *193*, 199; transmission and retransmission, 15, 60, 89, 92. *See also* playback
Texas Archive of the Moving Image (TAMI), ix, xii
Texas Broadcast Museum, 151
Theatre X, 204, *217*, 217–18
ThinkAbout (1979), 63, 65, 68, 69, 77
third university, 232
Thompson, Marshall, 191, 192
Tillstrom, Burr, 156, 158–59
Today Show, The, 41, 42–43, 52, 160
Tourtellot, Arthur, 102
Traeger, Irving, 49–50
trans archive, 224, 226, 230–31
transcription discs, 115
trans people, 228–29, 230–31, 233, 237–38, 239n1; transvestite usage and, 234–35
transphobia, 230, 234, 237
Trump administration, xi
Trussel, Vance, 117, 118
TVO, 75, 80, 81n2
Type C tapes, 203, 208, *212*, 214

UCLA Film and Television Archive, 16, 95, 110n72, 150, 229–30, 251
U-matic, 16, 123, 203, 207, 208, 212, 214
unarchivable, the, 20, 229–30, 235, 238
United Artists collection, 185, 186, 197, 201n1
University of Georgia (UGA): Grady College of Journalism, 116–19, 120, 127; Libraries and Media Archives, 116, 117–20, 121–27, 128n17. *See also* Peabody Awards Collection
University of Maryland (UMD). *See* Library of American Broadcasting Foundation; National Public Broadcasting Archives
University of Wisconsin–Madison, 14, 21, 183, 184, 186, 195, 197
University of Wisconsin–Milwaukee: film studies program, 216; preservation of campus tape collection, 203, 204–10, 221n21; television studio and productions, 203, 204–10, 220n13,

220n15; Theater X and Willem Dafoe, 216–18, 220n18
Uricchio, William, 13

value: classification of, 92, 99–101; evidentiary, 8, 9, 10, 17, 94, 243, 244; historical and cultural, 2, 16, 19, 87, 93, 94, 97–98, 105; informational, 13; local/regional television, 130–31, 133–34, 135–36, 143; long-term, 198, 204, 217, 220n17, 243; national television, 132–33; of newsfilm, 18, 30, 31, 32, 36–38, 49–51; of Peabody Awards Collection, 116; post-broadcast, 91–92, 101, 104, 106; systems, 232
VanCour, Shawn, 92
Vanderbilt TV News Archive, 16, 110n72, 150, 162n2
Vevier, Charles, 204
VHS, 80, 81n2, 120, 212, 214, 225
videotape, 72, 76, 94, 96, 167, 171; home recording, 151; rerecording over, 119–20, 132; UW-Milwaukee's collection of, 203, 210–19, *212*, *213*. *See also* playback; *and specific videotape type*
visual effects, *192*, 192–93, *193*, 199
Vogan, Travis, 56n3

Walters, William L., 206
Wasson, Haidee, 12–13
Weiner, Barbara, 32
Welbon, Yvonne, 228
Wells, Herman, 73, 77
Wheatley, Helen, 248, 249
white-normativity, 227, 231, 234–35, 236–37, 238
Widdicombe, John, 175
Williams, Karen, 232, 236
Williams, Mark, 230
Williams, Raymond, 3
Wilson, Chuck, 75
Wisconsin Center for Film and Theater Research (WCFTR), 19, 183–84, 251; copyright and, 194–96; scanning/digitization process, 194–96; television collections at, 184–88
Wisconsin Historical Society, 184
World of Giants (1958), 183–84; about,

274 INDEX

191–94; copyright status, 198; digitization of, 183–84, 194–96

Yemm, Rachel, 139, 146n27
YouTube, 84n41, 227, 229, 233, 252; Dafoe clip, 218; free access of, 148–49, 241, 245; uploads per day (in 2006), 151

Ziv, Frederick, 185
Ziv-TV, 185–87, *187*, 191–94, 198, 199, 200–201

Printed in the United States
by Baker & Taylor Publisher Services